821.8
T

Tennyson : a collection of critical essays / edited by Elizabeth A. Francis. -- Englewood Cliffs, N.J. :
Prentice-Hall, c1980.
220 p.
(Twentieth century views) (Spectrum
book)

ISBN 0-13-902353-4 : 10.95
[ISBN 0-13-902346-1 (pbk.)]

1.Tennyson, Alfred Tennyson, Baron,
1809-1892--Criticism and interpreta-
tion--Addresses, essays, lectures.
I.Francis, Elizabeth A.

26630
                              Ja81

80-19288
CIP MARC

COPY 73

TENNYSON

A COLLECTION OF CRITICAL ESSAYS

Edited by
Elizabeth A. Francis

Prentice-Hall, Inc.　 A SPECTRUM BOOK　*Englewood Cliffs, N.J.*

Library of Congress Cataloging in Publication Data
Main entry under title:

TENNYSON: A COLLECTION OF CRITICAL ESSAYS.

(Twentieth century views) (A Spectrum Book)
Bibliography: p.
1. Tennyson, Alfred Tennyson, Baron, 1809-1892—
Criticism and interpretation—Addresses, essays,
lectures. I. Francis, Elizabeth A.
PR5588.T44   821'.8   80-19288
ISBN 0-13-902353-4
ISBN 0-13-902346-1 (pbk.)

For my children

MAR 1 7 1981

C . 73

The excerpts from Tennyson's "Armageddon" on page 170 are used by permission of the Trustees (through Lord Tennyson) and of the Masters and Fellows of Trinity College, Cambridge.

The excerpt from Georges Poulet, *Studies in Human Time,* translated by Elliott Coleman — Copyright 1956 by Georges Poulet — is used by permission of The Johns Hopkins University Press.

Editorial/production supervision by Betty Neville
Cover design by Stanley Wyatt
Manufacturing buyer: Barbara A. Frick

10   9   8   7   6   5   4   3   2   1

PRENTICE-HALL INTERNATIONAL, INC. *(London)*
PRENTICE-HALL OF AUSTRALIA PTY. LTD. *(Sydney)*
PRENTICE-HALL OF CANADA, LTD. *(Toronto)*
PRENTICE-HALL OF INDIA PRIVATE LIMITED *(New Delhi)*
PRENTICE-HALL OF JAPAN, INC. *(Tokyo)*
PRENTICE-HALL OF SOUTHEAST ASIA PTE. LTD. *(Singapore)*
WHITEHALL BOOKS LIMITED, *Wellington (New Zealand)*

3 9082 05360252 3

Contents

Introduction

by E. A. Francis

I

In 1923 Harold Nicolson set out to disengage the "essential" Tennyson from the bias of nineteenth-century opinion:

> Of these many mythologies it was perhaps the Tennyson legend which attained the most exaggerated proportions. For over fifty years [the poet's] votaries prostrated themselves before the shrine which they had built for him, and he, moving a little clumsily at times within his sacerdotal vestments, became inevitably less and less the lyric poet, and more and more the civic prophet—the communal bard. There were grave disadvantages in this process. In the first place, it has rendered him, for some at least of the successors of his own generation, an object of derision and even of dislike. And, in the second place... it hampered seriously the expression of his own essential genius. For whereas Tennyson was an extremely good emotional poet, he was, unfortunately, but a very second-rate instructional bard.[1]

From Nicolson's standpoint the task of the twentieth-century critic was to free Tennyson's "best"—that is, lyric—poetry from the barrenness of prophecy. Nicolson incorrectly presumed that Tennyson's commitment to prophecy was a late growth, induced by the poet's response to his culture and therefore a denial of his native bent. In his effort to free the poet from the limitations of his artistic environment, Nicolson took "destruction" as the method of his constructive task, setting a limited group of poems apart from the rest for the attention of the twentieth-century reader and thus inaugurating a habit of "judgment" characteristic of critical studies that were

[1] Harold Nicolson, *Tennyson: Aspects of his Life, Character, and Poetry* (London, 1923), p. 5.

1

to follow. Auden's selection, published in 1946,[2] echoed Nicolson's notion of the correctly "pruned" corpus, and his introduction exaggerated Nicolson's attack upon Tennyson's powers of thought. Eliot had already lent himself to this view, concluding his trenchant and otherwise sympathetic analysis of *In Memoriam* with the damning lines, "and having turned aside from the journey through the dark night, to become the surface flatterer of his own time, he has been rewarded with the despite of an age that succeeds his own in shallowness."[3]

The result of such commentary was a reevaluation of Tennyson's lyric poetry at the expense of his narrative and public forms. "Songs" from *The Princess* were anthologized when the narrative was not. *In Memoriam* could be read as discrete and separable entries in the "diary" of grief rather than as a structured whole.[4] Justifiable as this view was in some respects, it obscured concerns for language and voice which partially unify the poem within its pastoral frame. Indeed selections from Tennyson's poetry which concentrated on the short dense lyrics and portions of the larger pieces constituted a program of reading for many students during the middle years of this century. With some obvious exceptions critical discussion also centered on a comparatively limited group of familiar poems: *The Lady of Shalott; The Lotos-Eaters; The Palace of Art; Mariana; Ulysses; Break, Break, Break; Tears, Idle Tears;* and the *Morte d'Arthur* prominent among them. New work on Tennyson's troubled upbringing at Somersby and on issues of faith and doubt in *In Memoriam* coincided with Nicolson's discussion of Tennyson's nature to support the view that the poet's bent was naturally lyrical and that communal and prophetic strains in his work were late accretions. An emphasis upon Tennyson's lyric voice and family background, received notions of the effects of Hallam's death upon the poet, and the necessity for excision established a legacy of issues with which criticism still struggles and which it has recently sought to transcend.

Certain studies from the middle years of this century deserve notice in that they stand apart from the main thrust of post-Nicolson criticism and illuminate issues which the work of the past fifteen years has begun to consider in depth. J. F. A. Pyre's study of diction,

[2]W. H. Auden, ed., *Tennyson: An Introduction and Selection* (London, 1946).
[3]T. S. Eliot, *Essays Ancient and Modern* (London, 1936), p. 190.
[4]*Ibid.*, p. 183.

meter, and image in Tennyson's poetry from 1827 to 1855 (*The For-mation of Tennyson's Style* [Madison, Wisc., 1921]), a detailed ac-count of Tennyson's linguistic development, underlies the con-temporary work of Alan Sinfield and W. David Shaw. Pyre sought to discriminate the stages of Tennyson's linguistic growth from one another and to present them chronologically. By contrast, Douglas Bush sought to identify Tennyson's early and abiding relationship to the classical heritage. Like W. P. Mustard (*Classical Echoes in Tennyson* [New York, 1904]) before him, Bush identified the genesis of certain Tennyson lines in classical sources, but he went on to state succinctly the effects of those sources on important poems. Bush's study of *Lucretius* is included in this collection.

Where Pyre sought keys to Tennyson's development in language and Bush sought them in the poet's early classical study and life-long commitment to classical literatures, W. D. Paden found sources for the poet's mature work by studying the earliest poems Tennyson had published. Paden's excellent and exhaustive study of the 1827 *Poems by Two Brothers* (*Tennyson in Egypt: A Study of the Imagery in His Earlier Work* [Lawrence, Kan., 1942]) identified patterns of image and argument in Tennyson's juvenilia which are in fact central to the structure of the poet's major works. Examining the notes for *Poems by Two Brothers,* he found keys to the boy's early reading in Sir William Jones and Savary, in classical geography and Biblical sources, in the English poets, and in typological writing. Paden's statements about the "mask of age" and the "warrior of God" have perceptibly and imperceptibly entered the language of Tenny-son criticism. The implications of Paden's research are only now being fully recognized.

The biographical research of Sir Charles Tennyson, particularly his account of the poet's life at Somersby (*Alfred Tennyson: by His Grandson* [London, 1949]), amplified the standard account of Ten-nyson's life written by the poet's son Hallam Tennyson (*Alfred Lord Tennyson: A Memoir* [2 vols., London, 1897]). Together with the socio-literary work of John Killham (*The Princess: Reflections of an Age* [London, 1957]) and the biographical research of Ralph Wilson Rader (*Tennyson's Maud: The Biographical Genesis* [Berkeley, Calif., 1963]), Charles Tennyson's biography has solidified knowl-edge of the poet's early experiences and affections, as well as his confrontation with social and political issues. E. D. H. Johnson's essay on Tennyson in *The Alien Vision of Victorian Poetry* (Princeton, 1957) made a different kind of contribution. Johnson placed the subjective elements of Tennyson's poetry in a nineteenth-century philosophical and poetic framework, emphasizing their participation in a general cultural heritage.

The years 1960-1963 marked a watershed in Tennyson criticism. J. H. Buckley's *Tennyson: The Growth of a Poet* (Cambridge, Mass., 1960) related the whole of the poet's life to his art. John Killham's *Critical Essays on the Poetry of Tennyson* (London, 1963) collected much of the best that had been written in the twentieth century to that date.

Two essays published in 1950, both collected by Killham, are central to innovations in Tennyson criticism from 1965 to the present. In "Tennyson and Picturesque Poetry," H. M. McLuhan identified the brilliance of Hallam's understanding of the implications of English impressionist criticism (directed to landscape painting) for poetry, particularly the poetry of Tennyson. McLuhan saw that Hallam's aesthetic theory resulted from "studying Dante through the poetry of Keats," and was therefore in some sense a meeting of Renaissance and Romantic poetic assumptions. Claiming that Hallam's essay for the *Englishman's Magazine* of 1831 was as important for its time as Wordsworth's "Preface" to *Lyrical Ballads* had been in 1798 or Eliot's "Tradition and the Individual Talent" was to be in 1917, McLuhan said that it implied

> ...the Symbolist and Imagist doctrine that the place of ideas in poetry is not that of logical enunciation but of immediate sensation or experience. Rhetoric must go, said the Symbolists. Ideas as ideas must go. They may return as part of a landscape that is ordered by other means. They may enter into a unified experience as one kind of fact. They may contribute to an aesthetic emotion, not as a system of demonstration but as part of a total order which is to be contemplated.[5]

McLuhan's study is important not only as a proper evaluation of Hallam's criticism but also as a statement about the place of Tennyson's poetry, especially its surface style, in an aesthetic tradition that stretches from the mid-eighteenth to the mid-twentieth century. Although McLuhan overemphasizes the effect of Hallam on the structures of Tennyson's major poems, thus reinforcing a notion that Tennyson's mature poetics resulted primarily from his rela-

[5]H. M. McLuhan, "Tennyson and Picturesque Poetry," *Essays in Criticism*, 1 (1950), 263.

tionship to his friend and that friend's death, he does permit us to
see Tennyson's poetry in its largest historical contexts and to seek
its meanings in the fusion of thought and image. McLuhan's wish
to see the Romantic tradition as a whole announced a critical stance
that underlies the very different assessments of Tennyson's early
poetry by Shaw, Bloom, Ricks, and Sinfield in this collection.

Arthur J. Carr in "Tennyson as a Modern Poet" also sees Tennyson as "our true precursor," the precursor of the modern age:

> He shows and hides, as if in embryo, a master theme of Joyce's
> *Ulysses* — the accentuated and moody self-consciousness and the sense
> of loss that mark Stephen Dedalus. He forecasts Yeats's interest in the
> private myth. He apprehended in advance of Aldous Huxley the uses
> of mysticism to castigate materialistic culture. And in *Maud*, at least,
> he prepared the way for the verse of Eliot's "Preludes" and "Prufrock."[6]

Carr recognized the importance of the theme of loss for Tennyson
before the death of Hallam, and the degree to which Tennyson's
"occasions" were, despite appearances, private rather than public
affairs.[7] Noting a significant connection between "the damming up
of desire" in such poems as *Mariana* or *Fatima*, and "a Keatsian
lushness of imagery and diction,"[8] and invoking Freud's insights
to support his case, Carr offered an analysis of Tennyson's "ornate"
style which builds on Walter Bagehot's earlier commentary and
leads to the work of Bloom reprinted below:

> Tennyson had learned to embody a problem in a mood and the mood
> in evocative, concrete, and disturbed imagery. To this ability he
> would soon add the use of myth and legend that made a hard and bril-
> liant surface of traditional substance under which the private sensi-
> bility moved as if through water.[9]

Carr's assessments of individual poems, brief as they often are, remain "irrefutable"; so too does his sense of the significance of
Tennyson's poetry for its age:

> Tennyson had forged a poetic instrument out of the themes of loss
> and recovery through regression into dream and vision. Death and

---

[6]Arthur J. Carr, "Tennyson as a Modern Poet," *University of Toronto Quarterly,*
19, (1950), 361.

[7]*Ibid.,* p. 364.

[8]*Ibid.,* p. 370.

[9]*Ibid.*

fear were established as the conventions that rule the dialectic of sense and conscience. This instrument became his means of apprehending the rational problems of his experience also, and lent them the deep sense of crisis that accorded well with the feelings of his class and of his age. The future of art, the nature of society, and the issues of science and religion, take the colors and disposition of his subjective life.[10]

Nicolson's opinions have come full circle, for contemporary criticism, building on the work of McLuhan, Carr, and others, attempts to see the lyricist in relation to the bard, the allegorist of sense and conscience in relation to the repressed but vital dreamer. The essays which follow represent the range of Tennyson criticism during the past forty years and major developments from it during the past decade. In conjunction with other essays listed in the selected bibliography at the end of the volume they raise significant questions for future Tennyson criticism. Some of the pieces collected in this volume are readings, but most are efforts to place Tennyson in a critical context or to place a given poem in the corpus. The emphasis upon recent work recognizes the acceleration of interest in Tennyson during the last fifteen years and a corresponding increase in the strength of Tennyson criticism. Two short pieces from earlier periods—notably those by Eliot and Bush—have been chosen because they are classical essays in the field. Bush's piece has been a model for other critics. Eliot's has been fount or antagonist of much that has been written about *In Memoriam* since 1936.

The early section of the book deals with Tennyson in relation to his romantic heritage. W. David Shaw builds on the insights of F. E. L. Priestley and the arguments of Alan Sinfield and J. F. A. Pyre as he studies the rhetoric of *The Lady of Shalott* and *The Lotos-Eaters*. For Shaw, Tennyson is a "transitional" poet, concerned with "transition" both in terms of the language and content of selected poems. Bloom's essay "Tennyson: In the Shadow of Keats" extends McLuhan's grasp of the relation of both Hallam and Tennyson to the whole romantic tradition and states the usefulness of Freud's insights on the nature of repression for a study of Tennyson's erotic surfaces. The essay exemplifies Bloom's theory of the nature of poetic influence.[11] It drives beneath what Carr has called the hard surface of Tennyson's poetry to some of the impulses which moti-

[10]*Ibid.*

[11]Cf. especially Harold Bloom, *The Anxiety of Influence* (New York and London, 1973).

vate its deepest structures. Christopher Ricks' essay, "Poems from Hallam's Death till the End of 1834," epitomizes the results of careful editorial discrimination and research. Like the book from which it comes, the essay reads the interface between Tennyson's life and art.

A. Dwight Culler, writing on *The English Idyls,* and F. E. L. Priestley, writing on *The Princess,* both consider Tennyson's innovative handling of traditional genres. Culler reads Tennyson's domestic poems in terms of their visual, romantic, and classical heritage, providing readings for poems too long ignored in the criticism.[12] Culler discusses at length Tennyson's persistent habit of "framing" poems, this time in terms of the relation between the contemporary and the received in Tennyson's verse. The delicate mirroring, laughter, and understatement in *The English Idyls* becomes abundantly clear. F. E. L. Priestley's essay also concerns Tennyson's remarkable ability to innovate within the patterns of received genres. Where Culler sees *The Princess* as an elaboration of the idyl, Priestley understands it as a revision of romance. He delineates the "strange diagonal" between comedy and romance that defines the narrative's tone and inhabits its deliberately apologetic structure.[13] J. H. Buckley's short piece on *Maud,* set later in the collection, also deals with generic issues.[14] In it Buckley writes: "Tennyson's distaste for all false convention determines the themes and penetrates the very texture of *Maud,* which is at once the most dissonant of all his major works and the most varied in its rich operatic harmonies." Buckley's sense of musical structure in *Maud* anticipated in general terms Culler's formal and historical analysis of the differences between monodrama and dramatic monologue published in 1975.[15]

[12]Cf. John Dixon Hunt, "Story Painters and Picture Writers: Tennyson's Idylls and Victorian Painting," in *Writers and Their Background: Tennyson,* ed. D. J. Palmer (Athens, Ohio, 1973); and Thomas J. Assad, "On the Major Poems of Tennyson's *Enoch Arden* Volume," *Tulane Studies in English,* 14 (1965), 29-65.

[13]Cf. especially James Kincaid, "The Princess," in *Tennyson: The Major Poems* (New Haven, 1975); and John Killham, *Tennyson and 'The Princess': Reflections of an Age* (London, 1958).

[14]Cf. also Ralph Wilson Rader, mentioned earlier; Humbert Wolfe, *Tennyson* (London, 1930); and Jonas Spatz, "Love and Death in Tennyson's *Maud,*" *Texas Studies in Language and Literature,* 16 (1974), 503-10.

[15]A. Dwight Culler, "Monodrama and the Dramatic Monologue," *Publications of the Modern Language Association,* 90 (1975), 366-85.

James Kissane's piece, "Tennyson: The Passion of the Past and the Curse of Time," serves as a transitional essay in the collection. Building on the insights of Carr, Kissane studies a range of Tennyson's early and middle poems with respect to recurrent themes of loss and begins to consider their implications, with respect to a reading of *In Memoriam*. As theme criticism the piece contrasts strongly with Eliot's appreciation of the elegy and Sinfield's analysis of its language. For Sinfield, writing very recently, *In Memoriam* is at once a meeting of classical and romantic tradition, and a text open to intensive linguistic examination. In *"In Memoriam:* The Linnet and the Artifact," Sinfield presents the context within which close consideration of the poems' diction, syntax, and verbal relationships can take place. The essay printed here will introduce readers to a study which should be read in its entirety.

The final essays in this collection deal with continuities. The first of the *Idylls of the King* were published in 1859, but Tennyson had considered the possibility of treating the Arthurian legends in one form or another since late boyhood. Written plans for such a work exist in manuscript, dating from about 1833. John Rosenberg, in the penultimate selection below, describes the evolution of the poem's form in terms of the history of its composition (see primarily Kathleen Tillotson, "Tennyson's Serial Poem," in *Mid-Victorian Studies* [London, 1965, pp. 80-109]), but also as a considered growth from Tennyson's deepest convictions and themes. Rosenberg's essay can be read profitably in relation to Kissane's, for it also treats ideas of time, rise, fall, and crisis in Tennyson's poetry. My own essay on Tennyson's late work considers the effects of Tennyson's habits of retrieval and reconsideration on the shape of *Demeter and Other Poems* and on the content of *The Death of Oenone.*

II

In their separate ways all the pieces collected in this book touch upon Tennyson's constantly renewed interest in the nature of poetic voice and the outlets for that voice in formal structures. Indeed there is an underlying tension in Tennyson's canon between privately defined and idiosyncratically used poetic structures and the great received genres of the tradition. This issue underlies the juxtaposition of radically different kinds of song in *Poems, Chiefly Lyrical*

(1830), Ida's understanding of herself and her capitulation to marriage in *The Princess,* and the movement of short poems within overarching structures in *Idylls of the King.* It is given its most complex and perhaps most satisfying scrutiny in *In Memoriam,* where the question of the poet's separate voice is bound to the evolving shape of the elegy. There the history of Tennyson's grief for Hallam becomes both trope and occasion for the poet's appraisal of his artistic history to date, his assessment of the strength, direction, and worth of his art. Traditional attributes of elegy shape, and are reshaped by, both the speaker's varying attitudes toward a lost human friend, and his need to define the force of words and the poet's power to speak. I turn briefly to certain difficult passages from *In Memoriam,* especially XCV and CIII, which illustrate these precepts and thus lead us to consider central concerns of the poetry as a whole.

At *In Memoriam* XXXVI the griever presumes to celebrate Christ, whose life was the union of "Word" and deed:

> And so the Word had breath, and wrought
> With human hands the creed of creeds
> In loveliness of perfect deeds,
> More strong than all poetic thought;
>
> Which he may read that binds the sheaf,
> Or builds the house, or digs the grave,
> And those wild eyes that watch the wave
> In roarings round the coral reef.   (XXXVI, 9-16)

The lines complete a series of poems which begins with the description of Lazarus at XXXI, a series in which the speaker emulates Hallam's powers of abstract thought in his effort to unite himself with the lost beloved. The tone of XXXVI is certain, elevated, prophetic as it asserts the power of language to overcome the barrier between word and fact. But the poet's vaunt is swiftly rebuked:

> Urania speaks with darken'd brow:
> "Thou pratest here where thou art least;
> This faith has many a purer priest,
> And many an abler voice than thou.
>
> "Go down beside thy native rill,
> On thy Parnassus set thy feet,
> And hear thy laurel whisper sweet
> About the ledges of the hill."

And my Melpomene replies,
   A touch of shame upon her cheek:
   "I am not worthy ev'n to speak
Of thy prevailing mysteries;

"For I am but an earthly Muse,
   And owning but a little art,
   To lull with song an aching heart,
And render human love his dues;

"But brooding on the dear one dead,
   And all he said of things divine,
   (And dear to me as sacred wine
To dying lips is all he said),

"I murmur'd, as I came along,
   Of comfort clasp'd in truth reveal'd;
   And loiter'd in the master's field,
And darken'd sanctities with song."   (XXXVII)

At its surface the passage disciplines the speaker to the language and decorum of pastoral elegy. At its depths the statement is one of the most profound in Tennyson's poetry. "Give over the effort to speak in Hallam's tongue, with Hallam's strength. Pastoral, not prophecy, is your proper mode." The speaker confesses his artistic and spiritual limitation. He subordinates his powers with respect to those of the dead beloved, chooses English earth as the proper source and domain of his poetry, and thus eschews the prophetic mode of speech which had been his own earliest poetic stance. *In Memoriam* sustains the conventions of pastoral elegy as it innovates within the features of the received tradition. But it is also about, and structured about, the poet's deep ambivalence toward the sources and strengths of his own art.

The speaker's apprehension of pastoral develops, within the fiction of the elegy as arranged for publication in 1850, from the unwilled "I pipe but as the linnets do" of XXI and the rebuke of XXXVI/XXXVII to the rich aubade of LXXXIII and the delayed sweet advent of spring in XC-XCIV. Then, speaking from the garden of Somersby at XCV, the griever at last retrieves the dead beloved's presence, something he seeks throughout the elegy to this point. The night is calm—"the brook alone far-off was heard" (l. 7) —the poet in the company of others to whom old songs come without pain:

> While now we sang old songs that pealed
> From knoll to knoll, where, couched at ease,
> The white kine glimmered, and the trees
> Laid their dark arms about the field. (ll. 13-16)

Such pastoral is sufficient and purposeful, the protective and certain context from which the poet's reach for presence begins. The speaker's "hunger" for the beloved's restoration can be satisfied briefly when the range of pastoral broadens to include the possibility that the beloved's words "renew" as do living forms in nature:

> A hunger seized my heart; I read
> Of that glad year which once had been,
> In those fallen leaves which kept their green,
> The noble letters of the dead. ... (ll. 21-24)

> So word by word, and line by line,
> The dead man touched me from the past,
> And all at once it seemed at last
> The living soul was flashed on mine. ... (ll. 33-36)

Whereas Urania's rebuke in XXXVII separated the language of pastoral from the prophetic language of the dead beloved, XCV permits a new reconciliation between them. Hallam lives in the "word," where word and nature are at one. "Leaves" renew and the "glad year" keeps its color. Given Tennyson's description of the whole poem as a "commedia" beginning with a funeral and ending with a marriage,[16] it is appropriate that critics have described Hallam in this moment as Beatrice to Tennyson's Dante,[17] as divine illumination.[18] It has also been noted that the final lines of XCV echo two of Tennyson's earliest poems,[19] but the significance of that echoing has not been clear. At XCV, 33-43 the speaker achieves Hallam's presence in the elevated language of Tennyson's earliest poetry, language strictly disciplined in favor of pastoral by Urania's rebuke

[16]Hallam Tennyson, *Memoir,* 1, 304-5.
[17]Ward Hellstrom, *On the Poems of Tennyson* (Gainesville, Fla., 1972); and Gordon D. Hirsch, "Tennyson's Commedia," *Victorian Poetry,* 8 (1970)
[18]Cf. Alan Sinfield, "Matter-Moulded Forms of Speech: Tennyson's Use of Language in *In Memoriam,*" in *The Major Victorian Poets: Reconsiderations,* ed. Isobel Armstrong (Lincoln, Neb., 1969), pp. 51-67.
[19]Cf. Arthur J. Carr, *op cit.,* p. 376; and Christopher Ricks, ed., *The Poems of Tennyson* (London, 1969), p. 947, note XCV, 54-55.

at XXXVII. Now memory yields to presence in the colors but not
the wildness of XXXIV, and the sudden flash of Hallam's soul "on
mine" deeply resembles the flash of the Seraph upon the soul of the
human prophet-poet in Tennyson's early poem *Armageddon:*

> So word by word, and line by line,
>   The dead man touched me from the past,
>   And all at once it seemed at last
> The living soul was flashed on mine,
>
> And mine in his was wound, and whirled
>   About empyreal heights of thought,
>   And came on that which is, and caught
> The deep pulsation of the world,
>
> Aeonian music measuring out
>   The steps of Time—the shocks of Chance—
>   The blows of Death.   (ll. 33-43)

Hallam's presence is not reached by abstractions modeled on Hallam's critical and theological writing, but in the context of landscape and by the evocative power of the dead man's written words.
The importance of this moment cannot be missed in terms of a reading of Tennyson's early poetry, for these lines couch the poet's young
aspiration in a new and personal form; indeed that aspiration is given
to us as the first stage of the *peripeteia* upon which the resolution
of the whole elegy is to be based. The poet's desire for the beloved
merges with his desire to reattain the immediacy of early inspiration. What has changed is the landscape of pain the speaker
traverses in his quest for vision.

That vision is tragically momentary. Joy ceases abruptly as did
the speaker's joy in Tennyson's early account of the meeting between
prophet and Seraph, struck through by an internal doubt:

> At length my trance
> Was cancelled, stricken through with doubt.   (ll. 43-44)

"Presence" dies as dreams do in the tragedy of waking, a second,
characteristic pattern of Tennyson's earliest verse. His vision "can-
celled," the speaker's eyes turn gradually outward to the white kine
and the embrace of trees in a pastoral dawn:

> Vague words! but ah, how hard to frame
>   In matter-moulded forms of speech,
>   Or even for intellect to reach

Through memory that which I became:

Till now the doubtful dusk revealed
    The knolls once more where, couched at ease,
    The white kine glimmered, and the trees
Laid their dark arms about the field:

And sucked from out the distant gloom
    A breeze began to tremble o'er
    The large leaves of the sycamore,
And fluctuate all the still perfume,

And gathering freshlier overhead,
    Rocked the full-foliaged elms, and swung
    The heavy-folded rose, and flung
The lilies to and fro, and said

"The dawn, the dawn," and died away.   (ll. 45-61)

Tennyson adopts these lines from another early poem, *In Deep and Solemn Dreams,* in which dreamed visions of the heavenly city and of pastoral joy are both lost at dawn, stricken through by doubts (imaged by silent sea and whirlwind) which rise within the dreamer's (that is the speaker's) sleeping brain. The lines quoted above are adopted from the second dream of *In Deep and Solemn Dreams,* with the critical difference that the tragedy of waking to loss is gone. At *In Memoriam* XCV the speaker need not beg his "brothers" to "keep the sacred charm" of sleep,[20] for this version of pastoral is one of waking beyond dream. Immediate "presence" is not to be sustained. The speaker will know the beloved within nature directly perceived, and in a "kinship" he asserts between nature's green and the constant revision of poetic language. The resolution of grief in the dawn of XCV is a resolution of opposed tropes in Tennyson's poetry as well as a perfection of pastoral form. At the end of XCV there is no division between life and death, the apocalyptic colors of the West and the rosy promise of the East. The speaker attains knowledge of earthly horizons and their fruitful obliteration:

[20]Yet a little, brothers, keep
    The sacred charm of tearless sleep—
    Oh unkind! What darkening change
    Hath made your features dim and strange!

Dear lips, loved eyes, ye fade, ye fly,
    Even in my fear ye die,
    And the hollow dark I dread
    Closes round my friendless head.   (ll. 53-60)

>   And East and West, without a breath,
>   Mixt their dim lights, like life and death,
>   To broaden into boundless day.   (ll. 62-64)

In Memoriam XCV affirms Urania's critique in XXXVII but with joy. The poet's knowledge is not Hallam's, but Hallam — example of prophetic inspiration — is immanent in memory, place, and language. He is to be known through the animating 'motion of the breeze that affirms the goal of his aesthetic — that sense and emotion cohere in images which can be read. Subtly Tennyson unites his own poetics with the values expressed by Hallam in his essay for the *Englishman's Magazine* of 1831: at this dawn there is no simple "mingling" of lights but their mixture, their fusion. In these special terms Tennyson achieves his own version of the moment of romantic illumination and makes an artifact that recreates the moment for the attentive reader. He defines the relations between the language of *Armageddon* and that of *In Deep and Solemn Dreams,* those seminal early formulations of the poetic act, formulations Tennyson set at the core of every major poem he was to write.

The reconsideration of the language of early poems, the sequence of visions achieved and released at *In Memoriam* XCV, permits the elegist's turn from grief to the world. This is marked by a move away from Somersby and the landscape in which one hears the "native rill" to places that do not so easily demand or evoke the details of memory. In the passage from XCV to CIII a profound alteration of voice occurs, marked especially in CIII which, by contrast with XCV, the first turning point of the elegy, is to be read as a parable about art. *In Memoriam* CIII is presented as a dream, a dream which gives the poet sufficient comfort and courage to leave the landscape of home. Begun in a setting which recalls the features of Tennyson's poems of art written in the early 1830's, the landscape of *The Lady of Shalott* and *The Palace of Art,*[21] the dream becomes a vision epic in its aspirations, tinged by the colors of apocalypse. The poet, accompanied by veiled ladies, goes out upon a river as the Lady of Shalott once did. The figures of the dream grow to epic proportions as the speaker attains the embrace of the beloved on a ship which rests at the border of land and sea. The significance of the enlargement is obvious enough. It fulfills a promise given at the end of *In Memoriam* LXIII: "Abide a little longer here,/ And thou shalt take a nobler leave." It serves as justification for a shift

[21]Cf. Carr, p. 377.

from pastoral to epic modes, a shift that was to issue, historically, in *Idylls of the King*. I would claim further that its placement in the published elegy is consistent with principles of revision that govern the whole work. It can be shown that poems about art written comparatively late in the history of *In Memoriam*'s composition were deliberately placed in the finished whole to permit an overlying discussion of art to govern the arrangement of poems. CIII formally marks a shift from grief to promise, from tears to heroic energies, in the elegy's fiction. Parable is an alternate formulation of the relations between vision and dream given at XCV. It notes the possibilities for narrative in Tennyson's work; it is a "representation" of meaning rather than its confession.

At the end of *The Lady of Shalott* the singer, having seen Lancelot in her mirror, goes out upon the river at day's end and in autumn, white-robed against the colors of sunset. For her to go out upon the river is to die, and to die singing. Not only does the weaver-singer die outside the protective towers of artistic isolation, she *forms* her death in doing so, making a visual representation of her meaning. A "fairy"—or romance—voice at the beginning of the poem, she becomes a "seer" or prophet as she moves, her words and their meaning inaccessible to those who hear her from the riverbank. By the time she reaches Camelot she is an artifact of herself, a visual icon of the song that can no longer be heard. All that remains of the voice and its history is the colorful representation the singer has made. *The Lady of Shalott* is, among other things, about the nature and limits of artistic representation. It views the poem as the sign of the voice. At *In Memoriam* CIII this despairing image of river and representation receives a more affirmative interpretation. Now the exodus from subjective and private song to public speech is but a movement toward the embrace of the beloved, a justifiable transition from lyric to prophetic and epic modes.

It should be clear, then, that *In Memoriam* is not only a tribute to Hallam and a recreation of the conventions of pastoral elegy, but an account of development within the poet's voice. That account issues in the complex linguistic reconciliations which occur in the final sections of *In Memoriam* as arranged for publication in 1850 —especially CXVIII, CXXVII, and the sequence from CXXIX to the Epilogue, where single tropes serve many purposes. So at CXXVI it is the "tempered" spirit, born like the earth itself of fire and bathed in "hissing" tears, that represents the maturing poetic voice. The trope of geological change includes reference to Hallam's critical writing and early poetry as well as to the speaker's strong need for a separate voice.[22] So at CXXIX/CXXX the poet who passionately recognized the limits of sudden illumination at XCV evokes Hallam for the last time with renewed reference to poetry of vision (reference as in XCV to the Seraph of *Armageddon*) and the intimacy of dream (coined from a reference to *In Deep and Solemn Dreams*).[23] When the speaker turns away from his work in the Epilogue, casting himself as surrogate father for a bride and predicting the birth of a child, his feet stand firmly upon the surface of graves, his hands bless a living union, and his mind looks to a visionary last event. He prophesies from within the human frame, himself the "body" of his representation.

For Tennyson the issue of proper voice was considered only secondarily in terms of the differences among pastoral, romance, and epic modes. From the beginning of his career the desire for prophetic strength coincided with his choice of private poetic forms that were ultimately to underlie traditional genres in his major poems. Indeed a partial misunderstanding of Tennyson's commitment to prophecy has lain at the heart of twentieth-century Tennyson criticism and its habits of excision and judgment. For Tennyson the essential contrasts between lyric and prophecy, attraction to the past and commitment to the present, came to determine the structure of major poems less in terms of the abstract notions "lyric" and "prophetic," "past" and "present," "memory" and "hope," than in terms of the actions of certain early poems treated and re-treated across time. Those actions reflect major differences in poetic voice. They predict the course of a poem's argument more certainly than does its narrative surface. The earliest poems were characterized by patterns of coming and departure, dream and walking, a troubled relation between word and deed, and a sense of limitation and loss. Tennyson's *personae* speak in memory or anticipation; they are

[22]With CXVIII compare Ricks' commentary on CXXVII (*The Poems of Tennyson*, pp. 976-77) and its reference to Hallam's *A Farewell to the South* and *The Influence of Italian upon English Literature* (both printed in T. Vail Motter, ed., *The Writings of Arthur Hallam* [London, 1943]).

[23]Compare CXXIX, 5-12 with the visions of *In Deep and Solemn Dreams* and CXXX, 1-4, 13-16 with the Seraph and his reinterpretation in *Timbuctoo*. For an account of apocalypse and dream in Tennyson's early poems *Armageddon* and *Timbuctoo*, see David Goslee, "Spatial and Temporal Vision in Early Tennyson," *Victorian Poetry*, 11 (1973), 323-29.

creatures of absence, not presence. As I have tried to show in the brief commentary on *In Memoriam* above, these patterns of the earliest poetry have the force of private "genres." They interact with Tennyson's ability to make rich surfaces, his apprehension of generic traditions, and his concern for contemporary social and literary issues. Tennyson's major poems are only at their narrative level linear in structure. In terms of the history of their composition and their habits of statement and style, *The Princess, In Memoriam, Maud,* and *Idylls of the King* are all palimpsests. Each of Tennyson's major poems marks a stage in the self-conscious and self-consciously portrayed history of a poet's voice. The details of that history are still to be fully understood.

Much that has been written about Tennyson during the last fifteen years sharpens and simplifies earlier critical assessments, but many questions remain. What was the "picture" for Tennyson as a visual image and abstract representation? What is the rhetoric of Tennyson's public forms in relation to public forms of discourse in his own day? What is the nature of poetic structures made by accretion and superimposition rather than by linear compositional techniques? What was the force of Tennyson's poetry as a model for contemporary artists in his own and other media? How did Tennyson's practice encourage the development of small "genres" in the art and literature of the late century?

Throughout his career Tennyson sought power. Despite the complexity of some of his works, he also sought simplicity and the ability to live in a constantly moving and tangible present undeterred by regret for the past or longing for future joy. Mediating the claims of weaver, singer, dreamer, and bard upon his art, his goal was at last the middle voice, best sign of the tempered spirit. This we recognize and heed in his work, in the poems that express it directly, and in those which reach toward it in less than perfect form.

Rites of Passage:
"The Lady of Shalott" and "The Lotos-Eaters"

by W. David Shaw

The qualities that Sir Henry Taylor[1] criticizes in Romantic poetry are exactly the qualities that Arthur Hallam praises in his review of Tennyson's *Poems, Chiefly Lyrical* of 1830.[2] In poets of "sensation" like Tennyson and Keats, as distinguished from a "reflective" poet like Wordsworth, Hallam praises the ability to live "in a world of images" and to make poetry a means of escape from the impermanence of life. Hallam fails to observe that even in these early poems Tennyson seldom records his sensations without refracting and refining them or without expressing, like Keats himself and Tennyson's Victorian contemporary Taylor, an inability to disengage himself completely from the "agonies, the strife/ Of human hearts" ("Sleep and Poetry," 11. 124-125). Just as the early Victorian age is torn between a Philistine worship of facts and a Romantic pursuit of beauty, so Tennyson wavers between his impulse to write poems of pure sensation, such as "Recollections of the Arabian Nights," and his impulse to test and enlarge his poetry. He writes his way out of the Romantic into the new Victorian age, just as Yeats, sixty years later, writes his way out of the nineteenth into the

[1]Preface to *Philip Van Artevelde* (London, 1834). This important document of literary history is reprinted in *Victorian Poetry and Poetics,* ed. W. E. Houghton and Robert Stange (Boston, 1968), pp. 861-865.

[2]"On Some of the Characteristics of Modern Poetry and on the Lyrical Poems of Alfred Tennyson," *Englishman's Magazine* (August 1831); reprinted in *Victorian Poetry and Poetics,* ed. Houghton and Stange, pp. 848-860. The distinction between ideas of sensation and ideas of reflection originates in Book II, chapter vii, of John Locke's *Essay Concerning Human Understanding* (1690).

twentieth century. Even as a poet of sensation the young Tennyson anticipates, like Yeats, a return from the autonomous Romantic "world of images" to a world of quick, unpredictable decay or change and the claims of the human heart.

The fear that poetry will yield to empiricism and technology is typically Victorian. The idea appears in Thomas Love Peacock's anti-Romantic manifesto, *The Four Ages of Poetry* (1820), and, most notably, in Macaulay's *Essay on Milton* (1825). For Macaulay the conflict between poetry and science raises the question, not merely of poetic decline, but of poetic survival. Tennyson knows that every transition of the spirit of poetry into a new age and place may also mean the death of poetry. As a poet of transition he succeeds in adapting his Romantic heritage only when he presents his sensations as half-seen shapes and wavering forms. Tennyson is a poet of the not-quite-living and the not-yet-perished. He leaves many of his speakers poised at transitional moments, suspended like Tithonus between heaven and earth. Ulysses is about to sail to his death; Menoeceus, in "Tiresias," is to be fed to the dragons; and the souls of saints and suicides—St. Simeon, St. Agnes, and the crazed Lucretius—are about to rise into heaven, or alternatively, "fly out...in the air" ("Lucretius," 1. 273) and perish there. Transition is a recurrent fascination of Tennyson. Cultural transition is also what the *Poems, Chiefly Lyrical* of 1830 and the *Poems* of 1832 typify in the literary history of the age. They mark the same type of transition at the beginning of the period that Yeats's volumes of 1899 and 1904 mark at its end. ...

"The Lady of Shalott" may be analyzed, like many popular ballads, as a metaphor without a tenor, as a symbol which speaks for itself. The poem tells a story: a lady grown tired of shadows leaves her tower, but on entering the world she is destroyed. At a more abstract level, the poem is about thwarted transition: the failure to develop a merely potential existence into an actual one. It sings of the irreversible departure from the mysterious lure of beauty and shadows, and the process of becoming vulnerable and human. Each reader will experience the poem at his own level of experience or at several levels. The poem is like a stone thrown into a pond, causing ever widening circles of meaning to go out from the center.

How does Tennyson hint of significance and make his narrative mean more than it says? Answers can be found in a study of his revisions. In the 1832 version the poet of sensation could not resist a complete account of the Lady's wardrobe. She wears a "cloudwhite crown of pearl" (1. 126), and after her death she is described, starkly, as a "corpse" (1. 156). The scenario is bizarre. In revising his poem Tennyson never allows the Lady to assume an individualized form. As James Spedding notes in a contemporary review, she is "stript of all her finery."[3] She moves into the background and becomes a figure of mystery — both a spirit and a human being, but not quite either. Also, in the 1842 version, the strict separation of the sensuous world of Sir Lancelot from the wan world of the Lady gives symbolic force to their final, fatal commingling. In revising, the poet of sensation gains a compression of substance that amounts to a fact of form. In his new form he discovers a tenor for his metaphor. He still speaks through a concrete representation, but he speaks also to and for our common humanity, and for something universal.

A popular ballad like "Sir Patrick Spens" commemorates a public event. But the values of Tennyson's heroine are too intrinsic for publicity. A source of major pathos in the poem is that its significant truths are all private truths. In the end the Lady is alone; and her poem, like her life, never tells more than half. The poem's mixture of lyric and ballad forms has therefore less in common with a popular ballad, or even with Wordsworth's *Lyrical Ballads,* than it has with Blake's parable "The Book of Thel." Working in harmony with this parabolic form, with this metaphor without a tenor, is the mystery of the mirror. In the 1832 version the mirror was an incidental feature of the Lady's surroundings, no more important than the tinkling sheep bell. In the 1842 version the mirror moves to the head of the stanza, and a long, colorful procession of churls and abbots is reflected from its surface. The tapestry the Lady weaves is a reflection of reflections; if the Lady is at one remove from the world, her art is at two removes. The Lady's mirror also reflects the knight's reflection in another mirror — the river (ll. 105-6).

The unstable world of mirrors, which breaks apart solid sensation, is rendered even more unstable by the wavering grammar. The fifth stanza abounds in hypothetical clauses and subjunctives: "If she stay," "the curse may be"; and in syntactic uncertainty: "if she stay/ To look down to Camelot" (ll. 40-41). Does "stay" mean "remain" or "refrain from"? From certainty to probability, from past to present

[3]*Edinburgh Review* (April, 1843); quoted by Hallam Tennyson, in *Tennyson: A Memoir,* I (London, 1897), 191.

tense, the fluidity of mood in Part II commits Tennyson to nothing but hypotheses. If Tennyson were to keep the past tense, such a construction would imply that the actions had been completed and their results known. But the pervasive mingling of tenses implies that the results of past events are not yet known. The pathos of the questions—"But who hath seen her wave her hand?/ Or at the casement seen her stand?/ Or is she known in all the land?" (ll. 24-26) and "Who is this? and what is here?" (l. 163)—comes not only from the constraint and wishful yearning but also from the incongruity between the phrases "known in all the land" and the harshly empirical "what is here?" W. H. Empson analyzes the first set of questions as an example of sixth-order ambiguity: "The poet poses questions whose answers are both yes and no. ...[The Lady] is not known personally to anybody in the land, but everybody knows she is a legend."[4] The Lady's personal history and meaning, even though they imply obligations and fates of an interior kind, are never safe from questions. The inquisition of innocence makes the whole poem tend toward incongruity and pathos.

Though Tennyson's form is enigmatic, the conclusiveness of the poem's conclusion seems predetermined. "The Lady of Shalott" is a fated and, in a sense, a suicidal poem. The self-imposed poverty of its rhyme words ("lie," "rye," "sky," "by," for example [ll. 1-4]), their diminution in number from four to three ("go," "blow," "below" [ll. 6-8]), to two ("Camelot," "Shalott" [ll. 5, 9]); the quick descent of each stanza to the stability of the refrain—all these features are designed to secure the conclusiveness of the outcome. The separation of private and public worlds in the first three parts seems fated to will, in a destructive commingling of these worlds in Part IV, the suicidal completion of the poem's design. All the energy of Tennyson's parable is directed toward its own termination. The Lady's cry "The curse is come upon me" (l. 116) echoes the shriek of Blake's Thel. The Lady's shriek is that of "the disappearing ghost or the uprooted mandrake," as Northrop Frye observes of Blake's heroine; "and her tragedy could be anything from a miscarriage to a lost vision."[5] By concealing his meaning elliptically in a narrative form, Tennyson the poet of sensation is able, not merely to describe a special fate, not merely to tell a story of unrequited love like "Lancelot and Elaine," but to give a general representation of the

[4]*Seven Types of Ambiguity* (London, 1932), p. 182.
[5]*Fearful Symmetry: A Study of William Blake* (Princeton, 1947), p. 233.

process of dying into nature, of trying to acquire a stable human form. Tennyson is engaged in a lifelong search for stable identity. Renouncing the mysterious lure of a beautiful realm, a shadow world of "negative capability," Tennyson is fully aware that a death of the imagination such as Wordsworth suffered is the price the poet may have to pay for trying, like the Lady of Shalott, to make his world human. The memorial of Tennyson's poet might well be the epitaph of Wordsworth's "Elegiac Stanzas": "A power is gone, which nothing can restore;/ A deep distress hath humanized my Soul" (ll. 35-36).

Nowhere is the young Tennyson's ability to refine sensation, refracting it through thought, better demonstrated than in "The Lotos-Eaters." Whereas "The Lady of Shalott" presents the failure to carry alive the imagination of innocence into the stable forms of nature, "The Lotos-Eaters" illustrates the opposite problem: the failure to take the lessons of the wavering world outside, the world of quick decay and change, back into the timeless land of lotos. There are two rites of passage in the poem: one explicit, and the other merely proleptic, or ironically foreshadowed. The first rite occurs when Ulysses' men discover the essential anguish of being in time—the torment of "ever climbing up the climbing wave" (l. 95)— and they decide to escape into a changeless world. But lotos land is not paradise. It is to the garden in *Maud* what Blake's Ulro is to Beulah: its satisfactions are enervating and narcotic. The mariners will have to undergo a second rite of passage by returning to their oars; there is no refuge from what Yeats calls the "murderous innocence of the sea" ("A Prayer for My Daughter," l. 16).

In the proem of "The Lotos-Eaters," as mid-morning aspects of the world deepen into half-lights and shades, Tennyson dwells on forms that are tremulous and enigmatic. He qualifies his assertions by repeating "seemed," the verb of illusion, six times—twice in its emphatic form, "did seem" (ll. 9, 32). He also stresses the qualifications by once shifting the accent to the second syllable—"seemed" (l. 4)—and by once using the verb at the end of the alexandrine, the position of greatest prominence (l. 9). Most of the other verbs are in the past tense, as if to consign the mariners to legendary time. When infinitives such as "fall and pause and fall," or "mourn and rave," momentarily replace these verbs, any impression of timelessness is carefully qualified by the use of the illusory "seemed." Though the drift is from the less certain to the more certain, Tennyson blunts the force of the concluding "will," in both the proem and the song—"we will no longer roam" (l. 45); "we will not wander more" (l. 173)—by playing off these volitional forms against Ulysses' opening use of the simple future tense: "will roll us shoreward soon" (l. 2). Ulysses' commanding future, ringing through the rest of the poem, presents the beauties of lotos land as of unreal duration, as a fracture in the midst of normal life. As Bagehot notes, "Illusion, half belief...are as much the proper sphere of ornate art, as an inferior landscape is the proper sphere for the true efficacy of moonlight." The half-lights of lotos land are a great "equaliser of beauties."[6] They win temporary credence for premises and moods that could not survive severer light.

One of the marvels of "The Lotos-Eaters" is the way the chorus, no less than the proem, foreshadows the mariners' return to sea even as it celebrates their life on land. To show that the mariners are temperamentally unsuited to a life of ease the poem presents a paradox: if inhabitants of lotos land are incapable of action, how can they be roused to sing their hymn? How can they muster enough energy to celebrate even their own lack of energy in a choric song? The mariners' analytic intelligence is constantly at work; their rhetorical skill denotes an intellectual power that could never be exercised if the "land of streams" had already been possessed as their rightful home. Since the mariners know they must return to sea, where they will be torn to pieces by the gods they are indicting, their torment turns their blasphemy into a heroic enterprise, combining the grand cosmology of Lucretius' *De rerum natura* with the introspective "heresies" of the Book of Job. In their cosmological vision of the "Gods together, careless of mankind" (l. 155) the lotos-eaters pervert the traditional religious yearning for divine union. Their oath of renunciation is a parody of religious ritual, substituting for a community of believers a conspiracy of hedonists. And what begins as a prayer of praise and thanksgiving for the pleasures of mankind ends as a denunciation of man's "endless anguish" (l. 169).

The irony of an argument that loses direction reminds the reader that there is no refuge in lotos land from the fear of welter, from the fear of quick, unpredictable decay and change. Because the Choric Song is polemical as well as lyric, it reinstates the rational imagination, and it reaffirms the assertive, unstilled desires of the human heart, in ways that a pure lyric could never do. The even-numbered stanzas refract through thought the very sensations that the odd-numbered stanzas celebrate. Dislodged accents and explosive con-

[6]*Literary Studies*, ed. R. H. Hutton, II (London, 1898), 374-375.

sonants stumble over strongly marked caesuras; the t
even-numbered stanzas is fretful and agitated. A syntax o.
participles and of impersonal constructions creates a sense o
weighed upon and oppressed. But there is also an active, more
sonal syntax in the poem. Unlike the verbs of the proem—the in-
transitive "came," "did go," and the reflexive "sat them down"—the
verbs of the chorus call for active human subjects—"toil," "ever
climbing," "cleave"—and for value words—"let us swear." Qualify-
ing the general passivity are transitive verbs like "give" and "lend,"
which demote lotos land's narcotics, the subject of most of the sen-
tences in the proem, to the tertiary status of indirect objects. The
succession of adjectives—"mild-eyed melancholy Lotos-eaters"
(l. 27)—which originally muffle a human subject in a blanket of
alliterating sounds turns in the chorus into the phrase "of mild-
minded melancholy," which modifies the indirect object of an infinitive of active choice: "To lend our hearts and spirits wholly/ To the
influence of mild-minded melancholy" (ll. 108-109). The effect is not
to drug the lotos-eaters, as it is in the proem, but to intensify their
action. This syntax gives the impression of assertiveness and force.
The actors are not weak, as the original grammar affirms, but strong
for the struggle.

Ironically, just as the mariners are drifting back to dreamy meditation, their rhetorical energy begins to contradict their stated goal
of withdrawing into an artificial paradise. To relieve the horror of
existing in a present without duration, the lotos-eaters develop the
coda's long epic simile, in which they continue to acquire divinity
(ll. 155-170). For the gods there is also, traditionally, no past or
future. But as the analogy carries them away, it gradually changes
direction. The illusion of the mariners' union with the gods becomes
the certainty of separation; and the simile ends, not with a reassuring
analogy between the lotos-eaters and the gods, but with a disturbing
contrast. The simile finally opposes the cruel indifference of the
gods to the struggles, not just of the lotos-eaters, but of all mankind.
The logical reversal is signaled, not simply by the initiation of a
pattern of triple rhymes: "we," "free," "sea" (ll. 150-152), but also by
the syntactic device of starting and ending line 150 with the same
word. For the first time in the chorus the passivity of undirected
"motion" is "framed" and controlled by active subjects: "*We* have
had enough of action, and of motion *we* " (l. 150—my italics). What
begins in comfortable complacency, like Browning's Johannes Agri-

cola in Meditation," ends with the angry protest of his Caliban or the biblical Job. For mariners who have had "enough...of motion" the heroic blasphemies of the final version are deftly ironic; and to my mind, the blandness of the gods at the beginning of the simile provides the "subtly apt" counterpoint to rant that Christopher Ricks finds lacking.[7] Instead of being crudely anticlimactic, the weakly repetitive "Surely, surely" (l. 171) points the reader beyond the poem. It dramatizes a desperate effort to create certainty where only uncertainty exists.

The long epic simile combines with a striking shift in rhythm to dramatize the main irony in the poem: "like Gods together.../ Till they perish and they suffer—some, 'tis whispered—down in hell" (ll. 155, 168). In their simile the mariners do not come out where they have planned, and it is clear from the beginning that they will not remain in lotos land, as they have planned. Because of this reversal the outcome of the poem, though predestined from Ulysses' first staccato words—"'Courage!' he said,.../ This mounting wave will roll us shoreward soon' " (ll. 1-2)—is also unforeseen. The poem is not a trick poem that saves its best thought for the end. As Robert Frost would say, it is "a series of revelations, as much for the poet as for the reader."[8] Step by step, as the wonder of unexpected discovery keeps growing, the mariners come to realize that their impulse to emulate the gods is servile and self-hypnotic. The sensitivity of the soul is an unpardonable blot upon the hedonists' scheme, and for their philosophy an unexplained enigma. Like disappointed and rebellious children, the lotos-eaters are citics of their parent, Nature. Because they see, like T. H. Huxley, that cosmic nature is "no school of virtue, but the headquarters of the enemy,"[9] they judge the morals of its gods to be detestable. Their thrill of discovery is the surprise of remembering something they are not aware they know. Like the poem which is "a series of revelations," the Choric Song is always hurling insight ahead of the lotos-eaters so that they may strike new lines of purpose across it. Ironically, the last verb of a

[7] *Tennyson* (New York, 1972), p. 91.

[8] "The Figure a Poem Makes," in *Selected Prose of Robert Frost,* ed. H. Cox and E. Lathem (New York, 1968), p. 19.

[9] T. H. Huxley, "Evolution and Ethics," in *"Evolution and Ethics" and Other Essays,* ch. ii (New York, 1897), p. 75: "The pertinacious optimism of our philosophers hid from them the actual state of the case. It prevented them from seeing that cosmic nature is no school of virtue, but the headquarters of the enemy of ethical nature."

poem that renounces all volition is introduced by an auxiliary of volition: "we *will* not wander more" (my italics). The lotos-eaters will leave lotos land, not because they are too weak to keep their oath, but because they are too strong. The desire to become gods is unworthy of them.

Tennyson: In the Shadow of Keats

by Harold Bloom

Freud, in his essay on "Repression" (1915), says that psycho-analysis shows us:

> ...that the instinct-presentation develops in a more unchecked and luxuriant fashion if it is withdrawn by repression from conscious influence. It ramifies like a fungus, so to speak, in the dark and takes on extreme forms of expression, which when translated and revealed to the neurotic are bound not merely to seem alien to him, but to terrify him by the way in which they reflect an extraordinary and dangerous strength of instinct. This illusory strength of instinct is the result of an uninhibited development of it in phantasy and of the damming-up consequent on lack of real satisfaction.

Freud emphasized that repression manifested itself particularly in hysteria, but added that it could be observed in "normal" psychology also. Any definition of Freud's notion of "repression" should make clear that what is repressed is not an instinctual drive or desire, but rather the representation of it *in an image*. The repressed image is not wholly confined to the unconscious. However, some aspect of it is, an aspect which distorts, expands, intensifies the aspect still apparent in consciousness. Freud began by using "repression" and "defense" as though they were synonyms, but defense was necessarily always the wider term. Yet, of all the defenses, repression is most sharply differentiated from the others, and again it is the most elaborate of the defenses, being a three-phased process:

1. Primal Repression, directed against representations, but not against the instinct that remains fixated to the representations.

2. Repression proper, which Freud calls "after-pressure."

3. The Return of the Repressed, as dream, or symptom, or lapse in speech or behavior.

Since only representations or images can be repressed, but not desire or drive, we can wonder what motives Freud could ascribe to repression? There can be no repression unless the image threatens unpleasure, Freud insists. We approach therefore, particularly in the context of poetry, a fundamental question, which is doubtless fundamental for psychoanalysis also, but that is not *our* concern. Why must the ego be defended from the representations of its *own* desires? Whatever the answer is in a psychoanalytic context (and Freud is evasive in this area), I am certain that in the context of poetry the answer has to do with the anxiety of influence. The representations that rise up from the id are not wholly the ego's own, and this menaces the poetic ego. For the precursor poem has been absorbed as impulse rather than as event, and the internalized precursor thus rises, or seems to rise, against the ego from what appear to be the alienated representations of the id. It is in this strange area of identity-and-opposition that unpleasure in one's own images becomes a burden for the poetic ego, a burden that provokes defense, which in poetry means misprision, or the trope as a misreading of anteriority.

This essay is to be a discourse on Tennyson and not on Freud, however analogically, and yet I want to keep us in the gray area where poetry and psychoanalysis compete, for a while longer. My concern will be with Tennyson's revisionist genius for internalizing Keats, a process we might have thought impossible but for Tennyson's incredible rhetorical skill. That particular act of revisionary genius, on Tennyson's part, changed poetic history, for it was Tennyson's transformation of Keats that was the largest single factor in British and American poetry from about 1830 until about 1915. I am thinking not only of such various literary phenomena as the Pre-Raphaelites, Pater, aspects of Yeats, and of Wilfred Owen and other Georgians, and Trumbull Stickney and the early Stevens in America, but of hidden, crucial influences such as that of Tennyson on Whitman, and then of Tennyson and Whitman together upon Eliot. ...

...Tennyson was surely one of the most sublimely repressed poets in the language. It is no accident that Tennyson, like his precursor Keats, and like their common ancestor, Spenser, is one of the three most authentically erotic poets in the language. I commence with a marvelous poem of enormous erotic repression, *Mariana,* where I will ask: What does this erotic repression itself repress? Let us recall Freud's profound theory of desire, which speculates that desire always tries to bring about an identity between a present state of nonsatisfaction, and a past state that is recalled as satisfaction, whether truly it was that or not. I am afraid that Freud implies that what desire desires is desire, which means that desire never can be satisfied. On Freud's view, the unconscious component in desire dooms all erotic quests to the worst kind of repetition. Tennyson was the peculiar master of this insight, and I suggest now that Tennyson's mastery in this regard came out of a beautiful misprision of Keats. With all this as prologue, I come at last to the superb *Mariana,* a genuine perfection of strong poetry, and a work as genuinely alarming in its deepest implications as are even the darkest speculations of Freud.

The "sources," in a conventional sense, of *Mariana* are traditionally and rightly held to include Keats, particularly his rather dreary poem *Isabella,* which the young Tennyson loved rather more than anyone else has since. Here are stanzas XXX through XXXIV of *Isabella:*

> She weeps alone for pleasures not to be;
> 　Sorely she wept until the night came on,
> And then, instead of love, O misery!
> 　She brooded o'er the luxury alone:
> His image in the dusk she seem'd to see,
> 　And to the silence made a gentle moan,
> Spreading her perfect arms upon the air,
> And on her couch low murmuring, "Where? O where?"
>
> But Selfishness, Love's cousin, held not long
> 　Its fiery vigil in her single breast;
> She fretted for the golden hour, and hung
> 　Upon the time with feverish unrest—
> Not long—for soon into her heart a throng
> 　Of higher occupants, a richer zest,
> Came tragic; passion not to be subdued,
> And sorrow for her love in travels rude.
>
> In the mid days of autumn, on their eves
> 　The breath of Winter comes from far away,
> And the sick west continually bereaves
> 　Of some gold tinge, and plays a roundelay
> Of death among the bushes and the leaves,

To make all bare before he dares to stray
From his north cavern. So sweet Isabel
By gradual decay from beauty fell,

Because Lorenzo came not. Oftentimes
    She ask'd her brothers, with an eye all pale,
Striving to be itself, what dungeon climes
    Could keep him off so long? They spake a tale
Time after time, to quiet her. Their crimes
    Came on them, like a smoke from Hinnom's vale;
And every night in dreams they groan'd aloud,
To see their sister in her snowy shroud.

And she had died in drowsy ignorance,
    But for a thing more deadly dark than all;
It came like a fierce potion, drunk by chance,
    Which saves a sick man from the feather'd pall
For some few gasping moments; like a lance,
    Waking an Indian from his cloudy hall
With cruel pierce, and bringing him again
Sense of the gnawing fire at heart and brain.

Keats's distressed lady is waiting for a murdered man; Shakespeare's
Mariana is waiting for a deceiver, who has no intention of arriving.
All that Tennyson really wants from *Measure for Measure* is that
moated grange; we *know,* all through the poem *Mariana,* that her
lover *could* not arrive, even if he willed to, and that what reverberates in Tennyson's ear are a few lines from *Isabella:* "She weeps
alone for pleasures not to be;/ Sorely she wept until the night came
on.../ And so she pined, and so she died forlorn." Besides Keats,
Virgil is the presence almost always haunting Tennyson, and somewhere in the background we see Dido resolving to die, and hear the
ominous line: "She is weary of glancing at the curve of heaven"
(Aeneid IV, 451). But these "sources" have little to do with the truly
deep or repressed literary anxieties of the poem *Mariana,* just as
the tags from Keats scattered through are essentially ornamental
allusions ("athwart the glooming flats," line 20, goes back to
"athwart the gloom" of *Sleep and Poetry,* line 146, while "Upon the
middle of the night" suggests "Upon the honeyed middle of the
night" in *The Eve of St. Agnes,* line 49). Such echoes, as I keep saying, are not matters of poetic influence, nor is style much the issue
either. A profound ambivalence towards Keats's influence is the true

subject of Tennyson's poem and the rich repression that fascinates
the reader throughout is part of the defensive pattern of misprision
clearly at work in the poem. To get at that pattern, we need ask only:
why does this poem fascinate so much, what makes it as strong and
memorable as it is, why is it so important a poem? Important it
certainly is; as much as any poem, it can be said to have invented
that whole mode of poetry which in the next generation was called,
so very oddly, Pre-Raphaelitism. What is the new, uncanny element
that we hear in Tennyson's first stanza?

> With blackest moss the flower-plots
>   Were thickly crusted, one and all:
> The rusted nails fell from the knots
>   That held the pear to the gable-wall.
> The broken sheds looked sad and strange:
>   Unlifted was the clinking latch;
>   Weeded and worn the ancient thatch
> Upon the lonely moated grange.
>   She only said, "My life is dreary,
>   He cometh not," she said;
>   She said, "I am aweary, aweary,
>   I would that I were dead!"

There are the naturalistic particularities of Keats, as globed and
tactile as they are in the ode *To Autumn,* yet we are troubled by the
impression that what we confront is not nature, but phantasmagoria,
imagery of absence despite the apparent imagery of presence. The
troublesomeness comes from a sense of excess, from a kind of imagery of limitation that seems to withdraw meaning even as it thickly
encrusts meaning. The rusted nails appear no more nor less a morbid growth than the moss does, and the overwhelming impression of
absence seems irreversible. We are drawn into an internalization that
has brought phantasmagoria very close, yet the language gives such
pleasure, such a frustrate ripeness, that we are anything but sorry
to be so drawn. We have here, I think, a kind of catachresis imposed
upon a rhetorical irony, or psychically Tennyson's reaction-formation to the fascination that Keats had for him.

Catachresis is not so much a trope in itself as it is an abuse of the
other tropes. It is a kind of tautology to speak of a "false figure,"
since all figures are necessarily false, but a catachresis, skillfully
used, is a subtly imperfect trope, or a peculiarly extended trope, or a
forced one. Derrida seems to suggest that all philosophical tropes

are catachreses; Tennyson is not a philosophical poet, but he is peculiarly conscious of his own poetic belatedness from the start, and his rhetorical resources were enormous. In one sense, the whole poem of *Mariana* is an exquisite catachresis of Keats's own modification of the Wordsworthian crisis-poem, but we will come to that sense later. First, let us break from the sequence of *Mariana,* so as to consider its seventh and last stanza:

> The sparrow's chirrup on the roof,
> The slow clock ticking, and the sound
> Which to the wooing wind aloof
> The poplar made, did all confound
> Her sense; but most she loathed the hour
> When the thick-moted sunbeam lay
> Athwart the chambers, and the day
> Was sloping toward his western bower.
> Then, said she, "I am very dreary,
> He will not come," she said;
> She wept, "I am aweary, aweary,
> Oh God, that I were dead!"

This stanza is manifestly obsessed with time, and indeed with belatedness. But what kind of belatedness is this, erotic or poetic? If there is any validity at all to my theory of misprision, then sexual anguish, in a belated poetic text, would be, frequently, a mask for influence-anxiety, if only because an erotic blocking-agent, if it is to be handled by a poem, must be treated as though it also was a Covering Cherub or precursor-text doing the work of double-binding.[1] Let me again beat upon the obvious; I am *not* taking away from the poem *Mariana* the fine anguish of Mariana's erotic frustration. But I recur to a point I made about the poem in an earlier essay ("Tennyson, Hallam and Romantic Tradition" in *The Ringers in the Tower):* this Mariana is herself a poetess, her true affiction is the Romantic self-consciousness of Keats and Shelley as solitary questers made yet one generation more belated, and no bridegroom, if he ever arrived, would be able to assuage her malaise. Without pulling the poem into our contemporary areas of the war between men and women, we can still note that what Mariana is longing for is not her belated swain but a priority in poetic invention that would free her from her really deadly obsession that nevertheless is giving her an intense quasi-

[1][For discussion of these terms and their implications for criticism see Harold Bloom, *The Anxiety of Influence* (New York: Oxford University Press, 1973). — Ed.]

sexual pleasure, a kind of sublime perversion that no sexual satisfaction could begin to hope to match. Mariana is much more than
half in love with easeful death, and in the poem's closing lines she
all but identifies death with her own primal narcissism.

I urge us, however, in the final stanza, to concentrate on the astonishingly strong but psychically costly transumption or metaleptic
reversal of the most characteristic of Keatsian metonymies, which is
the substitution of a near-stasis or slow-pacedness for the language
of the sense, for the sounds and sights of passing time. To Mariana,
the sparrow's chirrup, the clock's ticking, the poplar's erotic cry in
response to the wind's cry, all "confound her sense," which recalls
Shelley's transumption of Wordsworth, in *The Triumph of Life,*
when he has Rousseau speak of "many sounds woven into one/
Oblivious melody, confusing sense." So Mariana also achieves a
synaesthetic vision, yet more in Rousseau's victimized way than in
Wordsworth's mode of tranquil restoration. What she hates, the
poem ends by telling us, is that final near-stasis of light, when the
sunbeam holds on, as thick-moted as the harsh luxuriance that
opened the poem. Reversing Keats's heroic and proleptic naturalism,
she projects and so casts out all past time, which means all erotic
otherness, and introjects death, her own death, in despair of present
as of the past. The poem is more deliciously unhealthy than all its
Pre-Raphaelite and Decadent progeny were to be, and remains the
finest example in the language of an embowered consciousness
representing itself as being too happy in its unhappiness to want
anything more.

Whatever canonical interpretation has said to the contrary, what
he does so superbly in *Mariana* is Tennyson's peculiar greatness as a
poet. I want in this discourse to trace that greatness now in a sequence of poems: *The Hesperides, Ulysses* (though very briefly,
since I have mapped *Ulysses* in *A Map of Misreading),* and then
most elaborately in *Tithonus,* with an after-glance at *Tears, Idle
Tears,* after which I will conclude with a reading of Tennyson's repressive masterpiece, "Percivale's Quest," as I have called it, ex-
cerpting it from *The Holy Grail* in the *Idylls of the King.* But I will
begin this sequence with a final glance at *Mariana,* so as to attempt
some conclusion about the nature of Tennysonian repression in that
poem. Let us look at that celebrated poplar tree, which Leslie Bris-
man notes as itself deriving from *Sleep and Poetry,* lines 277-78. It
enters in the fourth stanza, dominates the fifth, vanishes in the sixth,

and acquires an erotic voice in the seventh. Let us dismiss the grotesque notion that it is a phallic emblem; it is a very lone tree, and it represents the Sublime, so that we can call it, grimly and accurately, itself an emblem of repression, of purposeful forgetting or afterpressure, which always leaves a residue or some slight element of return. Far from being a representation of the lover who will not arrive, the poplar represents the Sublime or repressed element in Mariana herself, her own uncanny solipsistic glory. Its shadow falls not only "upon her bed" but significantly "across her brow" as well. As the solitary height above the level waste, the poplar is the precise equivalent of Childe Roland's dark tower, the internalized negative sublime that the quester will not see until it comes upon him or her. In the final stanza, what is the poplar but the High Romantic aeolian harp, or Mariana's song gathered together in its condensed glory?

What then is Mariana repressing? Why, that she doesn't want or need the other who cometh not. What would she do with him, what mental space has she left for him? And what is Tennyson the poet repressing? Only that the most dangerous and powerful and authentic part of his own poetic mind would like to be as perfectly embowered as Mariana's consciousness is, but of course it can't. And yet, Tennyson *has* surpassed Keats in his misprision of Keats's mode, for even Keats is not, could not be, the sustained artist that Tennyson is. To get beyond *Mariana,* as a poem, you must go the way of Dante Gabriel Rossetti, but that is another story, a story of still greater repression.

Before going on to an even more gorgeous triumph of repression, *The Hesperides,* let us worry the notion of repression just a bit longer, by returning to Freud's central essay on the subject:

> The process of repression is not to be regarded as something which takes place once for all, the results of which are permanent, as when some living thing has been killed and from that time onward is dead; on the contrary, repression demands a constant expenditure of energy, and if this were discontinued the success of the repression would be jeopardized so that a fresh act of repression would be necessary.

The emphasis here is on energy expended, again and again, and that is how we have got to think of repression, particularly in the context of strong poetry. Repression is, as Derrida surely remarks somewhere, a difference in contending forces, and so necessarily is a strong poem such a difference. It is the constant renewal of repression that is, I am convinced, the clue to the magnificence of Tennyson's style. No poet in English, not even Milton, is so consistently Sublime. Tennyson's most characteristic trope is not even the hyperbole, but is a catachresis or extended abuse of that trope of overthrow or overemphasis. Tennyson never stops exaggerating, yet never stops giving pleasure by his leaps beyond limits. Take the Miltonic closing trope of *Mariana:* "and the day/ Was sloping towards his western bower." It is an elegant allusion to line 31 of *Lycidas,* where the evening star "Toward heaven's´ descent had sloped his westering wheel," but Tennyson's or rather Mariana's sun is lingering belatedly, so that the sloper, when he gets there, will be in much the same closed-in condition as the embowered Mariana, so that we are compelled to see that solipsistic damozel as being rather a sloper herself. Keats, in a pungent and somewhat ungracious letter to Shelley, had urged his swifter colleague to be an artist and so serve Spenser's Mammon: load every rift with ore. Tennyson betters Keats's instruction and, as Keats's ephebe, word-paints himself into the most densely inlaid art in the language.

Mariana, as I suggested earlier, can be regarded as a catachresis of the Romantic crisis-ode, as a hyperbolic version of Coleridge's *Dejection* or Keats's *Nightingale.* The catachresis here is the hothouse-forcing of the crisis-situation, since it would be difficult to image a more extreme state of self-consciousness than the one that Mariana so dialectically enjoys. But note Tennyson's curious staging of the poem; he narrates, and she speaks, and yet we find it difficult to keep the narrative and the embowered voices separate from one another. A descendant, odd as it must seem, is Stevens's *Sunday Morning,* where again the narrator and the occasionally speaking woman tend to merge in heightened passages. Let us think of Mariana as Tennyson's Stevensian Interior Paramour or Shelleyan epipsyche, and be prepared to find her hovering elsewhere in his poetry.

It is at the catachresis of internalized quest or Keatsian revised romance that Tennyson is most gifted, a wonderful instance being *The Hesperides,* a poem that the poet always insisted upon suppressing. Why? I suppose because here the repression is not strong enough, so that there is a dangerous and, evidently to Tennyson, disconcerting partial or apparent return-of-the-repressed. Here is the incantation of the repressive daughters of Hesperus at its properly apocalyptic climax:

Holy and bright, round and full, bright and blest,
Mellowed in a land of rest;
Watch it warily day and night;
All good things are in the west.
Till midnoon the cool east light
Is shut out by the round of the tall hillbrow;
But when the fullfaced sunset yellowly
Stays on the flowering arch of the bough,
The luscious fruitage clustereth mellowly,
Goldenkernelled, goldencored,
Sunset-ripened above on the tree.
The world is wasted with fire and sword,
But the apple of gold hangs over the sea.
Five links, a golden chain, are we,
Hesper, the dragon, and sisters three,
Daughters three,
Bound about
All round about
The gnarlèd bole of the charmèd tree.
The golden apple, the golden apple, the hallowed fruit,
Guard it well, guard it warily,
Watch it warily,
Singing airily,
Standing about the charmèd root.

Though this lovely song intentionally induces a languorousness in its readers, it requires of its singers a continual expenditure of repressive energy. As these ladies had sung previously, trying no doubt to keep their drowsy dragon awake:

If ye sing not, if ye make false measure,
We shall lose eternal pleasure,
Worth eternal want of rest.

The pleasure they value so highly must be their pride as poets and as performers, as weavers of an enchantment so sinuous as to block all questers from fulfillment in an earthly paradise. Their closing stanza is a celebration of belatedness, of being perpetually "after the event" by virtue of always being poised in front of it. As a transumption, this is a catachresis of the Keatsian trope that unheard melodies are sweeter, and the Hesperides arrive at a stasis that introjects lateness ("All good things are in the west"). There is an implication, throughout, that poetry and repression are an identity, but there is also a manifest anxiety as to the palpable misprision of Keats that is being enacted. The end of quest is to be not in the quester's merging in the identity of others, or of the poethood, but in the perpetual stasis of an earthly paradise preserved by enchantment from the single gratification it affords, and which would end it.

We pass to mature Tennyson, but before turning to *Tithonus,* where the Keatsian influence is so wonderfully engaged and held to a draw, I want very briefly to reexamine *Ulysses,* which is a companion-poem to *Tithonus.* It would seem odd to speak of repression in regard to a poem like *Ulysses,* whether we mean in the speaker of this dramatic monologue, or in Tennyson himself, for however one wants to interpret the poem, it offers us a vehement and highly expressive selfhood. Whether this Ulysses is a hero, or more likely a hero-villain, or whether he is Tennyson knowing he must go on after Hallam's death, or a more equivocal Tennyson confronting his own ambivalences, in any of these cases he would appear to be a consciousness that has forgotten nothing, even unconsciously. Indeed he seems a total purposefulness, fretting at inaction, and far from burying the representations of any impulse, he seems a man who in the drive to fulfill *all* impulses would welcome all self-representations whatsoever. What can this most sublime of questers not know, or not wish to know, whether about himself or about his relation to others? And, if this is somehow Tennyson himself, why ought we to associate the poem with defensive processes of any kind? Finally, what sort of a poem is this *Ulysses* anyway? Where are we to find its p. ecursors, its brothers, its descendants, in our own quest for those inter-poetic relationships and juxtapositions by which meaning is produced?

Vico, more directly than any other theorist, associated meaning with survival, and rhetoric with defense. Tennyson's Ulysses is not interested in mere survival (thus his heartfelt scorn "as though to breathe were life!") but he cares overwhelmingly about *what he means,* and whether he still means what he used to mean. His rhetoric defends against meaningless or mere repetition, against the reduction of life to the metonymy of breath. In the deep sense, his quest for continued meaningfulness is Vichian, for the meaning he seeks will guarantee his survival as the hero, the perpetually early wanderer, rather than the belated, aged king he has become when we meet him at the opening of his monologue. Surely, this Ulysses is strikingly like one of those magical formalists that Vico describes the primitive godlike men as being. As their lives were what Vico called "severe poems," so this Ulysses had lived a severe poem, and now cannot bear the life he has come home to, in what has turned out to be a mockery of the fulfilled quest. Can it be that by successfully returning home, this Ulysses has understood himself too well, and thus destroyed his own quest for meaning? In Vichian terms, the poet's quest for divination has been ruined in this quester, which is why he must set out again if he is to survive.

I want to quote part of one of what Vico calls his "Corollaries concerning Poetic Tropes, Monsters, and Metamorphoses," because I believe that Vico is a much better guide than Freud to the curious affinity or even identity between strong poetry and a kind of repression. Vico, in his axiom 405, notes that in language most of the expressions relating to inanimate things are formed by metaphor from the human body, senses, or passions. He then cites his own axiom 120: "Beware of the indefinite nature of the human mind, wherever it is lost in ignorance man makes himself the measure of all things." Even so, Vico says, man through rhetoric "has made of himself an entire world." In what follows, Vico suddenly achieves an astonishing insight:

> So that, as rational metaphysics teaches that man becomes all things by understanding them, this imaginative metaphysics shows that man becomes all things by *not* understanding them; and perhaps the latter proposition is truer than the former, for when man understands he extends his mind and takes in the things, but when he does not understand he makes the things out of himself and becomes them by transforming himself into them.

Behind this axiom is the central Vichian principle: you only know what you yourself have made, which means that to know yourself is to have made yourself. Whatever one thinks of the truth of Vico's vision, it certainly applies to Tennyson's Ulysses, who is a severe poet and a Vichian primitive solipsist. When Tennyson's quester says: "I am a part of all that I have met" he means: "I understand only myself, and so everything I have met I have made out of myself, and I have become all things by transforming myself into them." One step further on from Tennyson's Ulysses is Browning's Childe Roland; another step on is Pater's Marius, and the final step is taken by the Hoon of Wallace Stevens who can proclaim triumphantly:

I was the world in which I walked
And what I saw or heard came not but from myself
And there I found myself more truly and more strange.

What Vico saw is that truly poetic metaphysics was founded upon
a sacred solipsism, which Vico called "ignorance," or rather that
imagination takes its flight when the mind *represses* its own knowing and its own understanding. What Tennyson's Ulysses represses
is his own knowledge, of himself and of his relation to others, so
that by this repression he can be driven out, away from home, to
seek knowledge again. To *know* is to have become belated; not to
know, not to understand, is to become early again, however self-
deceivingly. What is the relation between this odd catachresis of a
transumptive stance, and the celebrated Negative Capability of
Keats? Keats spoke of "when man is capable of being in uncer-
tainties, Mysteries, doubts, without any irritable reaching after
fact & reason" and added that one must be capable "of remaining
content with half knowledge." This is the wisdom of the *aporia,*
of knowing we must end in uncertainty, and surely Tennyson's
Ulysses is a grand parody of such intellectual heroism. Ulysses
asserts he wants full knowledge, and actually wants no knowledge
at all, except the Vichian transformation of the self into everything
unknown, meaning into everything encountered.

With *Tithonus,* the Vichian repression of understanding achieves
an even more intense version of the Sublime, yet one that is also
more recognizably in the shadow of Keats. Vico, if I understand him
(which in my own terms means if I misread him strongly enough),
is saying that poetic repression is a mode of Knowing, or even that
rhetoric is a mode of knowing *by negation.* The absolute exquisite-
ness of the rhetoric of Tennyson's *Tithonus* may mask a profound
loss of the self by way of a negation of knowing that becomes a new
kind of repressive knowing. Or, more simply, what is Tithonus
repressing?

The woods decay, the woods decay and fall,
The vapours weep their burthen to the ground.
Man comes and tills the fields and lies beneath,
And after many a summer dies the swan.
Me only cruel immortality
Consumes: I wither slowly in thine arms.
Here at the quiet limit of the world,
A white-haired shadow roaming like a dream

> The ever-silent spaces of the East,
> Far-folded mists, and gleaming halls of morn.

Ostensibly, both *Ulysses* and *Tithonus,* like *Tears, Idle Tears* and the whole of *In Memoriam,* are poems of grief at the loss of Hallam, and of guilt for going on living without Hallam, the guilt of being a survivor, of being humanly as well as poetically belated. We might apply here the insight of Freud, in his "Mourning and Melancholia" essay, that melancholia begins, like mourning, in the loss of the beloved object, but this loss is not the real cause of the melancholia. Instead, the ego splits, with one part attacking the other, and the attacked portion becomes the repressed representation of the lost object (through "identification"). What is thus exposed is the narcissistic element in the love felt for the lost object, so that mourning becomes a process in which self-love is transformed into self-hatred. *Tithonus* shows a pattern not wholly unlike this Freudian insight, but I want to place our emphasis elsewhere, upon Vico again, and therefore upon the repression that makes Tithonus the extraordinary poet he is.

Or, should we say "aesthete" rather than "poet," just as we should say "hero-villain" rather than "hero" when we speak of Ulysses? I want to approach *Tithonus,* including its surpassingly beautiful opening passage, by way of *Tears, Idle Tears,* a closely related poem, and also like *Tithonus* an act of defense against the composite precursor, Keats-and-Wordsworth. Just as any sensitive reader will hear Wordsworth's Simplon Pass (from *The Prelude*) in the opening of *Tithonus,* so he or she will be haunted by *Tintern Abbey* while brooding upon *Tears, Idle Tears:*

> Tears, idle tears, I know not what they mean,
> Tears from the depth of some divine despair
> Rise in the heart, and gather to the eyes,
> In looking on the happy Autumn-fields,
> And thinking of the days that are no more.
>
> Fresh as the first beam glittering on a sail,
> That brings our friends up from the underworld,
> Sad as the last which reddens over one
> That sinks with all we love below the verge;
> So sad, so fresh, the days that are no more.
>
> Ah, sad and strange as in dark summer dawns
> The earliest pipe of half-awakened birds

To dying ears, when unto dying eyes
The casement slowly grows a glimmering square;
So sad, so strange, the days that are no more.

Dear as remembered kisses after death,
And sweet as those by hopeless fancy feigned
On lips that are for others; deep as love,
Deep as first love, and wild with all regret;
O Death in Life, the days that are no more.

Cleanth Brooks has devoted some brilliant pages in *The Well Wrought Urn* to uncovering the motivation of Tennyson's weeper. I myself would say that we cannot uncover the motivation, because of the patterns of repression in the poem. Whatever else we read it as being, *Tears, Idle Tears* is a lament of belatedness, in which part at least of the poet's burden is his inability to achieve any priority in the wording of his own very authentic grief. The dominant imagery of the poem is hyperbolical *depth*, buried passion, and buried in more than one sense, though the poem's largest trope of representation is the Virgilian noble synecdoche, in which weeping for a particular loss is a part of which the tears of universal nature are the whole. In the poem's closing lines, Tennyson tropes upon Wordsworth's double trope in the *Intimations* 'Ode,' of "Heavy as frost, and deep almost as life!" that ends the first movement of the ode, and "Thoughts that do often lie too deep for tears," the ode's final line. The weight that Wordsworth called "custom," a death-in-life, lay deep almost as life, until it was transumed by thoughts of such depth that they transcended tears. But Tennyson beautifully reverses the trope, by metalepsis; the depth greater than "custom" and greater than thoughts of human sympathy, is the repressed depth of lost first love, the true death-in-life that cannot be reversed into an earliness: "the days that are no more."

Though Tennyson defends against Wordsworth's presence, in a poem actually composed at Tintern Abbey again, the tropes of limitation he employs defend rather against Keats, whose ode *To Autumn* is more deeply involved in the lyric repressions of *Tears, Idle Tears.* In *his* ode, Keats looks on the happy autumn fields, and does not weep, does not lament the loss of earliness, the absence of the songs of spring. The bird songs of late-summer/early-autumn intimate to Keats one of his liminal states, a threshold vision poised or held open to the possibility of tragedy, but above all *open,* to whatever may come. This *aporia,* or beautiful uncertainty, is too strong a limitation for Tennyson to accept. But for Tennyson the bird song is not another metonymy for death, like the glittering beam and the sail in the previous stanza, and like the strange metaphoric transformation of Keats's characteristic open casement in "when unto dying eyes/ The casement slowly grows a glimmering square." So gorgeous a lyric is *Tears, Idle Tears,* in its dark undoings of Keats's heroism, that we do not pause long enough to suspect a little how perceptive, how aesthetic a vision, is being achieved despite those tears. They are "idle" enough in that they do nothing to blind this weeper.

I think *that* is where the emphasis falls in Tennyson's even more beautiful reverie of a grieved aesthete, his *Tithonus,* where the mourning is necessarily more primal and terrible, being for the monologist's own lost youth and beauty. But, quite evidently, not for lost love, as the grand link between Tithonus and Ulysses is their palpable, solipsistic inability to have loved anyone but their own former selves. As I have said elsewhere, one would not wish to be in a boat with Tennyson's Ulysses, who has the knack of surviving while others drown. Equally, unlike poor Aurora, one wouldn't wish to be in the same bed with Tithonus. But of course it all depends on how one reacts to a really primal narcissism—which will involve another brief digression into how criticism might set about reclaiming the pirated poetic element from yet another of Freud's fundamental insights.

Freud's final insight in regard to narcissism was his realization that it was a defensive movement against the death-drive. His original insight had seen narcissism as the element in the ego that made the ego an image, an imaginary object, rather than an hypostasis of reason. In the subtle lights of Tennyson's *Tithonus,* it is fascinating to note that Freud began to brood upon narcissistic neuroses in order to explain the psychoses of hypochondria and megalomania, as Tithonus has more than a touch of each. We fall in love, according to Freud, as a defense against a narcissistic cathexis or self-investment when our passion-for-ourself threatens to go too far. But in such falling, we continue to love what represents ourself, whether what we were, or what we would like to have been. If Tithonus had fallen in love with Aurora at all, then it was only to the degree that she was a narcissistic representation of himself. But she has remained splendidly herself, he has withered, and now he loves only death.

I repeat Freud's belated insight, that ultimately narcissism is a defense against the death-instincts. If Tithonus genuinely wants to die, as he asserts, then he has ceased to be a poet (if ever he was one) and he has abandoned also the primal megalomania of his own narcissism. His monologue belies both these assertions, and so is either self-deceptive or rhetorically deceptive towards ourselves, or both together, as would be normal in the characteristic Browning monologue. Something is therefore very equivocal about this dramatic monologue, and so I want to return again to its really gorgeous opening lines. Let us regard this first verse-paragraph as the poem's *clinamen,* its swerve away from the naturalistic affirmations of Wordsworth and of Keats. What is absent in these opening ten lines is simply all of nature; what is present is the withered Tithonus. As Tennyson's reaction-formation against his precursors' stance, these lines are a rhetorical irony, denying what they desire, the divination of a poetic survival into strength. Behind these lines are Wordsworth on the Simplon Pass ("The immeasurable height/ Of woods decaying, never to be decayed") but more crucially the entire vision of an early cosmos in Keats's *Hyperion.*

I think that the five remaining verse-paragraphs of *Tithonus* will be found to reveal, in sequence, the five expected revisionary ratios, rather too neatly, but I don't think that this is merely my own compulsion or misprision-neurosis working out; rather it is another indication that *Tithonus* truly is a High Romantic crisis-poem, masking as a dramatic monologue, so that its patterning of defenses, tropes, and images closely follows the models of poems like *Tintern Abbey, Intimations of Immortality, Dejection,* the *Ode to Psyche,* and all their companions. Rather than trace the next five verse-paragraphs through my map of misreading, I will leave that operation to my readers' curiosity or skepticism. Let us assume that my apprehension of the patterns of misprision here will be confirmed. What will that tell us about the poem?

In an essay on Christopher Smart's *Rejoice in the Lamb,*[2] Geoffrey Hartman speaks of Freud as our latest doctor of the Sublime, as a diagnostician of "the pathology of ecstasy," the true culminator of the tradition that goes from Boileau on Longinus through Vico and Edmund Burke on to Kant and Schopenhauer. Hartman's laconic

[2][Geoffrey Hartman, "Christopher Smart's *Magnificat:* Toward a Theory of Representation," in *The Fate of Reading and Other Essays* (Chicago: University of Chicago Press, 1975), pp. 74-98.—Ed.]

point against a view of defense as a primary phenomenon, whether in the psyche or in poems, is made rather aggressively and ironically when he observes: 'Defense mechanisms cannot blossom when there is nothing—no fire or flood—to defend against." Against this, I would name, for Tennyson, Keats as the fire and Wordsworth as the flood. *Tithonus,* as a poem, is at once a narcissistic apotheosis and a powerful repressive reaction against the greatest poets ever to have attempted a humanized Sublime, an attempt made by way of a humanization of the ancient poetic lust for divination. When Tithonus defensively turns against himself, he turns against the whole heroic enterprise that would single out the poet as a candidate for survival:

> ...Let me go: take back thy gift:
> Why should a man desire in any way
> To vary from the kindly race of men,
> Or pass beyond the goal or ordinance
> Where all should pause, as is most meet for all?

This is a dark synecdoche, reminding us that the burden of a trope is pathos, and that the ancient war between rhetoric and a more rational dialectic can never end. But though he yields to masochism as a vicissitude of instinct, we would do wrong to take *Tithonus* literally when he says "take back thy gift," since the gift of immortality in this poem is also the gift of divination, without which no one becomes, or remains, a poet. Against this momentary yielding to an instinctual vicissitude with its strong representation set against the self, Tithonus recoils with an obsessive force in a psychic defense of limitation, which in his case is a compulsive return to origins, a regression conveyed primarily by the metonymy of the Wordsworthian glimmer or gleam, but with a direct eroticism that derives from Keats:

> A soft air fans the cloud apart; there comes
> A glimpse of that dark world where I was born.
> Once more the old mysterious glimmer steals
> From thy pure brows, and from thy shoulders pure,
> And bosom beating with a heart renewed.
> Thy cheek begins to redden through the gloom,
> Thy sweet eyes brighten slowly close to mine,
> Ere yet they blind the stars, and the wild team
> Which love thee, yearning for thy yoke arise,

> And shake the darkness from their loosened manes,
> And beat the twilight into flakes of fire.

What is palpable in this lovely passage is that the sexual warmth
not only is but always *was* Aurora's, and also that the monologist, a
solipsistic aesthete, now and always was no part of "the wild team/
Which love thee." Even Ulysses is not so sublimely incapable as is
Tithonus of apprehending anyone's emotions except his own. Thus,
Aurora's tears are read by Tithonus as his own hysterical fear that
his now noxious immortality cannot be withdrawn (which, on the
level of Tennyson's own repressions, I would tend to interpret as his
own evaded realization that he is doomed to go on seeking to be a
strong poet, even though Hallam is dead). Again, in the fifth verse-
paragraph, there is the extraordinary passivity of Tithonus as a
lover, with its overwhelming emphasis not upon sexual pleasure or
fulfillment, but upon the monologist's heightened powers of
aesthetic perceptiveness while being embraced.

When, in the final verse-paragraph, we move into the area of
East and West, or early and late, the *aprophrades* or introjection of
the past has about it the peculiar and unnerving accents of paranoia
—not that of Tennyson, I hasten to say, but of the monomaniacal
Tithonus. What is most striking to me, about these lines, is their
cruelty as the masochistic Tithonus manifests a repressed sadism
towards the bereaved and loving Aurora:

> Yet hold me not for ever in thine East:
> How can my nature longer mix with thine?
> Coldly thy rosy shadows bathe me, cold
> Are all thy lights, and cold my wrinkled feet
> Upon thy glimmering thresholds, when the steam
> Floats up from those dim fields about the homes
> Of happy men that have the power to die,
> And grassy barrows of the happier dead.
> Release me, and restore me to the ground;
> Thou seest all things, thou wilt see my grave:
> Thou wilt renew thy beauty morn by morn;
> I earth in earth forget these empty courts,
> And thee returning on thy silver wheels.

Let us grant that the monologist's situation is extreme, but his
presumably unconscious cruelty transcends even that extremity. Is
it really necessary for him to assure her: "Thou seest all things, thou

wilt see my grave"? Need he finally assure her that, when he is "earth in earth," he will forget her? I do not believe Tennyson was aware of this cruelty, and I am suggesting that even in these glorious closing lines, a profound repression is at work. To grow endlessly more agèd while remaining immortal is an oxymoronic or belated version of the divination that is crucial to strong poetry. The hidden concern of the poem *Tithonus,* as of the poem *Ulysses,* is Tennyson's own belatedness as a poet, his arrival on the scene *after the event,* after the triumph of poetry of "reflection" in Coleridge and Wordsworth, and of poetry of "sensation" in Shelley and Keats, to use a critical distinction invented by Hallam. Hallam's enormous contribution to Tennyson was to overcome the poet's diffidence, and to persuade him that he could become a third, with Shelley and Keats. Hallam dead, Tennyson knew not only the guilt of a survivor but also the obsessive poetic fear of belatedness, the fear that torments his own Sir Percivale, that every repressed voice crying from within will proclaim: "This Quest is not for thee."

With Percivale's Quest from *The Holy Grail,* I come to my final text from Tennyson, and begin by dismissing as a palpable evasion his own weak misreading of his own text, in which Percivale and all the other knights, except Galahad, represent a flawed Christianity, flawed in Percivale's case by an ascetic, otherworldly mysticism, a sort of St. John of the Cross Catholic temperament. But the Percivale we meet in the poem is hardly a mystical ascetic, but rather a highly familiar compound ghost, the High Romantic antithetical quester, whose every movement is *contra naturam,* even in spite of himself. We are back in that central current that goes from Spenser, in the *Prothalamion,* and from Spenser's Colin Clout to the *Penseroso* of Milton and the equivocal heroism of Satan questing onwards through Chaos to reach Eden, the New World. These are Percivale's ultimate ancestors, but much closer are the Solitary of Wordsworth, and the Solitary's younger brothers in Childe Harold, Endymion, and, above all others, the doomed, driven Poet of *Alastor.* Contemporary with Percivale is Browning's Roland as well as Tennyson's Ulysses, while looming up are the Oisin and Forgael of Yeats, and the Nietzchean parody of all these in Stevens's Crispin, or the antithetical quester reduced to the state of *The Comedian as the Letter C.*

I am suggesting that, in Percivale, the repressed element in Tennyson's poethood emerges fully, in a fury of questing that

deforms and breaks all it encounters more devastatingly than even
Childe Roland's vision wrecks upon his world. Hypnotic and in-
cantatory as Tennyson is almost always capable of being, I know
nothing in him as phantasmagoric, as Sublime, as much charged
with a greatly controlled hysteria of repression as Percivale's
destructive quest:

> And I was lifted up in heart, and thought
> Of all my late-shown prowess in the lists,
> How my strong lance had beaten down the knights,
> So many and famous names; and never yet
> Had heaven appeared so blue, nor earth so green,
> For all my blood danced in me, and I knew
> That I should light upon the Holy Grail.
>
> Thereafter, the dark warning of our King
> That most of us would follow wandering fires,
> Came like a driving gloom across my mind.
> Then every evil word I had spoken once,
> And every evil thought I had thought of old,
> And every evil deed I ever did,
> Awoke and cried, "This Quest is not for thee."
> And lifting up mine eyes, I found myself
> Alone, and in the land of sand and thorns,
> And I was thirsty even unto death;
> And I, too, cried, "This Quest is not for thee."
>
> And on I rode, and when I thought my thirst
> Would slay me, saw deep lawns, and then a brook,
> With one sharp rapid, where the crisping white
> Played ever back upon the sloping wave,
> And took both ear and eye; and o'er the brook
> Were apple-trees, and apples by the brook
> Fallen, and on the lawns. "I will rest here,"
> I said, "I am not worthy of the Quest;"
> But even while I drank the brook, and ate
> The goodly apples, all these things at once
> Fell into dust, and I was left alone,
> And thirsting, in a land of sand and thorns.
>
> And then behold a woman at a door
> Spinning; and fair the house whereby she sat,
> And kind the woman's eyes and innocent,
> And all her bearing gracious; and she rose
> Opening her arms to meet me, as who should say,

"Rest here;" but when I touched her, lo! she, too,
Fell into dust and nothing, and the house
Became no better than a broken shed,
And in it a dead babe; and also this
Fell into dust, and I was left alone.

And on I rode, and greater was my thirst,
Then flashed a yellow gleam across the world,
And where it smote the plowshare in the field,
The plowman left his plowing, and fell down
Before it; where it glittered on her pail,
The milkmaid left her milking, and fell down
Before it, and I know not why, but thought
"The sun is rising," though the sun had risen,
Then was I ware of one that on me moved
In golden armour with a crown of gold
About a casque all jewels; and his horse
In golden armour jewelled everywhere:
And on the splendour came, flashing me blind;
And seemed to me the Lord of all the world,
Being so huge. But when I thought he meant
To crush me, moving on me, lo! he, too,
Fell into dust, and I was left alone
And wearying in a land of sand and thorns.

And I rode on and found a mighty hill,
And on the top, a city walled; the spires
Pricked with incredible pinnacles into heaven.
And by the gateway stirred a crowd; and these
Cried to me climbing, "Welcome, Percivale!
Thou mightiest and thou purest among men!"
And glad was I and clomb, but found at top
No man, nor any voice. And thence I past
Far through a ruinous city, and I saw
That man had once dwelt there; but there I found
Only one man of an exceeding age.
"Where is that goodly company," said I,
"That so cried out upon me?" and he had
Scarce any voice to answer, and yet gasped,
"Whence and what art thou?" and even as he spoke
Fell into dust, and disappeared, and I
Was left alone once more, and cried in grief,
"Lo, if I find the Holy Grail itself
And touch it, it will crumble into dust."

I have quoted all of this sequence, so as not to lose any of its cumulative force. But what is this force? I think we recognize in it, all of us, one of our own nightmares, the nightmare that is centered upon our own self-destructiveness, and so upon our own murderousness also, our aggressive instinct whose aim is the destruction of the object. As the greatest of modern moralists—true successor of Pascal, Montaigne, Schopenhauer, Emerson, Nietzsche—Freud is the inevitable authority to cite in any account of the aggressive instinct or drive-towards-death, though the poetic variant, in Tennyson, will hardly be an exact equivalent of the Freudian insights. Rather, Tennyson's vision of Percivale's Quest, and Freud's vision of the death instinct (particularly in *Beyond the Pleasure Principle)* will be found to have a troublesome resemblance suggesting that both are complex misprisions of a common precursor, of a larger mental form to which Vico remains the surest guide I have been able to discover.

Though Percivale's Quest might seem to sustain the analysis of the ascetic ideal as given by Nietzsche in *Towards the Genealogy of Morals,* this apparent similarity has more to do with Tennyson's overt intention than with his actual representation of Percivale, in the poem. What we encounter in Percivale, as in the wandering Poet of Shelley's *Alastor,* is a repressed aggressive instinct, or what Freud calls the death instinct directed outwards. But clearly, Percivale's deathliness intends to be directed against his own self. What does it mean that Tennyson is compelled to make of Percivale a consuming force that devastates everything it encounters?

Freud's very problematic final theory of the instincts posits a group of drives that work towards reducing all tensions to a zero-point, so as to carry everything living back to an inorganic state. Freud's formulation is difficult, because it suggests that a self-destructive drive back towards origins is a universal phenomenon. As a theory, Freud's notion here is frankly daemonic, and related to his dark insight that all repetition phenomena may mask a regressive element in every human instinct. To account for life's ambivalence towards itself, Freud resorted to a more radical dualism than he had entertained earlier. The id became the center for representing every instinctual demand, with none assigned to the ego, which means that ultimately every desire, whether for power or for sexual fulfillment, is in some sense linked to the desire for death. Without pretending to be summarizing the full complexity of Freud's speculations, I will leave the notion of the death instincts there, except to note that Freud was compelled to adopt a new formulation in this area, the Nirvana Principle, which he took from Schopenhauer by way of a suggestion of the English psychoanalyst Barbara Low.

The Nirvana Principle, introduced in *Beyond the Pleasure Principle* (1920), is the psyche's drive to reduce all excitation within itself, whether the origin of the excitation be internal or external, to the zero-level, or as close to zero as possible. I have invoked all of this Freudian speculation in order to get us to the Nirvana Principle, for that is the actuality of Percivale's Quest, despite Percivale's apparent intention and Tennyson's stated and overt intention. Percivale believes he is questing for the Holy Grail, but in reality he quests for Schopenhauer's quasi-Buddhistic Nirvana, where desire shall vanish, the individual self fade away, and quietude replace the strong poet's search for a stance and word of his own. Percivale, I am suggesting, is as close as Tennyson can come, not to a return of the repressed, but to an absolute or total freshening of self-repression. And though *The Holy Grail* is ostensibly a critique of Percivale and an exaltation of Galahad, and even of the humane and sweet Ambrosius, what any reader is going to remember is that sublime and terrific destructive march to the zero-point that is the litany of Percivale's quest. Reflect even upon the exchange between Ambrosius and Percivale that ends the account of Percivale's ruinous march. Ambrosius cries out, in the name of common humanity:

> "O brother, saving this Sir Galahad,
> Came ye on none but phantoms in your quest,
> No man, no woman?"
>
> Then Sir Percivale:
> "All men, to one so bound by such a vow,
> And women were as phantoms. ..."

How shall we read "such a vow"? Only I think, despite Tennyson's intentions, as the vow to be a strong poet, whatever the human cost. Percivale, in the deep sense, is Tennyson the poet, unable to get out of or beyond the shadow of Galahad, the quester who beholds and becomes one with a strength that resists the Nirvana Principle. I am not proposing any simple equation of Galahad = Keats, but a more complex formula in which Galahad does represent the High Romantic quest, and Percivale the belated quest of Victorian Romanticism.

Tennyson was too sublimely repressed a poet to develop very overtly his ambivalence towards his prime precursors, and the death of Hallam, who was the great champion of Keats, augmented the repression. But Tennyson too was a preternaturally strong poet, and we have seen something of his strength at misprision. The shadow of Keats never did abandon him wholly, and so the stance of belatedness became a kind of second nature for him. But what he may have lacked in priority of stance, he greatly compensated for in priority of style. He prophesies his true ephebe, the late T. S. Eliot, and time, I am persuaded, will show us how much stronger a poet Tennyson was than Eliot.

Poems from Hallam's Death till the End of 1834

by Christopher Ricks

In October 1833, the month after Hallam's death, FitzGerald wrote:

> Tennyson has been in town for some time: he has been making fresh poems, which are finer, they say, than any he has done. But I believe he is chiefly meditating on the purging and subliming of what he has already done: and repents that he has published at all yet. It is fine to see how in each succeeding poem the smaller ornaments and fancies drop away, and leave the grand ideas single.[1]

By December, Tennyson's brother Frederick was reporting that Alfred "will most probably publish again in the Spring."[2] His Cambridge friends were delighted that his spirits were not broken: "Tennyson has, I hear, so far recovered from the catastrophe in which his sister was involved, as to have written some poems, and they say, fine ones" (January 22, 1834).[3] Yet a more morbid urgency may be heard in the semi-apologetic letter which Tennyson wrote in April 1834 to "Christopher North," repenting of his epigram against the dreaded reviewer, and fearing that "Christopher North" was about to be spurred into a further critique by the polemics of one John Lake.

"Poems from Hallam's Death till the End of 1834." From Christopher Ricks, *Tennyson* (New York: Macmillan Publishing Co., Inc., 1972), pp. 118-34. Copyright © 1972 by Macmillan Publishing Co., Inc. Reprinted with permission of Macmillan Publishing Co., and Macmillan Press Ltd., London and Basingstoke.

[1] Edward FitzGerald, *Letters,* 2 vols. (London, 1894), I, 25; October 25, 1833.

[2] The Tennyson d'Eyncourt papers, at the Castle, Lincoln (Lincolnshire Archives Committee), H. 113/67; December 18, 1833.

[3] R. C. Trench, *Letters and Memorials,* 2 vols. (London, 1888), I, 84; December 2, 1833.

I could wish that some of the poems there broken on your critical wheel were deeper than ever plummet sounded. Written as they were before I had attained my nineteenth year they could not but contain as many faults as words. I never wish to see them or hear of them again—much less to find them dragged forward once more on your boards. . . .[4]

The creative revision of his early poems was a major undertaking. A more immediate effect of Hallam's death was a burst of imaginative energy that intensifies and corroborates the achievement of the previous year or so, and makes the years 1833-1834 the most remarkable flowering of Tennyson's genius. Following upon "The Two Voices" and "St. Simeon Stylites" (the distinctive feats of the months before Hallam's death), there came within a year a series of successes: some sections of *In Memoriam,* "Ulysses," "Tithon" (the early version of "Tithonus"), "Morte d'Arthur," "Oh! that 'twere possible," and "Break, break, break." Such achievements ought to make us receive with some skepticism—despite its apt reminder of the faults of his early poems—Tennyson's remark, "I suppose I was nearer thirty than twenty before I was anything of an artist."[5]

A cluster of poems responded at once and directly to Hallam's death. One of them, not published by Tennyson, incorporates a somber ambiguity in the words "Make me live," soliciting not only an animating energy from Nature but also a commanding refusal to permit the suicidal:

> From sorrow sorrow yet is born,
>   Hopes flow like water through a sieve,
> But leave not thou thy son forlorn;
>   Touch me, great Nature, make me live.
>
> As when thy sunlights, a mild heat,
>   Touch some dun mere that sleepeth still;
> As when thy moonlights, dim and sweet,
>   Touch some gray ruin on the hill.

A long series of disillusionments was distilled into the totality of melancholy, the limpid desolation, of that opening antithesis.

A similar tone informs "On a Mourner," written in October 1833 but not published till 1865. In revising it for publication, Tennyson

[4]Hallam Tennyson, *Alfred, Lord Tennyson: A Memoir,* 2 vols. (London, 1897), I, 96.
[5]*Memoir,* I, 12.

was to make it less directly personal. He veiled and objectified the poem by adding the title; by addressing it to another, changing "my" to "thy";[6] and by omitting two explicit stanzas about "that friend I loved in vain." The poem sets the essential limits to the consolatory power of the beauties of Nature; real though they are, they are ultimately ineffectual if Nature too is mortal. The poem begins with the delicate softness of Nature and "her airy hill"; it ends with quite other hills of craggy endurance, as the voices of Hope, Memory, Faith and Virtue enter,

> Promising empire; such as those
> Once heard at dead of night to greet
> Troy's wandering prince, so that he rose
> With sacrifice, while all the fleet
> Had rest by stony hills of Crete.

It is a consummate ending, a victory achieved, an empire over oneself, a rest that is beautifully played against the stony. And despite the finality (audible in the concluding hard-edged rhyme), the end is one which—like so many of Tennyson's endings—is poised, waiting.[7] The fleet will not have rest forever. The Virgilian ending anticipates Tennyson's translation from Homer (1863), where the last fourteen lines form a single sentence, culminating in a fateful pause and poise.

> ...So many a fire between the ships and stream
> Of Xanthus blazed before the towers of Troy,
> A thousand on the plain; and close by each
> Sat fifty in the blaze of burning fire;
> And eating hoary grain and pulse the steeds,
> Fixt by their cars, waited the golden dawn.

A more histrionic immediacy—grief rather than melancholy— is heard in the unpublished fragment which Tennyson's son was to call the germ of *In Memoriam,* "Hark! the dogs howl! the sleet-winds blow." A visionary flight snatches him up:

[6]In the late poem "Far-Far-Away" (written 1888), Tennyson was to change the manuscript first person to third person throughout.

[7]Allingham describes Tennyson reading, lingering with solemn sweetness on every vowel sound—a peculiar *incomplete* cadence at the end." (*Diary,* p. 158, August 25, 1867) [*William Allingham, A Diary,* eds. H. Allingham and D. Radford (London, 1907).—Ed.]

> I seek the voice I loved—ah where
> Is that dear hand that I should press,
> Those honoured brows that I would kiss?
> Lo! the broad Heavens cold and bare,
> The stars that know not my distress.

Tennyson's son, fearing a homosexual misconstruction, preferred not to print that third line, or the cry "I wind my arms for one embrace." Already, as in *In Memoriam* ("like a guilty thing"), there is an unexplained and perhaps inexplicable sense of guilt; the shadow of Hallam "bends his eyes reproachfully." Already there is mingled an awe of Hallam's new grandeur and a fear that such grandeur has outstripped Tennyson:

> Larger than human passes by
> The shadow of the man I loved.

That awe and that fear were to mingle, too, in *In Memoriam.* Tennyson set to work on the sequence (which was not to be published for seventeen years) in the month in which he heard of Hallam's death. The earliest group (in one of the notebooks now at Trinity College) consists of the following sections: XXX, "With trembling fingers did we weave"; IX, "Fair ship, that from the Italian shore"; XVII, "Thou comest, much wept for"; XVIII, "'Tis well; 'tis something"; a version of XXXI-XXXII, "When Lazarus left his charnel-cave"; LXXXV, "This truth came borne with bier and pall"; and XXVIII, "The time draws near the birth of Christ." The striking thing about this earliest group is that it evinces the less perturbed calm which *In Memoriam* mostly intimates to be an achievement slowly won rather than immediately entered upon. None of these sections shows dismay or dark questioning; already they proffer reassurance:

> This truth came borne with bier and pall,
>   I felt it, when I sorrowed most,
>   'Tis better to have loved and lost,
> Than never to have loved at all—

But when Tennyson sorrowed most, he was least able to confront the starkest heart searchings. As the years passed, he brought himself to contemplate more. The point is not about sincerity, but about intensity of meeting. The tender calm manifested so early in this first group (at its best in the two exquisite celebrations of the ship that is bringing Hallam's body) foreshadows the very latest stage of the poem's creation, and makes it unsurprising that at the very last moment in 1850—between the privately printed edition in March and the publication at the end of May—Tennyson added some of the most darkly penetrating sections of the poem. Likewise that he should subsequently have said to a friend, James Knowles, "It's too hopeful, this poem, more than I am myself."[8]

On this same occasion, Tennyson was to compare *In Memoriam* with "Ulysses": "There is more about myself in 'Ulysses,' which was written under the sense of loss and that all had gone by, but that still life must be fought out to the end. It was more written with the feeling of his loss upon me than many poems in *In Memoriam.*" Tennyson—and this is not surprising—found himself able to incorporate the direct sense of loss in the poems which by indirections found directions out.

"...But that still life must be fought out to the end." Yet are the terms of "Ulysses" fighting terms? It opens indeed with a chafing, a clipped impatience:

> It little profits that an idle king,
> By this still hearth, among these barren crags,
> Matched with an agèd wife, I mete and dole
> Unequal laws unto a savage race,
> That hoard, and sleep, and feed, and know not me.

The contempt is pervasive and energizing, with the "barren crags" leading from the "idle king" and leading into the "aged wife": the marriage match does harsh justice. Yet this stoniness is at once followed by a different kind of affirmation:

> I cannot rest from travel: I will drink
> Life to the lees: all times I have enjoyed
> Greatly, have suffered greatly, both with those
> That loved me, and alone; on shore, and when
> Through scudding drifts the rainy Hyades
> Vext the dim sea...

It has amplitude, the affirmation, but a plumped amplitude. "Far on the ringing plains of windy Troy": it rings, but with a strangely unstrange timbre which sounds thin beside that "dim sea." Yet this is not necessarily a failure in the poem, since what it truly aimed at may have been equivocal. "The feeling of his loss upon me" is also in the poem (which Tennyson wrote in the month when he heard of Hallam's death), tempering—or rather the opposite of tempering in the sense of steeling—the poem's staunchness and instead insinuates a deeper wanhope. That the feelings evinced both within and by the poem are ambiguous or paradoxical was noticed by Goldwin Smith in 1855:

> You may trace the hues of this character tinging everything in the poems. Even the Homeric Ulysses, the man of purpose and action, seeking with most definite aim to regain his own home and that of his companions, becomes a "hungry heart," roaming aimlessly to "lands beyond the sunset," in the vain hope of being "washed down by the gulf to the Happy Isles," merely to relieve his *ennui,* and dragging his companions with him. We say he roams aimlessly—we should rather say, he intends to roam, but stands for ever a listless and melancholy figure on the shore.[9]

The point is a telling one: it rightly refuses to believe, simply, what Ulysses tells his mariners. Robert Langbaum explores the paradox further:

> Most characteristic of Tennyson is a certain life-weariness, a longing for rest through oblivion. This emotional bias is all the more powerful because it appears to be subconscious. Not only does it conflict with the poet's often stated desire for personal immortality, but it even conflicts in a poem like "Ulysses" with what seems to be his intent.... The same weariness and longing for rest is the emotional bias of Tennyson's finest dramatic monologue, "Ulysses"; though here the emotion is couched in the contrasting language of adventure, giving an added complexity of meaning to the poem. To read "Ulysses" as a poem of strenuousness in the manner of Browning, as some critics have done, is to read with the head only and not the sensibility. For its music bears the enervated cadence of "Tithonus" and "The Lotos-Eaters."[10]

There are indeed cadences in the poem which are far from enervated, but are they not sapped and sopped by the insidious enervations ("The long day wanes: the slow moon climbs: the deep/

[9]*Saturday Review,* November 3, 1855; reprinted in John Jump, ed., *Tennyson: The Critical Heritage* (London, 1967), p. 188.

[10]Robert Langbaum, *The Poetry of Experience: The Dramatic Monologue in Modern Literary Tradition* (London, 1957), pp. 89-90.

Moans round with many voices") at the poem's center? The poem's last sentence has its urgency:

> Though much is taken, much abides; and though
> We are not now that strength which in old days
> Moved earth and heaven; that which we are, we are;
> One equal temper of heroic hearts,
> Made weak by time and fate, but strong in will
> To strive, to seek, to find, and not to yield.

It is a beautiful stroke that proffers "in *old* days" for what Tennyson elsewhere speaks of as "our younger days." And rippling underneath that final line, striving to utter itself but battened down by will, is another line, almost identical and yet utterly different: "To strive, to seek, to yield, and not to find."

Ulysses is old; he stands upon the shores of life. The poem conveys a dragging sense of inertia, of *ennui,* strangely matched (but not barrenly) with the vocabulary of adventure and enterprise. Goldwin Smith was right to sense that Ulysses "intends to roam, but stands for ever a listless and melancholy figure on the shore." For though the poem describes the passing of time, it does so with an oily stagnancy of shimmer:

> The lights begin to twinkle from the rocks:
> The long day wanes: the slow moon climbs: the deep
> Moans round with many voices. Come, my friends,
> 'Tis not too late to seek a newer world.

The rhythm and diction (long, slow) are narcotically oppressive. Can the single voice of Ulysses then outdo those "many voices"? Does not the last line poignantly convey a sense that "'Tis far too late to seek a newer world"? Enterprise draws, but experience drags.

> Yet all experience is an arch wherethrough
> Gleams that untravelled world, whose margin fades
> For ever and for ever when I move.

Matthew Arnold, in one of the most penetrating remarks ever made about Tennyson, observed: "It is no blame to their rhythm, which belongs to another order of movement than Homer's, but it is true that these three lines by themselves take up nearly as much time as a whole book of the *Iliad*."[11]

---

[11]*On Translating Homer* (London, 1861) III. It is true, too, that Arnold managed to misquote five words in these three lines.

Ulysses yearns to believe that his life is not just a past, that it still has a future. But that this is a yearning, and not a confident assurance, comes out in a ubiquitous feature of the poem's language: its reluctance—in a poem of such an adventurous setting forth, so strange as to deserve to be called morbid—to use the future tense. This stylistic tissue of the poem is remarkable—unobtrusive but potent. For this poem, which seizes the chance of a future, rises only at two points into future tenses, neither simple futures. At first, in: "I will drink/ Life to the lees," *will,* not *shall:* a determination, not a simple futurity. Near the end, with the future tenses all governed by—and attenuated by—the word *may:*

> It may be that the gulfs will wash us down:
> It may be we shall touch the Happy Isles,
> And see the great Achilles, whom we knew.

But of course the subject of "Ulysses" makes future tenses indispensable; Tennyson can dispense with them only by converting them into equivalents which yet minimize futurity. The characteristic line from "Ulysses" might be "Though much is taken, much abides," or "I am a part of all that I have met": past and present leaving no room for future. The equivalents (not, of course, equivalent to our sensibilities) are persistent, finding a variety of linguistic forms to express and to repress the future:

> ...Gleams that untravelled world, whose margin fades
> For ever and for ever when I move.

That world to be traveled, whose margin will fade... Not "Every hour will bring new things," but "every hour...A bringer of new things." "Something...may yet be done," not *will be.* "Until I die." And—most richly used of all—the infinitive, such as *to follow,* which is throughout an ambiguous equivalent for the future tense.

> And this gray spirit yearning in desire
> To follow knowledge like a sinking star...

It is not said that Telemachus will fulfill his labor, but that he is "discerning to fulfil" it, and to make mild, and to subdue, and not to fail, and to pay adoration. It is not too late to seek; Ulysses' purpose holds to sail; and the poem ends with a crescendo of such equivalents, which stand in for the future tense but also stand out against it: "but strong in will/ To strive, to seek, to find, and not to yield."

Yet one feature of the poem which many critics have found richly equivocal may be poorly so.[12] There is a recurring argument as to how much Ulysses himself is admired or endorsed by the poem. But this uncertainty seems less a matter of a valuable contrariety than of a weakness. The crucial passage is that in which Ulysses hands over the mundane responsibilities to his son Telemachus. But at this point something goes wrong in terms of the poem's addresses. "This is my son, mine own Telemachus": too staged, this invites a demeaning "How do you do." And Tennyson—elsewhere in the poem so subtly meticulous—allows a ruckle of the syntax: Telemachus is

> decent not to fail
> In offices of tenderness, and pay
> Meet adoration to my household gods,
> When I am gone. He works his work, I mine.

The sense is of course "decent not to fail...and decent to pay...," but a clumsiness is there. The apparent lordliness of "He works his work, I mine" (as who should say, "We are all doing God's work, you in your way, and we in His") seems therefore more the poet's lapse into misjudgment than Ulysses' lapse into an unattractive and significant hauteur.

The argument is a tricky one. But if the Telemachus lines are faultily wooden rather than dramatically revealing, this might be because of "This is my son. ...." At this stage of his life (perhaps throughout his life), Tennyson was not able to write with alert conviction about sons and fathers, especially about their mutual respect. Too much from his own life came in the way. St. Simeon Stylites can cry with conviction "O my sons, my sons," but that is because they are not literally his sons. And in "Tiresias," the prophet can address Menoeceus throughout with paternal tenderness as "my son" for exactly the same reason.[13] So the Telemachus passage is neither a fine ambivalence nor a merely technical flaw, but—given Tennyson's shadowing experiences—a recalcitrance deep in the material itself.

[12]The most scrupulous account of the arguments is by John Pettigrew, *Victorian Poetry*, I (1963), 27-45.

[13]In "The Ancient Sage" (written 1885 and—like "Tiresias"—published then), the sage likewise repeatedly calls his young companion "My son." For Tennyson one of the magnetisms of King Arthur was that probably he neither had, nor was, a father.

"Death closes all." How does the poem close—with the story's outcome? When Tennyson's friend J. M. Kemble sent the poem to another Cambridge friend, he said: "I will fill up my paper with a grand thing of Alfred's, unfinished though it be."[14] But the poem was already finished. For once again there is an interplay between the rich stagnancy of a Tennyson poem (Ulysses standing forever on the shore) and the known outcome of its borrowed story. Ulysses' last voyage is hinted at in the *Odyssey,* but it is related in Dante's *Inferno* (xxvi, 90ff.). In Dante, Ulysses speaks; Tennyson's indebtedness is open and full.[15] Cary's Dante gives us "But virtue to pursue and knowledge high" (Tennyson's "To follow knowledge like a sinking star"); within three lines in Cary, "To the dawn/ Our poop we turn'd"; and only ten lines later a whirlwind strikes and sinks the ship. "And over us the booming billow closed": so closes the canto of the *Inferno,* a close which follows hard upon Ulysses' speech to his mariners. Tennyson's "Ulysses" ends upon the brink of disaster; Ulysses' future may be real but it is desperately brief. "How dull it is to pause, to make an end." But how strange to use *pause* and *end* virtually as synonyms. The ship of death is poised to set sail. It is this full suspension, this imminence, which underlies Carlyle's very beautiful comment on those poignant lines which the known but silent outcome dooms to stoical wishfulness:

> It may be that the gulfs will wash us down:
> It may be we shall touch the Happy Isles,
> And see the great Achilles, whom we knew.

"These lines do not make me weep, but there is in me what would fill whole Lachrymatories as I read."[16]

"Ulysses" sought to meet Hallam's death (which it did not exactly confront) by seeking an assurance of the courage of life, life being worth the highest compliment: risk. "Tithonus," which Tennyson spoke of as a "pendant" to "Ulysses," meets Hallam's death at a

[14]*The Poems of Tennyson,* ed. Christopher Ricks (Longman Annotated English Poets, London, 1969), p. 560. "Unfinished" might possibly mean "without final revision"; but Kemble's text, apart from two slips, is that of the Heath MS, and the differences from Tennyson's final text, though of great interest, are few and are matters of detail.

[15]"Yes, there is an echo of Dante in it" was Tennyson's understatement (*Memoir,* ii. 70).

[16]*Memoir,* I, 214.

different angle: by envisaging and envisioning a situation in which immortality is no blessing. Tithonus was granted immortal life but without thought of immortal youth; he is now the ceaselessly withering lover of Aurora, goddess of the dawn. Tennyson wrote the first version of the poem "Tithon" in the closing months of 1833; he did not at first publish it, perhaps because it was too poignant, or not perfected, or too vulnerable in its longing for death. Twenty-six years later, his friend Thackeray badgered Tennyson for a contribution to his new magazine, the *Cornhill;* Tennyson ferreted out "Tithon," transformed it into "Tithonus" (twelve lines longer and revised with supremely creative fitness), and published it in the *Cornhill* in 1860.

"Tithonus" is not, either allegorically or symbolically, a depiction of Tennyson's love of Hallam. But the myth draws upon and is drawn by his mingled fear and love. Perhaps it was fed by the grief of Tennyson's sister Emily, Hallam's betrothed, who was to write to Tennyson: "What is life to me! if I die (which the Tennysons never do). ..."[17] Probably Tennyson felt as did their Cambridge friend Monteith, who wrote to him in 1833: "Since Hallam's death I almost feel like an old man looking back on many friendships as something bygone."[18] Certainly it grew from the same awed perturbation which Benjamin Jowett felt when years later he visited Hallam's grave; Jowett wrote to the Tennysons: "It is a strange feeling about those who are taken young that while we are getting old and dusty they are as they were."[19] "Tithonus" embodies a fear as to the *nature* of Hallam's immortality, a fear intimated in *In Memoriam,* XLI. His fear, says Tennyson, is rarely "that vague fear implied in death":[20]

> Yet oft when sundown skirts the moor
> An inner trouble I behold,

[17]*Memoir,* I, 135.

[18]*Memoir,* I, 500.

[19]Tennyson Research Centre, Lincoln; April 1, 1859. This preoccupation was to surface again in the late poem "Tomorrow" (written 1884), where the young lover of long ago is found preserved in the peat-bog: "Thin his Riverence buried thim both in wan grave be the dead boor-tree,/ The young man Danny O'Roon wid his ould woman, Molly Magee."

[20]See too the sections of *In Memoriam* which Tennyson did not publish, "Young is the grief I entertain," and "Let Death and Memory keep the face." Also Humphrey House, "*In Memoriam,*" *All in Due Time* (London, 1955), p. 134.

> A spectral doubt which makes me cold,
> That I shall be thy mate no more,
>
> Though following with an upward mind
>   The wonders that have come to thee,
>   Through all the secular to-be,
> But evermore a life behind.

Blake said that "Time is the mercy of eternity." To Tithonus, death was the mercy of eternity. The poem is Tennyson's subtlest and most beautiful exploration of the impulse to suicide. From the first words, the poem meets the inexorable with its own inexorability:

> The woods decay, the woods decay and fall,
> The vapours weep their burthen to the ground,
> Man comes and tills the field and lies beneath,
> And after many a summer dies the swan.
> Me only cruel immortality
> Consumes: I wither slowly in thine arms,
> Here at the quiet limit of the world,
> A white-haired shadow roaming like a dream
> The ever-silent spaces of the East,
> Far-folded mists, and gleaming halls of morn.

The first four lines breathe peace and equanimity; such a death is breath-less, not breathless. But the fifth line disturbs all this, first by its immediate inversion ("Me only..."), unlike anything in the previous lines; next with the epithet "cruel," which springs with further force because the previous lines had not contained a single adjective; and disturbs it finally by its predatory enjambment ("Me only cruel immortality/ Consumes"),[21] whereas the previous lines had all been self-contained sense-units with terminal punctuation. Tithonus, who is "Here at the quiet limit of the world," is so aged as to be at the limit of life and yet is cruelly denied the chance to cross that limit into grateful death. The sentiment is a desolate counterpart to the retreating limit of aspiration in "Ulysses":

[21]Yet the predatoriness is doubly paradoxical. First, in that to mortals it is mortality, not immortality, which would be thought of as cruel; so that the first four lines are now heard in the accents not solely of lament but of envy. Second, in that "Consumes," despite its urgent placing, reveals itself as no violent devouring — it consumes as consumption consumes, yet with no release into death: "Consumes: I wither slowly...."

> Yet all experience is an arch wherethrough
> Gleams that untravelled world, whose margin fades
> For ever and for ever when I move.

But Tithonus yearns to reach death, that untravelled world, that undiscovered country from whose bourn no traveler returns. Beauty and promise have become the bitterest of emptiness: the "gleaming halls of morn" can no longer promise any true dawn for Tithonus.

"The ever-silent spaces of the East": one hiding place of the poem's exquisite chill is its evocation of a silence which stands in a triple relation to the poem. It etherealizes the erotic relationship; it tacitly whispers of Tithonus's extreme age; and it is potently contrasted with the superbly mellifluous movements of the verse itself. The opening lines epitomize this ambivalence of silence and sound: the woods which fall evoke no crash; the "burthen" (not just "burden") which the vapors weep "to the ground"—*to* has a double sense—is a silent song, an eternal funereal refrain of silence; and when "After many a summer dies the swan," another silent song— that of the dying swan[22]—is evoked, the song elicited for us and then rescinded, unmentioned. The limit of the world is quiet; the spaces of the East are ever silent. In the past there was utterance, the only words of speech directly recorded in the poem:

> I asked thee, "Give me immortality."
> Then didst thou grant mine asking with a smile...

Not with words, but with a smile; and now that silent smile has been replaced by silent tears:

> Can thy love,
> Thy beauty, make amends, though even now,
> Close over us, the silver star, thy guide,
> Shines in those tremulous eyes that fill with tears
> To hear me?

We are in a world of impregnated silences: "A soft air fans the cloud apart"—and the air both suggests and denies a musical air. The heartbeat pulses beyond hearing; the hoofs of Aurora's team strike silent sparks from the unimaginable flint of the air, they convert sound into a glory of sight, "And beat the twilight into flakes of fire."

[22]See "The Dying Swan" (1830).

Aurora grows beautiful "In silence, then before thine answer given/
Departest." From the past of utterance there floats a "saying": "The
Gods themselves cannot recall their gifts" (where *recall* superbly
suggests not only "call back" but "recollect," an infinite divine
forgetfulness of extreme old age). How distant are the "days far-off"
when their love was real, its reality attested to by the only moment of
uttered audible beauty within the poem:

> ...while I lay,
> Mouth, forehead, eyelids, growing dewy-warm
> With kisses balmier than half-opening buds
> Of April, and could hear the lips that kissed
> Whispering I knew not what of wild and sweet,
> Like that strange song I heard Apollo sing,
> While Ilion like a mist rose into towers.[23]

No more sounds within the poem—only the final ambivalence
(chiming with that of the opening "burthen" and the swan's song)
by which the dawn's return is both glidingly silent and "silver," a
word traditionally apt to the mellifluous[24]: "And thee returning on
thy silver wheels." In this subtle and persistent paradox of silence
and sound, Tennyson found a thrust of relationship with his own
fineness of musical verbalism that makes "Tithonus" his most assuredly successful poem, at once quintessentially Tennysonian and
yet with its Tennysonian felicities of sound made stronger and more
poignant by its chill of silence, its desolated loss of that "strange
song" which had once animated its world. Made stronger, too, by
the sudden nakednesses of expression—the word "scare," for instance, so unprotected by mellifluousness, in "Why wilt thou ever
scare me with thy tears"; or the total simple urgency of the cry,
again unswathed, "Let me go."

The desolation of their love is no consequence of any faithless-
ness in Tithonus or Aurora. "I" and "me" echo through the poem,
but with an impotence that is manifest in the first of them: "I
wither slowly in thine arms." The suggestion there is of a passivity
that is eternally moribund, an embrace that goes on forever but as
a lacerating travesty of lovers' hyperbolical ecstasy: "Yet hold me

---

[23]Tennyson's genius in revising his talent is manifest in the fine eroticism of
"half-opening buds," rich without prurience; his earlier version had been simply
"opening buds."

[24]*Oxford English Dictionary*, "Silver," 13: "Of sounds"; from 1526, including
Milton and Pope.

not for ever in thine East"—the ambiguity there in *hold* (keep me forever, and embrace me forever) does indeed show that what Tithonus gained was loss. The only two occasions—in this love poem—on which *I* governs *thee* epitomize the bitter plot: "I asked thee, 'Give me immortality'"; and the future that ends the poem, "forget...thee":

> I earth in earth forget these empty courts,
> And thee returning on thy silver wheels.

Empty of what? The potent absence in the poem, its central emptiness, that which in Tennyson's most pained poems manifests itself as not just emptiness but emptiedness, is the lovers' word *we*. *We* does not come once; *us* comes only once, at the poem's central sadness:

> Can thy love,
> Thy beauty, make amends, though even now,
> Close over us, the silver star, thy guide,
> Shines in those tremulous eyes that fill with tears
> To hear me?

Given the pathos of Tithonus's plight, it invites wonder that the poem staves off self-pity. Again a skill in miniature—a pronoun—effects something not miniature at all. For to the withering Tithonus his past self is another person; the split is painful but free from self-pity because it is virtually unimaginable that so distant a past self is his self. Tennyson nets this by casting "I" as "he":

> Alas! for this gray shadow, once a man—
> So glorious in his beauty and thy choice,
> Who madest him thy chosen, that he seemed
> To his great heart none other than a God!...
>
> Ay me! ay me! with what another heart
> In days far-off, and with what other eyes
> I used to watch—if I be he that watched—
> The lucid outline forming round thee...

Tithonus seems doomed to the unending. His poem ends:

> Yet hold me not for ever in thine East:
> How can my nature longer mix with thine?
> Coldly thy rosy shadows bathe me, cold
> Are all thy lights, and cold my wrinkled feet
> Upon thy glimmering thresholds, when the steam

> Floats up from those dim fields about the homes
> Of happy men that have the power to die,
> And grassy barrows of the happier dead.
> Release me, and restore me to the ground;
> Thou seest all things, thou wilt see my grave:
> Thou wilt renew thy beauty morn by morn;
> I earth in earth forget these empty courts,
> And thee returning on thy silver wheels.

An eternal immobility meets the heavenly mobile. The effect is paradoxical, as Henry James remarked in praising this passage for "a purity of tone, an inspiration, a something sublime and exquisite":

> It is poised and stationary, like a bird whose wings have borne him high, but the beauty of whose movement is less in great ethereal sweeps and circles than in the way he hangs motionless in the blue air, with only a vague tremor of his pinions. Even if the idea with Tennyson were more largely dramatic than it usually is, the immobility, as we must call it, of his phrase would always defeat the dramatic intention. When he wishes to represent movement, the phrase always seems to me to pause and slowly pivot upon itself, or at most to move backward.[25]

But is the poem's end its outcome? Tithonus notoriously neither withers endlessly nor is granted "the power to die"—in the words of Tennyson's note, "He grew old and infirm, and as he could not die, according to the legend, was turned into a grasshopper." Unthinkable for *this* poem? Other early poems by Tennyson explicitly use the grasshopper legend, though,[26] and the problem—how can we accommodate such an outcome to such an ending?—recurs in many of Tennyson's best poems. We can neither happily bring in that merciful translation into a grasshopper, nor happily leave it out. "Earth in earth" is, as Tennyson says, Dante's *terra in terra* (*Paradiso,* XXV): "My body is earth in the earth, and it will be there with the rest till our number tallies with the eternal purpose." But

---

[25]*The Galaxy,* September 1875; "Tennyson's Drama," *Views and Reviews* (London, 1908), p. 171. James's sympathetic and acute account of Tennyson's "poised and stationary" style is the counterpart of his wittily malicious description of Tennyson's reading of "Locksley Hall," with James's all disingenuous disappointment at how the Laureate would "spout": "With all the resonance of the chant, the whole thing was yet *still,* with all the long swing of its motion it yet remained where it was—heaving doubtless grandly enough up and down and beautiful to watch as through the superposed veils of its long self-consciousness" *(The Middle Years).*

[26]Other early poems: *The Devil and the Lady* and *The Grasshopper.*

the eternal purpose for Tithonus will not leave the body as earth in earth. The contrariety of poem and outcome is here at its most perplexing; neither the tragedy of immortal age nor the tragedy of death will be available to Tithonus, but something much smaller, verging on the kindly ludicrous. Tennyson's poem proffers a world in which the ultimate further alternative to the cruel tragic alternatives is a miraculous but unmagnificent diminution: a grasshopper. What future for Tithonus? Neither of those which he fears. The poem potently eschews the future tense, which surfaces at only one moment, in those closing lines: "thou wilt see my grave:/ Thou wilt renew thy beauty"—and then, with a superb elision of the future tense, "I earth in earth forget. . . ." With a profound circularity of return, both "Ulysses"—which yearns to have a future—and "Tithonus"—which yearns to have no future—can find no room for the future tense of hope.

The English Idyls

by A. Dwight Culler

These little paintings in their costly frames.
DRAFT OF *The Gardener's Daughter*

"Of this *Second* Vol.," says FitzGerald of the *Poems* of 1842, "the Morte d' Arthur, Day-dream, Lord of Burleigh, & Dora, were in MS in a little red Book, from which they were read to me & Spedding of a Night, 'when all the House was mute,' at Spedding's House, Mirehouse, by Basanthwaite Lake, in Cumberland. Spedding's Father & Mother were both alive: and his Father, who was of a practical turn, and had seen enough of Poets in Shelley and Coleridge (perhaps in Wordsworth also)..., rather resented our making so serious a Business of Verse-making, though he was so wise and charitable as to tolerate every thing & Everybody — except Poetry & Poets."[1] FitzGerald goes on to say that the frame to the *Morte d'Arthur,* which was published in 1842 under the title *The Epic,* did not exist at this time and therefore must have been added sometime between May 1835, the date of the reading, and 1842.[2]

"The English Idyls." From A. Dwight Culler, *The Poetry of Tennyson* (New Haven: Yale University Press, 1977), pp. 106-28. Copyright © 1977 by Yale University. Reprinted by permission of the publisher.

[1]Edward FitzGerald's copy of Tennyson's *Poems* (1842), II, verso of last page (Trinity). On another occasion FitzGerald wrote, "I well remember that when I was at Merehouse (as Miss Bristowe would have us call it), with A. Tennyson in 1835, Mr. Spedding grudged his Son's giving up much time and thought to consultations about Morte d'Arthur's, Lords of Burleigh, etc., which were then in MS. He more than once questioned me, who was sometimes present at the meetings, 'Well, Mr. F., and what is it? Mr. Tennyson reads, and Jem criticizes: — is that it?' " (Hallam Tennyson, ed., *Tennyson and His Friends* [London, 1911], p. 402).

[2]"Morte d'Arthur when read to us from MS in 1835 had no Introduction, or Epilogue; which were added to anticipate or excuse the 'faint Homeric Echoes' &c."

Since the ostensible purpose of the frame, which describes the reading of the poem to a group of college friends at Christmastime, is to provide an embarrassed apology for a poem so little relevant to modern life, and particularly for the anachronism of the style— "faint Homeric echoes, nothing worth"—one may think that it derives from this reading and that Parson Holmes is a distant allusion to Mr. Spedding, Sr. Actually, of course, the effect of the frame is firmly to assert the poem's worth, for although the parson, who has been "Now harping on the church-commissioners,/ Now hawking at Geology and schism," fell asleep during the recital, this is a compliment rather than the reverse, and the other two listeners were deeply moved. Naturally, like the college youths they are, they will not betray their emotion. Francis Allen, "muttering, like a man ill-used,/ ...drove his heel into the smoulder'd log" and sent a blast of sparkles up the flue. The narrator was set by the tale to dream, but the real indication of his interest comes in the introductory part of the poem where, when mention is made that one book of Everard Hall's epic has survived, "I, tho' sleepy, like a horse/ That hears the corn-bin open, prick'd my ears," for he remembered Everard's college fame and recognized the true source of his spiritual nourishment. What they had been discussing, these three youths and Parson Holmes, was how "the old honour had from Christmas gone,/ Or gone, or dwindled down to some odd games/ In some odd nooks like this"—forfeits and kissing the girls beneath the sacred bush— and the parson, "taking wide and wider sweeps" through the various issues of the day, had finally settled down "upon the general decay of faith/ Right thro' the world...:'there was no anchor, none,/ To hold by.'" At this point Francis Allen, laughing, clapped his hand on Everard's shoulder and said, "I hold by him," and though Everard, ever playing the clown, says, "And I by the wassail-bowl," the clear implication of this is to anticipate Arnold's statement that in the modern world poetry will more and more take the place of religion. In the general decay of faith Francis Allen will hold by the poet, who will provide a new order, a new set of values, to replace the old.

This, as we have already seen, is what the poem does—not con-

(FitzGerald's copy of *Poems* [1842] , II, 1). See [Hallam Tennyson] *Materials for a Life of A. T. Collected for my Children* [n.p., n.d.] , I, 237; and Hallam Tennyson, ed., *Alfred Lord Tennyson: A Memoir* (London, 1897), I, 194.

fidently, for Tennyson with characteristic agnosticism mutes the thought of Arthur's second coming. But there is enough said to enable the youths to see that Sir Bedivere's problem is their problem and that the proper solution is not, as Holmes would say, blindly to cling to the old but through prayer, labor, and imagination to prepare for the new. Indeed, the narrator is so impressed that when he goes to bed he dreams that Arthur does come again; "like a modern gentleman/ Of stateliest port," and that all the people acclaim him. Now whether it be the stateliness of his port or the cheeriness of the church bells that ring him in, we feel that in this detail Tennyson has suffered a lapse of taste. His point, of course, is that, like Adam, the narrator awoke and found his dream was true. But the "dream" was the myth of Arthur embodied in Everard Hall's poem, and the youths found it true when, in their embarrassment, they kicked the log and acknowledged its bearing upon themselves. They did not need to dream it over again in the modern dress it had already assumed, and, in any case, if the modern gentleman is supposed to be Hallam, there is the objection that Hallam is dead and that it was his death and not his second coming that was the occasion of the poem. The last dozen or sixteen lines not only reduplicate the action unnecessarily, they also get ahead of the story.

Nonetheless, the frame is a real achievement. Without it Tennyson would have created a jewel, but with it he has placed this jewel in a setting which enhances its beauty by the play of reflected lights. It is not merely that the frame emphasizes the relevance of the Arthurian myth—though this has more point than usual because of the fact that the myth contains a cyclical view of history—but also that the *Morte d'Arthur* is transformed from the narrative of a king's death into a work of art, a poem. It is distinctly a piece of literature. It does not pretend to any other reality than this, that it is the eleventh book of an epic written by a young man and being read to an audience of which two are attentive and one is asleep. Thus, the poem as a whole is called *The Epic,* and its center is neither in the frame nor in the inset but somewhere between the two. It hovers back and forth between the reading of the poem, which is initiated by the first part of the frame, and its reception, which is detailed by the second—between these and the poem itself. Hence the poem's quality as art can actually be emphasized, and this is done by the heightened formalism and artificiality of the romance or epic style. Within the poem this courtly and ritualistic character—the archaic language, the epithets, the symmetry of the action, the repeated poetic formulas—is justified as the literary equivalent of the old order that is passing. But within the frame it constitutes a heightened and intensified beauty which is simply the beauty of art itself. For this reason the style of the frame is in sharp contrast with that of the inset—not archaic, formal, and ritualistic but the perfectly natural and cultivated language of Oxford and Cambridge undergraduates. At the same time there is nothing colloquial about it: it is limpid and graceful and it is written in blank verse. Thus, it too is art, though it is reality with respect to the artfulness of the inset, and so the whole question is raised, What is art and what is reality? What is the relation of the poet to society, of the myth to the moment? We are left with the impression that we do not know quite so clearly as we thought we did, and we are even aware that the problem does not stop here. For far within the center of the poem, dwelling "Upon the hidden bases of the hills," is another artist, the Lady of the Lake, who has fashioned in Excalibur a work of art that is far more dazzling even than the legend in which it is set. Yet this work of art is the means of the King's acting upon the world. So there is a work of art which impinges upon reality, which itself is a work of art which impinges upon reality, which, as we read it, impinges upon our reality again. By this device of a series of receding images—like the picture of an artist painting a picture of an artist painting a picture—Tennyson raises questions which he has been asking, but not so distinctly, from the very outset of his career.

He does this again in an even more complicated, though less substantial poem, *The Day-Dream,* which is precisely parallel to *The Epic* in that it too represents the poet as telling an old-world legend to a person who he at least hopes will be deeply affected by it. In this case the legend is that of the Sleeping Beauty and the person Lady Flora. The poem, which is a veritable *Tale of a Tub* for preliminary and concluding matter, consists of nine sections, which form an envelope structure in three stages successively recessed. It may be represented thus:

1. Prologue
2. The Sleeping Palace
3. The Sleeping Beauty
4. The Arrival
5. The Revival

The fascinating thing about this structure is that Tennyson wrote the poem from the middle out. The first section written was *The Sleeping Beauty,* which was published in the *Poems, Chiefly Lyrical* of 1830 and which would have taken its place there among the "lady" poems as a pure aesthetic image. It was feminine, passive, absolutely immobile—"A perfect form in perfect rest." Then, sometime between 1830 and 1834, when Tennyson had become more interested in the social uses of beauty, he added the surrounding legend, sections 2 and 4-6. Section 2 presents a picture of the Sleeping Palace which concludes with the words, "When will the hundred summers die,/ And thought and time be born again,/ And newer knowledge, drawing nigh,/ Bring truth that sways the souls of men?" The answer is given in the arrival of the fairy Prince, who, led by a "Magic Music" that has beat within his heart since childhood, comes, "scarce knowing what he seeks," and kisses the Sleeping Beauty. She and all the palace awake (though some of the king's councillors rather reluctantly), and he carries her off to his father's court: "Through all the world she followed him." He is, in other words, precisely the kind of lover that the Lady of Shalott and Mariana longed for and never had, and as a result the roles can be reversed. For where the Lady of Shalott was the artist and did not even have a sympathetic listener, the Sleeping Princess is Beauty itself, who is brought out of her hidden bower by the artist imbued with love.

> All precious things, discovered late,
>   To those that seek them issue forth;
> For love in sequel works with fate,
>   And draws the veil from hidden worth.

This was the state of the poem when Tennyson read it to FitzGerald and Spedding in the famous session of May 1835. At least when FitzGerald says that "the Prologue & Epilogue" were added after that date,[3] we must probably understand him as referring to all the

---

[3]"The Prologue & Epilogue were added after 1835, when we first heard it read in Cumberland; I suppose for the same reason that caused the Prologue &c. to Morte D'Arthur; giving a *Reason* for telling an Old-World Fairy Tale." Manuscript note in FitzGerald's copy of Tennyson's *Poems* (1842), II, 148.

preliminary and concluding matter, for the Moral and Envoi, which refer to Lady Flora, would not have been intelligible without the Prologue, which introduces her. In this outermost frame Tennyson is again practicing imitative form. For just as the Prince took the Sleeping Beauty out into the world, so Tennyson now takes the legend of the Sleeping Beauty out into the world by telling it to Lady Flora. For Lady Flora, who in the Prologue is dozing by an open lattice, is herself a Sleeping Beauty, and as the poet watches her, he too has a dream which is the "day-dream" of his title. He dreamed "until at last/ Across my fancy, brooding warm,/ The reflex of a legend past,/ And loosely settled into form." If she will but close her eyes he will tell it to her, but when he does, Lady Flora, whose "too earnest eyes" and "pensive mind" betoken a too serious approach to literature, demands the moral. The poet protests. "What moral is in being fair?" But if she will have one, let her consider how pleasant it would be to fall asleep for a hundred years, missing all the intervening wars and struggles, and then to wake upon a new state of science, poetry, and politics. So we should reap "The flower and quintessence of change." But really, anyone can make applications according to his humor, and to do so is to narrow art too much. Its use is in its beauty. In this case, where the poet would be the fairy Prince to his Lady Flora and wake her from the sleep of single life into the condition of wifehood, the poem is the kiss by which he would do it. Fashioned as a graceful compliment, it would itself accomplish the act of which it speaks. For it now appears that the Lady Flora is not merely dozing by the lattice, she is "all too dearly self-involved" and in that sense "sleeps a dreamless sleep to me"; and it is out of this solipsistic state that the poet, not entirely playfully, would wake her. Hence the rather frivolous poem. For just as the *Morte d'Arthur* provided for the young men the new order of imaginative experience which both they and Sir Bedivere required, so the legend of the Sleeping Beauty not only parallels Lady Flora's situation but is also the means of resolving it. And the resolution, as the poet is quick to point out, would combine her aesthetic with his, for if she would come out of her self-involvement into wifehood, that would be the "moral of [her] life" as it would be the "pleasure" of his.

Finally, Tennyson provided a brief frame for *Godiva,* written after passing through Coventry in June 1840. As so often, he throws the reader off the track by pretending that the poem is about some-

thing other than its true subject. Not only we, the modern generation, he says, who prate of rights and wrongs, have loved the people
well, but she, Lady Godiva, actually suffered for them a thousand
years ago and freed them from their tax. But when we come to the
passage that is the emotional center of the poem, that in which Lady
Godiva prepares to leave her inmost bower, and read the lovely
description of her tender, shrinking modesty, her sense of shame,
her reluctance to reveal her beauty to the world, then we realize that
we are reading of the artist and that Tennyson was getting ready to
publish once again. If one doubts this interpretation, one need only
consult the Trinity College manuscript, where Tennyson turned
Peeping Tom into the type of the critic.

> Nor do I trust the tale of peeping Tom:
> But if there were so gross a clown, be he
> Accursed! or if one of modern days
> Would turn this verse to scandal let him forge
> His own shame from it, Sathen helping him,
> Accursed! For she wrought a noble deed.[4]

Ultimately, Tennyson thought better about thus throwing down the
gauntlet to the *Quarterly Review* and told the story of Tom in its
traditional form. But he knew that by telling the story of Lady
Godiva he was exposing himself to the same kind of ribald laughter
that she had been exposed to in her ride. He thought, however, that
he was doing it for the same good purpose—to serve the people—
and hence the four lines of introduction:

> I waited for the train at Coventry;
> I hung with grooms and porters on the bridge,
> To watch the three tall spires; and there I shaped
> The city's ancient legend into this:—

The purpose of these lines is not, as Leigh Hunt says,[5] to inform us
how casually Tennyson writes his poetry but to reinforce the theme
of the poem by showing the poet mingling with grooms and porters,
as Lady Godiva did, and the train counterpointed by the spires of
the medieval cathedral.

   Though the true subject of this poem is the artist's sensitivity,

---

[4] *Trinity Notebook 26.*

[5] Leigh Hunt, *Church of England Quarterly Review* (October 1842), quoted in
Ricks [*The Poems of Tennyson* (London, 1969)] , pp. 731-32.

the mention of grooms and porters, trains and taxes, is not accidental. For beginning in the 1820s and continuing for perhaps thirty years there was a powerful demand on the part of many critics that the poet deal with the great realities of modern life instead of the outworn themes of Greece and Rome or the romance of the Middle Ages.[6] Trains and steam engines were as interesting as the monsters of antiquity, and the urban poor had their sorrows as well as the shepherds and shepherdesses of the Renaissance. Thus, when Elizabeth Barrett heard that Tennyson's new poem, *The Princess,* was "in blank verse & a fairy tale," she wrote, "Now isn't the world too old & fond of steam, for blank verse poems, in ever so many books, to be written on the fairies?"[7] And the *Westminster Review,* in noticing Tennyson's first volume, asked, "Is not the French Revolution as good as the siege of Troy?...The old epics will probably never be surpassed, any more than the old coats of mail; and for the same reason: nobody wants the article." The reviewer added that "a long story...is now always done, and best done, in prose."[8] Indeed, the real problem was not steam but the novel. The novel was usurping the dominant position previously occupied by poetry and was doing so precisely by its ability to deal, seriously and directly, with the issues of modern life. If the poet wished to compete with this rival, he would have to bestir himself. Hence some poets, such as Clough and Elizabeth Barrett, attempted the verse novel, whereas others, such as the Spasmodics, thought that a pretentious style and psychological violence would do the trick. Arnold, more thoughtfully, took the view in his Preface of 1853 that the important thing was not whether a subject was ancient or modern but that it involve actions which "powerfully appeal to the great primary human affections: to those elementary feelings which subsist permanently in the race, and which are independent of time."[9] He added that he was dropping his own *Empedocles on Etna* from his new volume not because it had an ancient subject but because it had a modern disease.

As usual, Tennyson took a mediatorial view. In his first two volumes there was little to provide comfort for the modernist, and

[6]For a good account see Walter E. Houghton, *The Poetry of Clough: An Essay in Revaluation* (New Haven: Yale University Press, 1963), pp. 93-99.

[7]*Letters of Robert Browning and Elizabeth Barrett Barrett,* ed. E. Kintner, [(Cambridge, Mass., 1969), 2 vols.,] I, 427.

[8]*Westminster Review,* 14 (January 1831), 212.

[9]*Poetical Works,* ed. C. B. Tinker and H. F. Lowry (Oxford, 1953), pp. xix-xx.

there is no question that in his heart he was deeply drawn to the
older legends and the traditionary forms. On the other hand, he
was a proponent of change, and he certainly would have been
startled by Elizabeth Barrett's remark, for in the "University of
Women," as *The Princess* was originally called, he at least thought
he was addressing the modern world. Aubrey de Vere, who heard
him read from it in the spring of 1845, found him "denouncing
exotics, and saying that a poem should reflect the time and place."[10]
Of course, the way in which he did this was to write an old-world
legend and place it in a modern setting, and we have already seen
that in so doing he was not merely answering the call for relevance
but was also devising complex poetic effects. He was, in fact, ap-
proximating a form which became one of the dominant forms of
the Victorian period and that with which his own name is particularly associated—the idyl. For the idyl, as employed by Theocritus
and Virgil, frequently involves two or three shepherds who come
together and speak in artless and simple language about their
everyday affairs. Then one asks the other to sing a song, or they
engage in a song contest, perhaps of the "amoeboean" variety in
which verse answers to verse, or they describe a beautifully carved
bowl or other work of art, and then, after a brief interval, they part
in subtly altered mood. It is difficult to say just what this Alexandrian
and Neoteric form meant, for the scholars who have studied it most
deeply are themselves not agreed. But one thing is certain: it was a
highly sophisticated, not a simple form, and it had more to do with
art than with shepherds. It was, indeed, a kind of coterie poetry,
written by learned and highly cultivated men for their friends, and
it was based on the premise that a delicate emotion expressed in a
pure style came closer to the aesthetic experience than the most
magniloquent emotion hammered home. It was, in other words, a
poet's poem, highly conscious of itself as art, and if the idyls of
Theocritus and the bucolics of Virgil have become world famous, it
is probably because quietude and charm, tenderness and pure
beauty, appeal as powerfully to the great primary human affections
as does heroic action. In any case, it was this form, which in Tennyson's work grew out of his use of the frame, that served as his means
of responding to the call for relevance.

The matter is paradoxical because, however "modern" or archaic
the poems of Theocritus and Virgil may have been, certainly by the

[10]Wilfred Ward, *Aubrey de Vere: A Memoir* (London, 1904), p. 74.

end of the eighteenth century the pastoral had acquired the name of the most sterile and artificial of poetic forms. It had been frozen in its own convention. Crabbe did the form a service by recalling it to truth and urging it to "own the Village Life a life of pain," and Wordsworth provided a new positive impulse to pastoralism by writing directly from nature. Indeed, when Wordsworth chose humble and rustic life as his subject because there the essential passions of the heart are more simply and accurately revealed, he was stating the true pastoral method. For pastoral is not a subject but a perspective. It is the perspective of one who has gone out of the city into the country and looks back upon his problems through the clear rural air. Hence, the tension of winter along with spring, of labor along with harvest, is essential, and these had always been included by Theocritus and Virgil. The latter especially found that he could treat vast social movements, such as the demobilization of armies, through the single instance of a shepherd threatened with dispossession of his farm. Through simple things, as Empson noted, complex things may be said.[11] Thus, when the impulse from a vernal wood which had been renewed by Romanticism met with the new industrialization and the urbanization of the early Victorian years, it was the perfect pastoral moment. On the one hand was the sense of a complex and sophisticated culture, of pressing national problems, and, on the other, of an older and greener world which was rapidly fading away but had not yet altogether been lost.

It is no wonder, then, that Theocritus came back into favor at this time, particularly at Cambridge. Asked whether Tennyson was a good classicist, the Master of Trinity is said to have replied, "He knew his Theocritus very well."[12] But so too did others. Among Tennyson's contemporaries at Trinity were a future translator of Theocritus and a future student of the Greek bucolic poets.[13] Possibly their attention was drawn to their subject by the publication in 1826-29 of a Cambridge reprint of the Kiessling edition of Theocritus, the most important English edition of the poet since Warton's in 1770. And of course all these men had known their Virgil since childhood. But the pastoral revival came from many

---

[11]William Empson, *English Pastoral Poetry* (New York, 1938), pp. 23, 137.

[12]Quoted in Douglas Bush, *Mythology and the Romantic Tradition* (Cambridge, [Mass.,] 1937), p. 204n.

[13]M. J. Chapman, the translator of Theocritus, Bion, and Moschus (1836), and Henry Alford, author of *Chapters on the Poets of Ancient Greece* (1842).

sources, one of them being Germany. For in 1756 Salomon Gessner published his *Idyllen* which, though retaining Greek names, added touches from a north European scene and infused into the poems a modern sentimentality and morality. These *Idyllen* were translated into English as the *Rural Poems,* and when Robert Southey heard about them from William Taylor of Norwich, he determined to imitate them.[14] His *English Eclogues,* nine in number, are doubtless the formal precedent for Tennyson's English Idyls, that is, for the recreation of the classical form with modern English characters and manners, but spiritually their flat prosaicism hardly provides a model. For that, for the freshness and beauty, the sentiment and charm of the English countryside, Tennyson was indebted, apart from his own observation, to the newly emerging prose idyl. For in 1843, in *A New Spirit of the Age,* R. H. Horne noticed that "Within the last half century a somewhat new class of writing has been introduced into this country with great success, and most fortunately for the public taste, as its influence is most healthy and sweet, most refreshing and soothing, most joyous, yet most innocent. It is that of the unaffected prose pastoral."[15] Citing the delightful papers and essays of Leigh Hunt, and particularly one little work *The Months,* he acknowledged that Miss Mitford was the undoubted leader of this school, though William and Mary Howitt were strong supporters. The latter's *Rural Life of England* (1838) in two volumes, and Miss Mitford's *Our Village: Sketches of Rural Character and Scenery* (1824-32) in five, make us aware that the idyl, or "little picture," when naturalized into English, takes the form of the "sketch." It is this form, halfway between an essay and a narrative, which seems to have just the flexibility and inconclusiveness demanded by these materials. What Lamb's essays and the *Sketches by Boz* did for London, and *The Sketch Book of Geoffrey Crayon, Gent.* for other parts of England and America, the sketches of Miss Mitford and William Howitt, of Charlotte Smith and Thomas Miller did for the English countryside. The danger of these works, as Horne's encomium indicates, is that they may fall into mere prettiness on the one side or heaviness on the other. For as the origin of the term *sketch* indicates, there was, quite apart from Gessner, a considerable Dutch or German element in these idyls, a kind of

[14]J. W. Robberds, *A Memoir of the Life and Writings of the Late William Taylor of Norwich* (London, 1843), I, 213.

[15]R. H. Horne, *A New Spirit of the Age* (Oxford, 1909), pp. 132-33.

domestic *Gemütlichkeit,* which made what had originally been an aristocratic into a middle-class form. The "little picture," in other words, may be a Cuyp instead of a Claude Lorraine, a Rembrandt instead of a Titian.

Tennyson did not altogether avoid these evils. *The May Queen,* which was universally beloved in the Victorian era, is to modern taste almost unreadable, and *The Lord of Burleigh,* though a fine "period piece," is also marred by condescension and superficiality. Even *Dora,* which many people admire, seems to me a mistake— not for Arnold's reason, that it sacrifices *simplicité* to *simplesse,*[16] but because its harsh Crabbean realism is at variance with the sentiment it ought to inspire. Tennyson's intention, in this tale adapted from Miss Mitford's *Our Village,* was to achieve the severity and simplicity of the Book of Ruth or the nobility of Wordsworth's *Michael.* But his harsh, bald style, in which (as in the third book of *Paradise Lost*) there is not a single metaphor or any descriptive passage, is the counterpart not of the loving mind of Dora but of the harsh vindictiveness of the old man. Since Dora's strategy is to soften the mind of her uncle by bringing the child to him in the midst of the harvest plenty, that strategy should also be practiced on the reader. Miss Mitford manages the matter better by having the tale told retrospectively by a feminine narrator in the midst of the harvest scene.

The best of Tennyson's English Idyls may be divided into two groups: on the one hand, *The Gardener's Daughter* and *The Miller's Daughter,* written about 1832-33, and on the other, *Walking to the Mail, Audley Court, Edwin Morris,* and *The Golden Year,* written about 1837-39. The former are dramatic monologues, focusing upon a feminine figure, and so closer to the poems of 1830-32; the latter involve a dialogue between two or more masculine figures and so are more Theocritean in structure.

The Gardener's Daughter is one of Tennyson's most luxuriant poems, but when we examine the manuscripts we find that it was once far more luxuriant, perhaps twice its present length and infinitely fuller not only of incident but also of description.[17] It was, indeed, not an idyl but a tale, precisely in the manner of *The Lover's Tale,* and so provides a link between that earlier Romantic mode

[16]Matthew Arnold, *On Translating Homer,* in *Complete Prose Works,* ed. R. H. Super (Ann Arbor: University of Michigan Press, 1960), pp. 206-7.

[17]*Trinity Notebook* 17 (23).

and the Victorian idyl. Then as now, it told of the narrator's wooing
of Rose, the gardener's daughter, but in the original there was much
more about the paintings of Eustace, the narrator's friend, about the
long-drawn-out difficulties of the courtship, and about the death of
a younger brother. Fortunately, at a certain point Tennyson had the
acumen to realize that the essence of his tale lay not in the narrative but in the picture which the narrator painted of Rose as she
stood in her cottage door. And so it is on that picture that the poem
focuses. We do not realize it at first, but by the end of the poem we
are aware that the tale is not addressed to us as readers but to some
unnamed auditor to whom the portrait is being unveiled by the
speaker years after his beloved's death. The poem thus belongs
with Rossetti's *The Portrait* and Browning's *My Last Duchess* as
a member of that Victorian subgenre, the portrait by the artist of a
dead girl. But whereas Browning is horrified at the thought of a
living woman being imprisoned in a dead work of art, and Rossetti is thrilled at the idea of a form which somehow imitates the
object without constituting it, Tennyson believed that the soul
could be captured in a portrait painted by Love.

For this portrait was so painted. The subtitle of *The Gardener's
Daughter* is *The Pictures*. The other picture is Eustace's portrait
of his betrothed, Juliet, of which the narrator said, "(half in earnest,
half in jest,)/ 'Tis not your work, but Love's.'" So the narrator is told
that he will paint his masterpiece when he goes to see Rose, the gardener's daughter. For, less in jest than in earnest, Tennyson believes that one does paint beautifully only that which one truly
loves. What does Tennyson love?

> Not wholly in the busy world, nor quite
> Beyond it, blooms the garden that I love.

Among all the rewritings and changes of the manuscripts these
lines remain unchanged. For though the gardener's daughter appears in a garden than has some resemblance to the bower of the
Sleeping Beauty or of the other sequestered maidens, it is not absolutely a *hortus conclusus,* cut off from the world. "News from the
humming city comes to it/ In sound of funeral or of marriage bells";
and although between the city and the garden lies a "league of grass,
wash'd by a slow broad stream," this stream creeps slowly down,
"Barge-laden, to three arches of a bridge/ Crown'd with the min-
ster-towers." Neither is Rose herself a Sleeping Beauty. True, "In

that still place she, hoarded in herself,/ Grew, seldom seen." Still, her fame was widespread, and when the narrator came to see her he found her, not warbling in her bower, but engaged in a useful domestic task. A storm the previous night had blown down one spray of a rose bush by the cottage door, and she, as he entered, was reaching up to replace it. Society ladies in those days assumed what they called "attitudes."[18] In a parlor or salon, before a cluster of admirers and arrayed in cashmere shawls or turbans, they threw themselves into a series of postures: they were now Niobe, lamenting her children, now Ariadne, gazing out to sea. "O Attic shape, fair attitude!" says Keats, but there is no fairer one than that into which Tennyson froze the gardener's daughter. For the real portrait is not that in pigments revealed by the narrator at the end of the poem but that in words revealed by Tennyson in the middle.

> For up the porch there grew an Eastern rose,
> That, flowering high, the last night's gale had caught,
> And blown across the walk. One arm aloft —
> Gown'd in pure white, that fitted to the shape —
> Holding the bush, to fix it back, she stood,
> A single stream of all her soft brown hair
> Pour'd on one side: the shadow of the flowers
> Stole all the golden gloss, and wavering
> Lovingly lower, trembled on her waist —
> Ah, happy shade — and still went wavering down,
> But, ere it touch'd a foot, that might have danced
> The greensward into greener circles, dipt,
> And mix'd with shadows of the common ground!
> But the full day dwelt on her brows, and sunn'd
> Her violet eyes, and all her Hebe bloom,
> And doubled his own warmth against her lips,
> And on the bounteous wave of such a breast
> As never pencil drew. Half light, half shade,
> She stood, a sight to make an old man young.

"It is the Center of the Poem," said Tennyson of the above passage; "it must be full & rich. The Poem is so, to a fault, I know: but, being so, this central Picture must hold it's [*sic*] place—"[19] That is

---

[18]See Kirsten Gram Holmstrom, *Monodrama, Attitudes, Tableaux Vivants: Studies on Some Trends of Theatrical Fashions, 1770-1815* (Stockholm, 1967), pp. 110-208.

[19]The note is in FitzGerald's copy of Tennyson's *Poems* (1842), II, 32.

why he pruned the poem so drastically, eliminating metaphors and descriptions, placing Eustace's self-portrait in an Ante-Chamber, ever, to FitzGerald's disgust, eliminating a lovely bit of autumn landscape which had been taken from Titian's *Three Ages of Man*.[20] For there are pictures within pictures within pictures in this poem. Like the Lady of the Lake and Godiva and the Sleeping Beauty, the Gardener's Daughter is framed within the narrative of her own wooing and by that successful wooing is brought out into the world. But then she is framed again by the husband's exhibiting her picture in later years and telling her story to the unnamed friend who listens.

The Miller's Daughter also focuses upon a picture, for as the squire, sitting over the walnuts and the wine, reminisces with his wife about their wooing, he recalls how, a listless and unhappy boy, he had thrown himself down one April morn by the mill pond. He had no thought of Alice but, like an absent fool, "angled in the upper pool." All seemed to be conspiring, however, to create their love. A love song he had somewhere heard beat time to nothing in his head, haunting him with the weary sameness of its rhymes. "Then leapt a trout." This was the precipitating moment, the tiny action, which, like the fluttering of the film of soot in Coleridge's flue, set the drama in motion. For as he watched the ripples clear, there in the level flood "a vision caught my eye;/ The reflex of a beauteous form"—Alice, who was leaning out of her casement to tend some flowers on the ledge. He raised his eyes and they met hers, so full and bright that he has never forgotten the scene. The entire poem is, indeed, a re-creation of that moment and of the mood of love which it inspired, for as the poem closes, the two wander out across the wold to the old mill, where they watch the sunset "fire your narrow casement glass,/ Touching the sullen pool below"—just as Alice had touched him long years before, just as the troubled waters, clearing to a mirror, had swept away the troubles of his youth.

[20]FitzGerald in his copy of *Poems* (1842) gives readings "from the MS as it stood for a long time, & so was known among us. In some respects I must like the old Reading best, though the Whole Poem is undoubtedly improved in Form & Matter. In particular, I never liked to lose the bit of Autumn landscape noted at p. 28— which I remember to have guessed—and rightly—to be taken from a Background of a Titian: I think, Lord Ellesmere's 'Ages of Man.'" The lines are given in Ricks, p. 517: "Her beauty ... fallows."

And yet, this life has not been free from trouble. As the scene opens the old Miller has just died, and this event diffuses a tender sadness over the poem. They have also lost a child, though, as so often in Tennyson, this event is so obscurely expressed that one is hardly aware it happened. And the circumstance which had made the youth so troubled in boyhood was the early death of his father, which made him fear that he too would die young. Life gives much, but more is taken away, opines the squire, and this truth is illustrated by the two songs inserted into the narrative, one, an imitation of Anacreon, which he made for their bridal day, and "That other song I made,/ Half-angered with my happy lot." The songs, so opposite in mood, re-create the pastoral structure, but this is perhaps even more effectively done by the second major picture of the poem, that of the old Miller himself. For though ostensibly irrelevant to the love that follows, it really establishes its mood. "I see the wealthy miller yet," begins the squire—

> In yonder chair I see him sit,
>   Three fingers round the old silver cup—
> I see his grey eyes twinkle yet
>   At his own jest—grey eyes lit up
> With summer lightnings of a soul
>   So full of summer warmth, so glad,
> So healthy, sound, and clear and whole,
>   His memory scarce can make me sad.

The poem is a little too sentimental, and one regrets the condescension of the mother, who, in learning of her son's choice, "wished me happy, but she thought/ I might have looked a little higher." But these are minor faults compared with the warm twilight glow that is diffused through the picture, the golden haze through which even trouble is seen by the eyes of love.

The idyls are so closely connected with painting that it is perhaps desirable to say a little about Tennyson's knowledge of this art. The great public galleries did not, of course, exist in those days, but Tennyson nonetheless had managed to see a good many pictures and to acquire a taste for both the Dutch and the Italian school. His father had collected a number of quite tolerable old masters on his visits to Italy and had written a manuscript treatise on oil painting, with a list of some two hundred of the most famous painters of all countries.[21] At Cambridge the collection bequeathed to the university by Viscount Fitzwilliam was at that time housed in a building lent by Caius College, where Tennyson presumably would have seen it. Later he visited the Dulwich Picture Gallery, at that time the principal public gallery in England, which housed a collection of nearly four hundred paintings, chiefly of the Dutch school, but with some French, Italian, and Spanish masters. The National Gallery was not opened until 1838, but Mr. Angerstein's collection of thirty-eight paintings, the nucleus of the collection, presumably could have been seen in his ill-lighted rooms in Pall Mall. Tennyson, in fact, preferred private collections. In 1833 he and Tennant went to see Samuel Rogers's gallery, in which there was a "superb Titian, very beautiful Raphael Madonna, and in fact all art gems." And in 1840, when he visited Warwick with FitzGerald, "nothing pleased me better on the whole than two paintings I saw in the castle: one, an Admiral van Tromp by Rembrandt, the other Machiavelli by Titian, both wonderful pictures, but the last grand beyond all words." Titian, indeed, was his favorite. "The first time he was in Paris," he told Miss Rundle, "he went every day for a fortnight to the Louvre, saw only one picture, 'La Maitresse de Titien,' the second time looked only at 'Narcissus lying by a stream, Echo in the distance and ferocious little Love.'" Hallam had somewhat broader tastes, and they used to argue about their favorites. "There is [at Cologne]," wrote Hallam to Emily Tennyson, "a gallery of pictures quite after my heart, rich, glorious old German pictures, which Alfred accuses me of preferring to Titian and Raffaelle." And in his last letter to Tennyson from Vienna, he wrote: "The gallery is grand and I longed for you: two rooms full of Venetian pictures only; such Giorgiones, Palmas, Bordones, Paul Veroneses! and oh Alfred such Titians! by Heaven, that man could paint! I wish you could see his Danaë. Do you just write as perfect a Danaë!" Tennyson's line, "Now lies the Earth all Danaë to the stars," is perhaps an answer to that request. It justifies Hallam's remark that "Titian's imagination and style are more analogous to your own than those of Rubens or of any other school."[22]

The later idyls are less dependent on painting than on poetry and song and so are more Theocritean in structure. E. C. Stedman,

[21]Sir Charles Tennyson, "Tennyson Papers, I: Alfred's Father," *Cornhill Magazine,* 153 (January-June 1936), 291.

[22]*Memoir,* L, 87, 103, 104, 175-76, 276-77.

indeed, has shown how many of them reproduce the basic formulas of Theocritus. The opening of *Godiva,* for example, uses the same device for entering on the story of Godiva as the thirteenth idyl uses for introducing that of Hylas: "Not we...but she."[23] *Audley Court* is modeled on the *Thalysia* (VII), in which Eucritus, Amyntas, and Simichidas, going to a harvest festival, meet the goatherd Lycidas, vie in pastoral song, and then, continuing to the feast, spend an evening of perfect content amid the opulent summer harvest. *Walking to the Mail* is Tennyson's version of Idyl IV, a gossipy conversation between two rustics, Corydon and Battus, about their neighbor AEgon, who has gone to compete in the Olympic games and whose cattle are growing thin. The social themes of Tennyson's idyls, however, derive less from Theocritus than from Virgil, where the troubled political background in connection with the confiscation of estates provided an analogy to the troubles of the Reform Bill. Indeed, the significant thing about Tennyson's use of both Theocritus and Virgil is that he could use them so freely, simply reviving their forms in order to accomplish an analogous purpose in his own day.[24]

Even under this aegis the danger is that the idyls will be considered merely trivial. In *Audley Court,* for instance, two young men walk across the fields to picnic at Audley Court. They talk, argue a bit, sing a few songs, and then return through the dark to their boat. What is so wonderful about that? Nothing, unless, as in a story or drama by Chekhov, the quality of the experience is everything, the sense of a mood delicately achieved that is very fragile. For the poem begins in bustle and confusion.

> "The Bull, the Fleece are cramm'd, and not a room
> For love or money. Let us picnic there
> At Audley Court."

And so the friends move off through the fields and, settling down upon the grass, create a kind of Victorian *déjeuner sur l'herbe.* Tennyson does not muff the occasion but, in almost pre-Raphaelite manner, produces an intensely wrought genre painting of a Victorian picnic hamper.

[23]Edmund C. Stedman, *Victorian Poets* (Boston, 1876), pp. 211-12; see Ricks [*The Poems of Tennyson*], p. 731.
[24]Stedman, *Victorian Poets,* p. 233.

> There, on a slope of orchard, Francis laid
> A damask napkin wrought with horse and hound,
> Brought out a dusky loaf that smelt of home,
> And, half-cut-down, a pasty costly-made,
> Where quail and pigeon, lark and leveret lay,
> Like fossils of the rock, with golden yolks
> Imbedded and injellied; last, with these,
> A flask of cider from his father's vats,
> Prime, which I knew; and so we sat and eat.

Under the genial influence of the cider they reminisce about old times, get onto the more dangerous present, argue heatedly about the Corn Laws, and come together again upon the king. For these youths, though friends from of old, are of diametrically opposed temperament and principles. The one, Francis Hale, is a farmer's son; the other, the narrator, "having wherewithal,/ And in the fallow leisure of my life," was a "rolling stone of here and everywhere." Thus, when they sing their songs, they are of sharply contrasting temper. Francis Hale's is a cynical drinking song—"But let me live my life"—for in his view army, shop, public service, and love are equally unrewarding. It is precisely the right song to modulate from the quarrel into a happy mood again, but the narrator's is precisely right to follow it. For it is a softly lyrical *nocturne,* probably adapted from an Elizabethan song, of his love for Ellen Aubrey. It modulates into the conclusion. For as they go back across the fields and drop down the headland to the quay, they find the town all hushed, the bay calm.

> the harbour-buoy,
> Sole star of phosphorescence in the calm,
> With one green sparkle ever and anon
> Dipt by itself, and we were glad at heart.

It was with these lines that the poem began. "This poem," says Tennyson, "was partially suggested by Abbey Park at Torquay. Torquay was in old days the loveliest sea village in England and now is a town. In those old days I, coming down from the hill over Torquay, saw a star of phosphorescence made by the buoy appearing and disappearing in the dark sea and wrote these lines."[25] Such serenity, however, required a discord to precede it, something to

---

[25][H. Tennyson,] *Materials,* 1, 239-40; *Memoir,* 1, 196. One wonders whether the title of the poem was not suggested by the well-known country house of Lord Bray-

suggest the commercialism that would later sweep over the town. And so in the original version of the idyl Tennyson gave a description of the snorting paddle boat on which Francis arrived, the crowded quay, the quacks and hawkers, the ranting showmen, and the squealing bagpipes. There was even a third character, "John the storyteller, John/ The talker, steering downward with a thumb/ In either armhole."[26] But all this was too much. The heavy picnic hamper was adequate balance to the elfin phosphorescence of the sea, for these are among the antinomies that had to be reconciled in the poem. The two youths are brought together, not simply by patriotism but by youth, friendship, song, and the beauty of the evening. The scene is the perfect equivalent of the serene harvest-festival at the farm of Phrasidamus in Theocritus's seventh idyl.

Walking to the Mail, like Theocritus's Idyl IV, turns even more on the subtly differing personalities of two friends. John, who is apparently visiting the district after being long away, is established as the pleasanter by his opening comment about the meadows. James, we gradually gather, is a somewhat less attractive figure, for he tends to pass harsh judgments on people and seems instinctively to believe in punishment. He alludes to the younker caught tickling trout—"caught *in flagrante*—what's the Latin word?—/ *Delicto*"—and even in reference to his own youthful escapades he seems to take satisfaction in the fact that he had to "pay." "There was law for *us;*/ We paid in person." Indeed, he generalizes his remarks into one simple principle:

> but, sir, you know
> That these two parties still divide the world—
> Of those that want, and those that have: and still
> The same old sore breaks out from age to age
> With much the same result. Now I myself,
> A Tory to the quick, [etc.]

The immediate occasion for these remarks is Sir Edward Head, whose house they are passing and for whom James feels a contempt because he allowed the Chartist violence so to infect his dreams

---

brooke, Audley End, at Saffron Walden near Cambridge. In 1836, just two years before the poem was written, Richard Lord Braybrooke published *The History of Audley End,* a topographical description and history, with plates, in which William Whewell and J. S. Henslow of Cambridge assisted.

[26]*Trinity Notebook* 26 (26).

that he could not sleep and ultimately left the country. John, though presumably a liberal, demurs at the harshness of this judgment and, turning to the pleasanter subject of Sir Edward's wife, whom he once knew as a slight, modest girl, is rebuffed by the phrase, "A woman like a butt, and harsh as crabs." For to James, who thinks in stereotyped phrases—"like breeds like," "Kind nature is the best"—such was bound to happen. She was a cottager's daughter and, marrying into the gentry, was unable to adjust: "Two parties still divide the world."

Indeed, the more we hear of James the less we like him. For one thing, his language is laced with cruelty. If he mentions a willow, it is "hump-back'd"; if a Chartist's pike, it is "venomous"; if Sir Edward is ill, he is "vexed with a morbid devil." This habit culminates when he unconsciously condemns himself by telling of a college prank. A farmer's sow was great with pig and several of them hauled her up the stairs of the college tower and hid her on the leads. When she littered, they killed the sucklings one by one and ate them—"till she was left alone..., the Niobe of swine." John makes no immediate comment on this but returns to Sir Edward.

> Well—after all—
> What know we of the secret of a man?
> His nerves were wrong. What ails us, who are sound,
> That we should mimic this raw fool the world,
> Which charts us all in its coarse blacks or whites,

—and then the reproof to James—

> As ruthless as a baby with a worm,
> As cruel as a schoolboy ere he grows
> To Pity—more from ignorance than will.

But then the mail appears, "as quaint a four-in-hand/ As you shall see—three pyebalds and a roan," which seems to support John's view that even in these days of Chartism and the Reform Bill, of Disraeli's Two Nations of the rich and poor, life is a mixed affair and people should strive to make it so, not by harsh, dogmatic judgments but by tolerance and reconciliation. Even the story of Jocky Dawes, which James tells, contributes to this interpretation. Jocky moved out of his house because it was haunted by a ghost, but when he found the ghost among the luggage, he decided to move back in and treat it like a familiar.

All the idyls share this spirit of reconciliation. *Edwin Morris,* written in 1839 against the background of the Llanberis lakes, contrasts two views of love, that of Edwin Morris, a kind of Admirable Crichton, too good to be true, who puts forth in languid aesthetic phrase a kind of Romantic Petrarchanism, and that of the fat curate Edward Bull, who declares that all this is nonsense: "God made the woman for the man,/ And for the good and increase of the world." The narrator, an artist, declares immediately that the curate pitches the pipe too low, but, though he is impressed by Morris's fine phrases, he is also a little resentful, for he thinks that he too has the seeds of a genuine love within him but also "something of a wayward modern mind/ Dissecting passion." This tinge of cynicism, mediating between the high-flown ideality of Morris and the gross materialism of Bull, will serve him well, for in his courtship of Letty Hill, ward of some cotton-spinning millionaires, he runs smack into the marriage of convenience. The episode is apparently the same as that which Tennyson treated more thunderingly in *Locksley Hall* and *Maud,* but here he treats it lightly. Despite the fact that the speaker has been hounded out of the country by the sheriff, he is not bitter. Indeed, as he begins to speak, he cries, "O me, my pleasant rambles by the lake,/ My sweet, wild, fresh three quarters of a year," and he shows a friend the sketches he made during that period. There are two, which comprehend the antithetical elements of the tale. One is of

> curves of mountain, bridge,
> Boat, island, ruins of a castle, built
> When men knew how to build, upon a rock
> With turrets lichen-gilded like a rock.

The other is of

> new-comers in an ancient hold,
> New-comers from the Mersey, millionaires,
> Here lived the Hills—a Tudor-chimnied bulk
> Of mellow brickwork on an isle of bowers.

Nature and commerce, the old and the new, gross materialism and romantic ideality have all found their place in art, and so even the false little Letty is forgiven. Mixed with his memories of that youthful time,

> She seems a part of those fresh days to me;
> For in the dust and drouth of London life
> She moves among my visions of the lake.

The Golden Year is a product of Tennyson's same visit to Wales in the summer of 1839. The poem is modeled on the singing match between two shepherds, though in this case the "song" of one of them, as befits his character, is in prose. For the contest is, in a sense, between prose and poetry, and the fact that Old James, the down-to-earth realist, begins his answer to Leonard "in mimic cadence" sufficiently indicates their parity. To make the contest fair, of course, it cannot take place under a hawthorn or in a bower. The speaker of the idyl had wished for Leonard when he and James had climbed Snowdon, for it was from that visionary height that a poet might be expected to speak. But they did not find him until they descended to Llanberis, and then the three of them crossed between the lakes and "clambered half way up/ The counter side." It was there, on the opposite side from Snowdon and only halfway up, that the debate took place. Leonard began in "measured words," by which one may gather that they were not only metrical but moderate. Indeed, Leonard was a poet who, like Tennyson himself, had been chided by his friends for not speaking out in these "feverous days," and his excuse had been that he was born too late, unsuited for modern times. Thus, when he comes to state the doctrine of progress, he does so in beautifully melodious but also muted phrase. As it is the law of all things to move, of the sun, the earth, the ocean, and the seasons, so it is man's law too; but it will be slowly, by ebb and flow, in a cyclical movement, that the Golden Year will come. Leonard looks particularly to the distribution of wealth, to education more widely disseminated, to less disparity between social classes, to free trade and universal peace. But Old James, who is a Carlylean curmudgeon with little faith in poets' dreams, "struck his staff against the rocks/ And broke it." "What stuff this is!" The ancient poets placed their Golden Age in the past, the modern in the future. Both are dreamers, for the true Golden Year is that, here and now, which is well spent in work.

> He spoke; and high above, I heard them blast
> The steep slate-quarry, and the great echo flap
> And buffet round the hills, from bluff to bluff.

It would be a wise judge who would award the prize in this song contest. The blasting, echoing like Old James's staff buffeted against the rock, does reinforce the doctrine of work, and one can hardly doubt that the true Golden Year is the present moment well used. But is it better used in poetry or blasting? On the one hand, it is by these practical means that the world will be transformed. But, on the other, one has a feeling that Leonard's song will reverberate longer, for, as Tennyson says in *The Princess,* "Our echoes roll from soul to soul,/ And grow for ever and for ever." In a passage not used by Tennyson, Old James leaves in the middle of the debate for some business in the town, and while he is gone Leonard privately expresses some doubts about his own doctrine. Would we be happier when the Golden Year comes? Even if we merged with the All would it be worth the loss of individuality? Tennyson was wise to omit this passage and simply allow the two "songs" to work themselves out within the dialectic of the poem.

Enough has been said to indicate that the English Idyls are not trivial poems but are works of a subtle and delicate art. In my opinion, they are among the finest of Tennyson's poems, certainly the most neglected in proportion to their merit of all of Tennyson's works. Their great value lies simply in the beauty and charm with which they invest their subject. There is a kind of golden haze, a lucent atmosphere, in which everything is enveloped. Though written at the same time as much of *In Memoriam,* they are by far the happiest of Tennyson's poems. The nostalgia and melancholy of the earlier lyrics is gone, the complacency of middle age has not yet descended. Preeminently they are poems of youth, of the heyday of one's existence, when love and art, nature and society are all clothed in a freshness which they will later lose. And yet they are not poems of escape. They solve the problem, better than Clough's *Bothie of Tober-na-vuolich* or Goethe's *Hermann und Dorothea,* of how to combine the persons and topics of everyday life with the heightened beauty which we look for in poetry. Granted that there are things they cannot do. Mystery and passion, ecstasy and magic they do not attempt, for they are poems of the middle range of life and of the middle class. But within these limits they are subtle and complex works, and they are not, as is sometimes said, of a cloying sweetness. Indeed, in their ironic juxtapositions and unresolved conflicts they have a dryness and classicality that is not achieved by any other of

Tennyson's poems. They are less the product of the muse than of one who is "bemused," who does not quite know what to make of modern life but whose artless statement of its problems comes nearer to the truth than other people's conclusions. ...

Style and Genre: *The Princess*

by F. E. L. Priestley

The Princess is perhaps unique among Tennyson's works in that its form is largely influenced by his didactic purpose. Elsewhere the experiments and innovations which characterize his poetic practice, the novel stanza forms, the unorthodox verse-lengths, the deliberate use of unexpected genre, or the mixture of genres, can be explained on purely aesthetic grounds, as attempts to widen the range of effects in English poetry. In *The Princess,* however, the aesthetic problem is a consequence of, or is at least inseparable from, the problem of his didactic strategy. The subject with which the poem deals, the rights of women, and the place of women in society, was one which seemed to foster "the falsehood of extremes." To many men, the struggle for female emancipation was purely and simply comic: to many women, deeply and fiercely tragic. Both extremes, of facetiousness and of earnestness, made for tightly shut minds. As Tennyson knew, a comic treatment would delight the men, infuriate the women, and confirm both sets of prejudice; a solemn one would please the women and disgust the men. His difficult task is to persuade both sides, to write something which both sides will read and which will moderate both extremes. This task obviously confronts him with a very difficult aesthetic problem.

In *The Rape of the Lock* Pope had faced a not dissimilar situation on a minor scale, but it was relatively easy for him to sacrifice the didactic purpose of healing the breach between Lord Petre and the Fermors to the aesthetic purpose of the pure genre, and the serious implications of the Cave of Spleen and the direct didacticism of Clarissa's speech are kept rigorously subordinate and even subservient to the single mock-heroic tenor of the poem. The importance

Tennyson attaches to the subject he is treating, and the much greater freedom he always shows in his approach to genre, make a treatment like Pope's an unlikely one for Tennyson, but the parallel, imperfect as it is, throws some light on Tennyson's procedure.

At the outset, he frees himself from the demands of any recognized formal genre by the device of the multiple narration; the poem has arisen from a game of impromptu storytelling by seven narrators who contribute successive parts. The conversation among these narrators before the story telling begins, and the description of their surroundings, prepare for a "medley" with a miscellany of subject-matter and tones. The device also frees the poet conventionally from responsibility for the substance of the story, although it is announced at the end that he was "to bind the scatter'd scheme of seven together in one sheaf" and, most important of all, to choose the style.

> What style could suit?
> The men required that I should give throughout
> The sort of mock heroic gigantesque,...
> The women...hated banter....
>   Why
> Not make her true-heroic—true-sublime,
> ...And I, betwixt them both, to please them both,
> And yet to give the story as it rose,
> I moved as in a strange diagonal,
> And maybe neither pleased myself nor them.

The image of the diagonal is a happy one: it suggests accurately the sense of linear continuity by which the poem moves—no poem gives actually less effect of chance or of haphazard direction—and at the same time suggests also an ironic ambiguity, since a diagonal may be thought of either as a straight line from one corner to its opposite, or as a line which retains a fixed distance from two sides perpendicular to each other. Tennyson's diagonal does not simply run from mock-heroic to heroic, from ridiculous to sublime; it operates in a delicate balance from the start.

It is indeed necessary to his purpose to avoid establishing an unequivocal tone at the beginning; he needs an unequivocally serious tone at the end, but not an unequivocally frivolous one at the first. And one has only to recall an example of the strict mock-heroic to realize within what limits Tennyson has confined the burlesque. In

The Princess, one looks in vain for the usual sequence of mock-epic conventions; there are no invocations, no epic catalogues, no supernatural machinery, no epic games.

The poem opens, indeed, with no suggestion of the mock-epic; the genre established with the first lines is that of romance, or of fairy-tale, rather than epic, and the style carries no suggestion of either epic or mock-epic:

> A prince I was, blue-eyed, and fair in face,
> Of temper amorous, as the first of May,
> With lengths of yellow ringlet, like a girl,
> For on my cradle shone the Northern star.
> There lived an ancient legend in our house...

The first-person narration, the conversational tone, the informal syntax, are as remote from epic style as the matter is remote from epic matter. The effect produced is, in a sense, neutral; neither serious nor comic, neither elevated nor low. The Prince goes on to speak of the "ancient legend" that

> Some sorcerer, whom a far-off grandsire burnt
> Because he cast no shadow, had foretold,
> Dying, that none of all our blood should know
> The shadow from the substance, and that one
> Should come to fight with shadows and to fall...

This establishes at the outset the theme of ambiguity, of shadow and substance, repeated from time to time throughout the poem. Each time this theme is introduced, it is brought in abruptly, so as to break the established mood and tone; it is made to interrupt a sharply focused scene and suddenly dissolve it, so that the reader, like the Prince, is momentarily caught up in uncertainty. It is only at the end of the poem, when the tone is to be clear and unequivocal, that the theme of ambiguity is resolved, and the Prince's "haunting sense of hollow shows" leaves him. I am concerned here, not with the meaning of the Prince's seizures, but with the effect of the passages describing them; with their function as interruptions to prevent an atmosphere from becoming too firmly established, and with their function as signposts to ambivalence.

As to Ida herself, in this opening section we are strongly influenced by the Prince's view of her:

> Still I wore her picture by my heart,
> And one dark tress; and all around them both
> Sweet thoughts would swarm as bees about their queen.
>   ...I rose and past
> Thro' the wild woods that hung about the town;
> Found a still place, and pluck'd her likeness out;
> Laid it on flowers, and watch'd it lying bathed
> In the green gleam of dewy-tassell'd trees...
> Proud look'd the lips: but while I meditated
> A wind arose and rush'd upon the South,
> And shook the songs, the whispers, and the shrieks
> Of the wild woods together; and a Voice
> Went with it, "Follow, follow, thou shalt win."

Humour is introduced very sparingly in the opening section, and never is allowed to touch Ida herself. The first light touches of the comic are applied to the two kings, fathers of the Prince and Princess. The Prince's father, inflamed with wrath by the letter announcing that Ida refuses to marry his son, tore the letter, "snow'd it down," "then he chew'd the thrice-turn'd cud of wrath, and cook'd his spleen." Ida's father, King Gama ("a little dry old man," "airing a snowy hand and signet gem,") vaguely remembers that there had been a compact, "a kind of ceremony—I think the year in which our olives fail'd." There is nothing in the presentation of the two kings to lend them dignity; Gama's account of his difficulties with Ida simply reinforces the impression of his own ineffectualness.

As the Prince writes seeking admission for himself and his friends, disguised as girls, to Ida's college, the touch of comedy in the description of his assumed lady-like back-hand script, "such a hand as when a field of corn/ Bows all its ears before the roaring East," follows a first description of Ida's college in which nothing of the comic is suggested, and which is rapidly modulated to a serious close:

>   We gain'd
> A little street half garden and half house;
> But scarce could hear each other speak for noise
> Of clocks and chimes, like silver hammers falling
> On silver anvils, and the splash and stir
> Of fountains spouted up and showering down
> In meshes of the jasmine and the rose:
> And all about us peal'd the nightingale,
> Rapt in her song, and careless of the snare. ...

> And then to bed, where half in doze I seem'd
> To float about a glimmering night, and watch
> A full sea glazed with muffled moonlight, swell
> On some dark shore just seen that it was rich.

This solemn coda to part one is, it will be recognized, in a different style from the fairy-tale opening, as well as from the comic passages. In its diction and in its rhythm, and in the solemnity of its mood, it prepares for the first of the lyrics, "As through the land at eve we went."

The dominant effect of the opening of the narrative is undoubtedly serious, in a rich vein of lyricism; the seriousness is continued into the first description of the college and of Ida herself. The style is here heightened to suggest the true heroic:

> Out we paced,
> I first, and following thro' the porch that sang
> All round with laurel, issued in a court
> Compact of lucid marbles, boss'd with lengths
> Of classic frieze...
> There at a board by tome and paper sat,
> With two tame leopards couch'd beside her throne,
> All beauty compass'd in a female form,
> The Princess; liker to the inhabitant
> Of some clear planet close upon the Sun,
> Than our man's earth; such eyes were in her head,
> And so much grace and power, breathing down
> From over her arch'd brows, with every turn
> Lived thro' her to the tips of her long hands...

This is as solemnly ornate as the descriptions in *Oenone,* and creates, especially as prepared for by the passages in part one, so dignified and lofty an impression of the Princess that nothing she says or does can seem to us merely comic. And the style of these passages, though elevated enough to suggest the heroic, is kept direct and restrained, almost entirely free of mannerism; and consequently entirely remote from the mock-heroic or burlesque.

By the beginning of the second part of the poem, then, we have been induced to think of Ida in poetic and dignified terms. As a result, when the comic is allowed to play on her, it can never reduce her to the ridiculous. At worst, her essential nobility can be seen to be touched here and there by folly; more properly, she can be seen as in the partial grasp of a noble wrong-headedness, a magnanimous eccentricity. The comic spirit can illuminate her defects of judgement, but not impugn her grandeur and rightness of intention.

We recognize the application of this principle in her first speeches. In her little speech of welcome to the disguised Prince and his friends, she first rebukes Cyril for using "the tinsel clink of compliment," but goes on to a statement of her aims, which the narrator describes, with no necessary suspicion of irony, as "those high words." And in her parting advice, although it begins with the at least half comic: "Ye are green wood, see ye warp not," and although her description of the college statues brings a comic reminder of how exclusively masculine is the history of the heroic as normally taught, she ends with a perfectly serious, and in the context moving injunction: "Better not be at all than not be noble."

The same method can be seen in her presidential address to the students. It starts by exploiting the comic effect of condensation and of translation of direct into indirect speech. This is, of course, one of Dickens's common devices, especially as applied to oratory. Ida's speech makes a rapid historical survey of the place of woman in society, starting with her favourite piece of science, the nebular hypothesis, and moving rapidly through evolution:

> ...The planets: then the monster, then the man;
> Tattoo'd or woaded, winter-clad in skins,
> Raw from the prime, and crushing down his mate...
> > Thereupon she took
> A bird's-eye-view of all the ungracious past;
> Glanced at the legendary Amazon
> As emblematic of a nobler age;
> Appraised the Lycian custom...
> Ran down the Persian, Grecian, Roman lines
> Of empire, and the woman's state in each,
> How far from just; till warming with her theme
> She fulmined out her scorn of laws Salique
> And little-footed China, touch'd on Mahomet
> With much contempt, and came to chivalry:
> When some respect, however slight, was paid
> To woman...
> However then commenced the dawn: a beam
> Had slanted forward, falling in a land
> Of promise; fruit would follow.

The passage manages to combine suggestions of a tub-thumping party speech, a lecture in a survey course, and a reporter's mangled account of a public address. Those who have had public lectures reported will particularly wonder whether the splendid mixture of metaphors at the end is really Ida's or the reporter's. But there is no doubt that so far the speech is presented in comic terms, just as though Ida's sentiments might be. But from this point on, the reporting of the speech changes its mode; it becomes less compressed, the ideas are given more elaboration, and are presented without the implicitly derogatory "glanced at," "appraised," "ran down," "fulmined." The presentation moves towards direct speech, and a direct and more persuasive style. As a result, when we come to the conclusion we are ready for actual direct speech, and ready also to take with a minimum of irony the introduction to these last words: "She rose upon a wind of prophecy/ Dilating on the future." And the quality of her last words enforces not only our agreement but again our respect for Ida:

> Everywhere
> Two heads in council, two beside the hearth,
> Two in the tangled business of the world,
> Two in the liberal offices of life,
> Two plummets dropt for one to sound the abyss
> Of science, and the secrets of the mind:
> Musician, painter, sculptor, critic, more:
> And everywhere the broad and bounteous Earth
> Should bear a double growth of those rare souls,
> Poets, whose thoughts enrich the blood of the world.

In each of the speeches the technique is the same, each moves towards an ending in which the serious sincerity of Ida's words is matched by the directness and simplicity of the style. We are returned always to the noble conception of Ida.

A great part of the comedy centres, of course, not directly about Ida but about the women's college, her scheme. Nearly all this comedy is double-edged, since it depends upon the simple situation of women aping men. It is not long before the question arises in the reader's mind whether a college which excludes every male creature is intrinsically any more ridiculous than one which excludes every female, and whether an education of fact-cramming or of superficial surveys is any more ridiculous for women than for men, and whether history from an exclusively feminine perspective is any more one-sided than from a masculine one. In so far as Ida's college is ridiculous, it may be because it imitates a ridiculous model. This is suggested by the Prince after half a day of attendance at lectures:

> We dipt in all
> That treats of whatsoever is, the state,
> The total chronicles of man, the mind,
> The morals, something of the frame, the rock,
> The star, the bird, the fish, the shell, the flower,
> Electric, chemic laws, and all the rest,
> And whatsoever can be taught and known;
> Till like three horses that have broken fence,
> And glutted all night long breast-deep in corn,
> We issued gorged with knowledge, and I spoke:
> 'Why, Sirs, they do all this as well as we.'

And again, as part two comes to an end, the comic modulates into the serious, first by the gentle idyllic description of the college gardens and finally of the night chapel, where

> the great organ almost burst his pipes,
> Groaning for power, and rolling thro' the court
> A long melodious thunder to the sound
> Of solemn psalms, and silver litanies,
> The work of Ida, to call down from Heaven
> A blessing on her labours for the world.

The day ends with a view of Ida as poet and priestess, holy and serious of purpose.

The lyric "Sweet and low" modulates from this solemn close to the high style of the description of morning which opens part three:

> Morn in the white wake of the morning star
> Came furrowing all the orient into gold.

There is hardly a note of comedy in this section, unless the reader is to be amused by feminine interest in geology, "chattering stony names/ Of shale and hornblende, rag and trap and tuff,/ Amygdaloid and trachyte." The dominant tone is set by two passages. In the first the Prince comments on Ida:

> "The crane," I said, "may chatter of the crane,
> The dove may murmur of the dove, but I
> An eagle clang an eagle to the sphere,

My princess, O my princess! true she errs,
But in her own grand way: being herself
Three times more noble than three score of men,
She sees herself in every woman else,
And so she wears her error like a crown
To blind the truth and me...whene'er she moves
The Samian Here rises and she speaks
A Memnon smitten with the morning Sun. ...."

In the second, Ida answers the Prince's question about evolution in a serious speech which undoubtedly represents Tennyson's own thoughts. She and the Prince have been looking at the fossil bones "of some vast bulk that lived and roar'd/ Before man was."

She gazed awhile, and said,
"As these rude bones to us, are we to her
That will be."

To which the Prince responds with the question: "Dare we dream of that.../ Which wrought us, as the workman and his work, that practice betters?" And she replies:

"Let there be light and there was light: 'tis so;
For was, and is, and will be, are but is;
And all creation is one act at once,
The birth of light: but we that are not all,
As parts, can see but parts, now this, now that,
And live, perforce, from thought to thought, and make
One act a phantom of succession: thus
Our weakness somehow shapes the shadow, Time;
But in the shadow will we work, and mould
The woman to the fuller day."

And this part closes with one of Tennyson's favourite and majestic symbols:

The Sun
Grew broader towards his death and fell, and all
The rosy heights came out above the lawns.

The first three sections of *The Princess,* then, contain little of the comic, and in style move mainly from the lyrically ornate style of romance to the direct rhetoric and simple diction of a true elevated style, with suggestions of the heroic in the Prince's description of

Ida. The "strange Poet-princess with her grand imagination" has been firmly established in a fitting stylistic context.

In the fourth part, the central one of the poem, the comic is allowed fuller scope, in a formula indicated by the Prince's words at the end of the section:

> The Princess with her monstrous woman-guard,
> The jest and earnest working side by side.

Thus the beautiful sunset lyric, "The splendour falls on castle walls," is followed at once by Ida's "There sinks the nebulous star we call the Sun,/ If that hypothesis of theirs be sound"; and the haunting "Tears, idle tears" is described by Ida as "moans about the retrospect." "O, Swallow, Swallow, flying, flying South" she dismisses as "a mere love-poem" which minds us of the time "when we made bricks in Egypt." If for a Poet-princess she here reveals an unexpectedly comic insensitivity to the lyrical, and an almost Philistine prosiness, we are soon made aware that she recognizes the beauty of the songs, but is (like many another critic) disturbed by the tendency of their themes:

> Thine are fancies hatch'd
> In silken-folded idleness; nor is it
> Wiser to weep a true occasion lost...
> But great is song
> Used to great ends: ourself have often tried
> Valkyrian hymns, or into rhythms have dash'd
> The passion of the prophetess; for song
> Is duer unto freedom, force and growth
> Of spirit than to junketing and love.

She is of sufficiently Wagnerian stature to make the notion of her Valkyrian hymns plausible rather than comic. The allusions also, of course, prepare us for her later fury and inflexibility. There is at the same time a serious side to these passages. As we have noted, the Prince describes Ida repeatedly in terms both of lyrical romance and of the heroic. She herself denies and tries to suppress the lyrical and romantic side of her nature, regarding it as weakness. The vigour of her expressions of contempt for the songs illuminates the vigour of her repression, and indirectly the power of the attraction she feels the songs exerting, and thus the hidden power of the lyrical in her. The Prince's assessment of her character is accurate.

The discovery of the disguised men, and their pursuit by the female proctors, move the tone towards the broad comedy of farce, and here for the first time mock-heroic style plays a considerable part in the pattern. But it is noticeable that there are no sustained passages of mock-heroic, and the mock-heroic is not applied to Ida herself. The images of the Princess that strike on our mind are serious heroic: she is "all the hopes of half the world"; her wrath is described in a true epic simile which suggests its justice:

> Over brow
> And cheek and bosom brake the wrathful bloom
> As of some fire against a stormy cloud,
> When the wild peasant rights himself, the rick
> Flames, and his anger reddens in the heavens...

Two other epic descriptions are applied to her some lines later:

> Not peace she look'd, the Head: but rising up
> Robed in the long night of her deep hair, so
> To the open window moved, remaining there
> Fixt like a beacon-tower above the waves
> Of tempest, when the crimson-rolling eye
> Glares ruin, and the wild birds on the light
> Dash themselves dead. She stretch'd her arms and call'd
> Across the tumult and the tumult fell.

And

> She, ending, waved her hands
>   ...then with a smile, that look'd
> A stroke of cruel sunshine on the cliff,
> When all the glens are drown'd in azure gloom
> Of thunder-shower, she floated to us...

Further, the Prince's speech to her is still in the lyrical style of romance, and continues the tone of part one:

> When a boy, you stoop'd to me
> From all high places, lived in all fair lights,
> Came in long breezes rapt from inmost south
> And blown to inmost north; at eve and dawn
> With Ida, Ida, Ida rang the woods;
> The leader wildswan in among the stars
> Would clang it, and lapt in wreaths of glowworm light
> The mellow breaker murmur'd Ida.

Part five of the poem is introduced by the lyric of battle, "Thy voice is heard thro' rolling drums," and by a brief interlude which returns us to the characters of the prelude, and which is designed to prepare us for a more completely serious treatment. And perhaps nothing could remind us more forcibly than part five that *The Princess* is not primarily mock-heroic. The battle here is not a parody of epic combat, but a serious battle over a serious issue, fought with real weapons and resulting in real wounds. The only elements indeed that might be considered comic here are the utterances of the two royal fathers:

> Look you, Sir!
> Man is the hunter; woman is his game:
> The sleek and shining creatures of the chase.
> We hunt them for the beauty of their skins;
> They love us for it, and we ride them down.

And

> Man for the field and woman for the hearth;
> Man for the sword and for the needle she;
> Man with the head and woman with the heart:
> Man to command and woman to obey;
> All else confusion.

But these crude expressions of male superiority, set in the context of preparation for war, and the determination to crush women by force, have a sardonic and grim effect far from the simply comic. The dominant tone begins to move towards the tragic; the pattern of action becomes indeed tragic in the strict sense. Ida is placed under an almost intolerable burden of gratitude to the Prince: "He saved my life: my brother slew him for it," yet her pride, after her defeat, makes surrender a very bitter sacrifice. The conflict in her spirit between love and hurt pride, between her sense of obligation and what she still sees as her duty, occupies the rest of the poem, and is intensely serious and moving. The tone and theme are both suggested by the invocation to her:

> O fair and strong and terrible!...
> But Love and Nature, these are two more terrible
> And stronger.

Elements of true epic style, and in particular the epic comparisons applied to Ida, become more frequent and more extensive, until they reach a climax at the moment of her greatest anguish:

> Seldom she spoke: but oft
> Clomb to the roofs, and gazed alone for hours
> On that disastrous leaguer...void was her use,
> And she as one that climbs a peak to gaze
> O'er land and main, and sees a great black cloud
> Drag inward from the deeps, a wall of night,
> Blot out the slope of sea from verge to shore,
> And suck the blinding splendour from the sand,
> And quenching lake by lake and tarn by tarn
> Expunge the world: so fared she gazing there...

This increasing note of the heroic is accompanied by a steady increase in the depth and complexity of the lyrics, culminating in the great Jungfrau song "Come down, O maid." At the same time, the lyrics become not only more serious and more complex, but more closely involved in the action, so that the heroic and the lyric become fused.

Tennyson's "strange diagonal," the line of tone and style through which he makes his poem move, is certainly not a two-dimensional one between a single pair of perpendiculars; it is indeed a strange diagonal, moving through a complex of dimensions, but like a true diagonal, moving surely and directly to an appointed terminus. ...

Tennyson: The Passion of the Past
and the Curse of Time

by James Kissane

> It is as if duration had been broken in the middle and man
> felt his life torn from him, ahead and behind. The ro-
> mantic effort to form itself a being out of presentiment and
> memory ends in the experience of a double tearing of the
> self.　　　—GEORGES POULET, *Studies in Human Time*

Tennyson confessed it, those who knew him remarked upon it,
and commentators have repeatedly emphasized it: a longing for the
"lost and gone" is the distinctive Tennysonian note. Looking back
through the years in the guise of "The Ancient Sage," Tennyson
pays the most solemn respects to his "boy phrase," "The Passion of
the Past," thereby showing that on this point the venerable Laureate
and the young Byronic melancholiac were at one.[1] James Spedding's
impressions of Tennyson in 1835 were dominated by the poet's
worship of the past and his "almost personal dislike of the present";[2]
and Carlyle depicted him, morbidly retrospective even though he
had been honored by the laureateship and blessed by marriage only
the year before, "sitting on a dung-heap among innumerable dead

"Tennyson: The Passion of the Past and the Curse of Time" by James Kissane.
From *ELH*, 32 (1965), 85-109. Copyright 1965 by The Johns Hopkins University.
Reprinted by permission of the author and *ELH*.

[1]"The Ancient Sage," ll. 216-228. All quotations from the poetry, unless otherwise
indicated, have been taken from *The Complete Poetical Works of Tennyson*, ed.
V. J. Rolfe (Cambridge, Mass., 1908).

[2]Hallam Lord Tennyson, *Alfred Lord Tennyson: A Memoir*, 2 vols. (London,
1897), I, 154.

108

dogs."[3] Nor has this passion of the past failed to receive due attention in Tennyson criticism. In a chapter titled "Tennyson: Memory and the Mystic Element," Solomon F. Gingerich anticipates some of the more recent commentary on the subject, and although neglect of the early poems causes him to place a misleading emphasis on Hallam's death as the origin of the Tennysonian *Sehnsucht,* there can be no quarrel with his contention that "the finest lyrics of a great lyric poet...have their chief motive in the infinite longing for the touch of a vanished hand and in an indescribable yearning for the days that are no more."[4]

If Gingerich's essay, by its assumption that the poet's proper business is to speak to and for his age, may be taken to represent criticism — old style, we surely have in Arthur J. Carr's "Tennyson as a Modern Poet"[5] an example of criticism — new style. And though Carr evokes a Tennyson who is more the precursor of Joyce, Yeats, and Eliot than one who (as Paull F. Baum wonderfully puts it) "applied himself earnestly to the duty...of playing demiurge to the *Zeitgeist,*"[6] he too finds nostalgia to be the poet's key "strategy." But the full importance of this strategy has yet to be demonstrated in detail. Gingerich's concern is mainly to relate Tennyson's passion of the past to his struggle for religious belief and to argue the validity of Tennyson's insight into the nature of mystical awareness. Carr, on the other hand, in perceptively asserting that the recurring emphasis upon memory and regret both "conceals and connotes anxiety" and "bind[s] together the elements of a divided sensibility,"[7] seeks to identify the biographical-psychological springs of Tennyson's poetry as essentially similar to those which generate the art of our own troubled century. In what follows, I do not mean to take issue with these approaches, which tend to examine the poetry for the sake of what it can tell us of the mind that created it. I wish,

[3]*Memoir,* I, 340.

[4]*Wordsworth, Tennyson, and Browning: A Study in Human Freedom* (Ann Arbor, 1911), pp. 130-131.

[5]*University of Toronto Quarterly,* XIX (1950), 361-382.

[6]*Tennyson Sixty Years After* (Chapel Hill, 1948), p. vi.

[7]*University of Toronto Quarterly,* XIX (1950), 368. W. D. Paden's *Tennyson in Egypt* (Lawrence, Kansas, 1942) should also be cited for its psychological treatment of Tennyson's attraction to the past. Carr uses Paden's term "the mask of age" for the poetic strategy in which longings toward the future and present frustration are presented as nostalgia.

rather, to extend and redirect somewhat the investigation of the theme of "the past" in an attempt to discern not so much its psychological implications as its artistic configurations. No distinctions between "life" and "art" beyond the absurdly obvious need be insisted upon; indeed, it is my point that precisely because Tennyson's passion of the past *does* "bind together the elements of [his] sensibility," more should be said about the function of this theme in certain characteristic poems and about its significance in the context of Tennyson's total work. A feeling that his great craftsmanship is not matched by a corresponding achievement of what might be called poetic vision remains the most serious obstacle to the repeatedly heralded rejuvenation of Tennyson's reputation as a poet. No doubt this feeling is too well-founded ever to be completely dissipated, but it can be justly modified, I believe, in the light of what his treatment of the theme of the past reveals: not the intellectual power that critics from Matthew Arnold to W. H. Auden have found wanting, but certainly more imaginative subtlety and intensity than one supposed Tennyson to possess. Whether the tracing of this theme shows Tennyson to be more the Victorian or more the modern, it does show him to be more the poet.

I

However much a sense of loss and a longing for the past must appear to us as a romantic commonplace, it cannot be denied that in Tennyson such feelings seldom failed to produce the richest and surest artistic response of which he was capable at any given stage in his development. The death of Hallam, in transforming, as it were, a poetic attitude into a biographical fact, undoubtedly wrought a crucial influence; but one finds, even amid the conventionalities of the very young poet, those distinctive configurations in which Tennyson expressed his passion of the past that give it, in the body of his work, much more than the status of an inherited cliché.

The "personal dislike of the present" which Spedding noted, whether symptom or cause, is an integral aspect of Tennyson's attraction to the past. The quality that, for Tennyson, most distressingly characterizes the present is its emptiness. Hence his aversion is experienced not as anguish but as a kind of numbness, for the present is a vacuum where nothing can be really *felt,* not even pain in the usual sense. "I never *liv'd* a day, but daily die," Tennyson wrote in a poem dating from his Cambridge period or perhaps earlier, "I have no real breath;/ My being is a vacant worthlessness."[8] Such a state differs from death itself only in being aware of its own emptiness. In *Maud,* the mad protagonist embodies this feeling in its extremest form when he imagines himself to be lying buried beneath the street (II, v). Here numbness has given way to a more acute suffering, but a sense of impotence still dominates.

Few poets equal Tennyson in his paradoxical power to evoke vividly the insipid desolation of the present, a power admirably revealed in the scenic descriptions of the early poem "Mariana." For Tennyson the passing moment is not ineffably palpable and intense, as it is for Keats, but insufferably drab:

> With blackest moss the flower-pots
> > Were thickly crusted, one and all;
> The rusted nails fell from the knots
> > That held the pear to the gable-wall.
> The broken sheds look'd sad and strange:
> > Unlifted was the clinking latch;
> > Weeded and worn the ancient thatch
> Upon the lonely moated grange.

This is the present as monotonous and attenuated temporality; time passes, but without meaning, without bringing with it the taste of being:

> The noise of life begins again,
> And ghastly thro' the drizzling rain
> On the bald street breaks the blank day.
>
> > > > (*In Memoriam,* VII)

Containing no quality that can be savored and hence eliciting no emotion, the present cannot be a realm of essential reality. "To me," Tennyson once wrote to Emily Sellwood, "the far-off world seems nearer than the present, for in the present is always something unreal and indistinct, but the other seems a good solid planet, rolling round its green hills and paradises to the harmony of more steadfast laws."[9] He found a formulation of his boyhood sentiments

---

[8]"Perdidi Diem," *Unpublished Early Poems (UEP),* ed. Charles Tennyson (London, 1931), p. 35. The editor suggests that these opening lines of the poem, at least, were written at Somersby.

[9]*Memoir,* I, 171-178.

and hopes in a passage from Addison (*Spectator,* No. 471), which he attached as an epigraph to a poem titled "Memory":

> "The memory is perpetually looking back when we have nothing present to entertain us: it is like those repositories in animals that are filled with stores of food, on which they may ruminate when their present pasture fails."[10]

Whereas the present seemed to Tennyson empty and unreal, the past, that "good solid planet," was a world of plenitude and stability. Moreover, it is the transient, evanescent present that is marked by dull reiteration ("never, never," "O sad *No More!* O sweet *No More!* O strange *No More!*" "I am aweary, aweary"); "the eternal landscape of the past" (*In Memoriam,* XLVI) on the other hand, though surely a land where all things always seemed the same, is in its very permanence tantalizingly fresh.

Most of the poetic guises the young Tennyson adopted express variously the longing of the empty present for the fullness of the past. His *personae* are commonly exiled, outcast, or—hardly surprising in view of the Rev. George Tennyson's misfortune—disinherited; they reflect, though seldom so gruesomely, the alienation represented in the poem "Perdidi Diem" by the image of "Young ravens fallen from their cherishing nest/ On the elm-summit," who

> flutter in agony
> With a continual cry
> About its roots, and fluttering trail and spoil
> Their new plumes on the misty soil,
> But not the more for this
> Shall the loved mother minister
> Aerial food, and to their wonted rest
> Win them upon the topmost branch in air
> With sleep-compelling down of her most glossy breast.
>
> (*UEP,* pp. 35-36)

Or, as Professor W. D. Paden has pointed out,[11] the young poet dons the mask of age, notably in "Ulysses" and "Tithonus," and so dramatizes the contrast between what is now and what once was. The forsaken lover and the bereaved mourner are also recurrent figures who register the same contrast. In the hero of *Maud* Tennyson

---

[10]The poem (*Works,* 755-756) was published in *Poems by Two Brothers.* The simile recurs in "The Lover's Tale," ll. 132-139.

[11]*Tennyson in Egypt,* p. 53.

weaves together many forms of loss, and "Morte d'Arthur" richly resonates with the surviving Bedivere's double loss of an old order and a beloved king.

Not the most artistically successful, but certainly among the most thoroughgoing of the earlier attempts to form his feelings concerning the past into a comprehensive pattern is "Locksley Hall." As the scene of the persona's reverie and the focal point of his memories, Locksley Hall becomes a veritable symbol of the past itself. The hall and its surroundings recall to the protagonist his "youth sublime,"

> When the centuries behind me like a fruitful land reposed;
> When I clung to all the present for the promise that it closed;
>
> When I dipt into the future far as human eye could see,
> Saw the vision of the world and all the wonder that would be.
>
> (ll. 13-16)

Thus the youthful bliss which the scene evokes is especially characterized by the seeming continuity of past, present, and future; the condition of happiness implies the perfect integration of the three temporal realms into a single bright vision.

> Love took up the glass of Time, and
>   turn'd it in his glowing hands;
> Every moment, lightly shaken, ran itself in golden sands.
>
> (ll. 31-32)

As in the state of prelapsarian innocence, time—in the past of Tennyson's imagination—was not distance but fulfillment. It will be remembered that the famous vision of futurity (ll. 119-130) culminating in the millennial Parliament of man and Federation of the world, is actually a conception recalled from the protagonist's youth; for a hopeful future is a thing of the past. That is to say it depends upon an accord between promise and realization such as is felt to have existed at a former time. In that condition a vital interrelationship would obtain between hope and memory which Tennyson refers to as "spouse and bride."[12] Thus in "Ode to Memory" Tennyson describes, by a more elaborate personification, memory's beneficent influence upon the prospect of the future:

> In sweet dreams softer than unbroken rest
> Thou leddest by the hand thine infant Hope.

[12] "On a Mourner," l. 23.

The eddying of her garments caught from thee
The light of thy great presence; and the cope
   Of the half-attain'd futurity,
   Tho' deep not fathomless,
Was cloven with the million stars which tremble
O'er the deep mind of dauntless infancy.

                                                            (ll. 29-36)

However, the Hamletesque hero of "Locksley Hall," to whose jaundiced eye "all things here are out of joint," sees himself trapped on the sterile promontory of the present as he grieves over the loss of his faithless Amy:

O my cousin, shallow-hearted! O my Amy, mine no more!
O the dreary, dreary moorland! O the barren, barren shore!

                                                            (ll. 39-40)

In the face of disillusionment, the authority of Addison's account of the sustaining virtue of memory, cited earlier, gives way to the more poignant insight of Dante; paraphrasing *Inferno,* V, 121, Tennyson's hero affirms "that a sorrow's crown of sorrow is re-membering happier things" (l. 76). From the first, Tennyson's attitude toward "blessed, cursed, Memory" is at best ambivalent, for he recognizes that the hope remembrance appeared to foster can be ironically transformed into despair:

Wherefore do I so remember
That Hope is born of Memory
Nightly in the house of dreams?
But when I wake at once she seems
The faery changeling wan Despair,
Who laughs all day and never speaks—
O dark of bright! O foul of fair!
A frightful child with shrivelled cheeks.

                                        ("Memory," *UEP,* pp. 33-34)

And in "Locksley Hall" Amy is urged to "drug thy memories" (l. 77) lest she too "hear the 'Never, never' whispered by the phantom years" (l. 83).

                                        II

Tennyson's overwhelming sense of transience, whose "never, never" destroys the temporal harmony by severing present from past, can be traced in poem after poem. But the importance of this theme is due not merely to its frequent occurrence, but particularly to the expression it receives in such great and familiar lyrics as this:

> Break, break, break,
>   On thy cold gray stones, O Sea!
> And I would that my tongue could utter
>   The thoughts that arise in me.
>
> O well for the fisherman's boy,
>   That he shouts with his sister at play!
> O well for the sailor lad,
>   That he sings in his boat on the bay!
>
> And the stately ships go on
>   To their haven under the hill;
> But O for the touch of a vanish'd hand
>   And the sound of a voice that is still!
>
> Break, break, break,
>   At the foot of thy crags, O Sea!
> But the tender grace of a day that is dead
>   Will never come back to me.

The poem's most striking effect is that of inner desolation surrounded by indifference,[13] and this is established by the contrast between the grieving persona and the images in the poem—the sea, the fisherman's boy, the sailor lad, and the stately ships—that are oblivious to him. The boisterousness of the children, the joy of the lad, the stateliness of the ships each emphasize the silent and abject longing of the mourner. But more decisive still is the relationship of these elements to the dominating image of the sea. Its rhythmic crash suggests the relentless surge of time itself.[14] The other characters of the poem are inseparably involved with the sea; it is their natural element. The shouting of the fisherman's boy and the singing of the sailor lad form a kind of antiphony with the voice of the sea, and the stately ships connote a prosperous voyage and snug harbor. Only the persona seems repelled by the sea, and he apos-

[13]An effect repeatedly encountered in Tennyson's works, notably in "Mariana," "Tithonus," and numerous cantos of *In Memoriam*.

[14]The association of the sea and related images with time is recurrent in Tennyson. Of particular relevance is the explicit symbolism of the following lines (134-135) from "The Passing of Arthur":

> And rolling far along the gloomy shores
> The voice of days of old and days to be.

trophizes it as if it were some implacable antagonist. Thus, on the one hand, we have images richly and variously suggestive of a harmony with temporal existence, arranged to suggest as well the increasing involvement in that existence from childhood to youth to maturity (play at the shore, sailing on the bay, voyaging in the sea). On the other hand, we feel the isolation of the mourner, who may see in the innocence and promise of youth and in the completion of a safe voyage cause for joy but who cannot share it. The shouting and the singing only bring into relief the "still voice" of the loved one and the poet's own unutterable sorrow; the ships' anticipated homecoming is the veritable antithesis of the poet's longing for the vanished hand.

Cleanth Brooks, in comparing this lyric with "Tears, Idle Tears," calls it "a much thinner poem," even a "coarser" and "more confused" one.[15] I do not find it so. The epithet "stately" is not, as Brooks contends, really irrelevant, in view of the way the ship image works in the poem. The final two lines, which Brooks regards as "frozen at the conventional prose level," are redeemed, I think, first, by the way in which the "day that is dead" establishes a stark opposition to images of life in process, and further, by the way the same phrase, in its metonymical relation to the death implied by the vanished hand and the still voice, actually associates the ideas of death and time most effectively. As a result, the poem becomes more than a personal lament; it is made an expression of the universal tragedy of temporal existence.

For ultimately it is not merely the vanished hand, nor yet the dead day itself that the poet mourns—time does not stand still, even for the fisherman's boy and the sailor lad. The real loss is the ability to recapture that day's tender grace, that grace (manifest in the boy and the lad) through which time seems fulfillment, not distance and deprivation.

> God gives us love. Something to love
>   He lends us; but when love is grown
> To ripeness, that on which it throve
>   Falls off, and love is left alone.
>
> This is the curse of time.

("To J. S.," ll. 13-17)

[15]*The Well Wrought Urn* (New York, 1947), p. 161.

Yet Brooks is quite right in saying that "Break, Break, Break" presents a more conventional response to the curse of time than does "Tears, Idle Tears." For all their similarities, the two poems are really on different subjects: in "Break" the persona is absolutely isolated from the past; in "Tears" he is haunted by it.

> Tears, idle tears, I know not what they mean,
> Tears from the depth of some divine despair
> Rise in the heart, and gather to the eyes,
> In looking on the happy autumn-fields,
> And thinking of the days that are no more.
>
> Fresh as the first beam glittering on a sail
> That brings our friends up from the underworld,
> Sad as the last which reddens over one
> That sinks with all we love below the verge;
> So sad, so strange, the days that are no more.
>
> Ah, sad and strange as in dark summer dawns
> The earliest pipe of half-awaken'd birds
> To dying ears, when unto dying eyes
> The casement slowly grows a glimmering square;
> So sad, so strange, the days that are no more.
>
> Dear as remember'd kisses after death,
> And sweet as those by hopeless fancy feign'd
> On lips that are for others; deep as love,
> Deep as first love, and wild with all regret;
> O Death in Life, the days that are no more!

Tennyson has recorded that this poem was written at Tintern Abbey, "full for me of its bygone memories."[16] Such "memories," we may suppose, were not merely personal; and might there not have been among his recollections some associated with that other great memory poem composed a few miles away? If so, perhaps he felt the deep incongruity between Wordsworth's "Lines" and his own mood that a comparison of the two poems reveals. For there is in Tennyson's poem none of his predecessor's serene confidence that "the wild ecstasies" of the past "shall be matured/ Into a sober pleasure" and that memory is but "a dwelling place/ For all sweet sounds and harmonies."[17] Wordsworth's poem is redolent of the

---

[16]*Memoir*, I, 253.

[17]"Lines Composed a Few Miles Above Tintern Abbey," ll. 138-139, 141-142.

communion between man and nature and between man and man, and in it meaningful existence is reaffirmed by a sense of the continuity of human experience. "Tears, Idle Tears," on the other hand, perhaps typifying a later stage of the romantic sensibility,[18] comes from an imaginative world where the self cannot know communion or continuity save in the unmitigable need to experience them.

Tennyson's assurance that the occasion of the poem is "not real woe,"[19] beyond its denial of biographical significance, suggests further that the tears have no specific cause. It is in that sense they are *idle,* and their source can only be identified as "some divine despair"—some transcendent sorrow of which individual grief is only a particular embodiment. These are the *lacrimae rerum;* they mourn the temporal process by which all things recede into the past. But if the poet's grief thus reflects what Graham Hough calls, in his analysis of the poem, "the pathos of history,"[20] its immediate occasion is the sight of "happy" autumn fields. The situation is reminiscent of that observed in "Break, Break, Break"; the autumn fields, "happy" in the sense that they represent fruition—the fulfillment of a temporal process, bring home to the persona by the force of contrast his own deprivation. Or, to put it more exactly, the contrast is between an existence in which the present constitutes the fullness of time and one in which the present's only content is an awareness of what is lost and gone.

Moreover, this disparity between the plenitude of external nature and the desolation of the conscious self is but the image of a cleavage within that consciousness. For the poem is concerned, in one sense, with the emotional dilemma implied by the dramatic contrast be-

---

[18]Georges Poulet, *Studies in Human Time,* trans. Elliott Coleman (Baltimore, 1956), pp. 25-29, deals with the shift in attitude I have in mind: "In communing with nature, in merging himself in love with a being similar but nevertheless different, man can project and find reflected again from without the total image of his being. .... More often still, by one of those abrupt returns of which Rousseau was the first to discover the enchantment and value, all at once the mind is able to feel an entire past reborn within itself. ... But this momentary possession ends in becoming a dispossession; it ends in the feeling of a loss renewed, in a consummate separation. An infinite distance separates afresh the present from the past. ... If one cannot feel, what good is it to recollect?" (pp. 27-28).

[19]*Memoir,* II, 73.

[20]"'Tears, Idle Tears.'" *Hopkins Review,* IV (Spring, 1951), 34. In addition to Hough's stimulating discussion of the poem, those by Cleanth Brooks (*The Well Wrought Urn,* pp. 153-162) and Leo Spitzer ("'Tears, Idle Tears' Again," *Hopkins Review,* V [Spring, 1952], 71-80) should be noted.

tween *looking* on the happy autumn-fields and *thinking* of the days that are no more. Sensation and reflection are disconnected, or if there is a relationship it is an ironic one in which the perception of "happiness" evokes sorrow in the percipient. Here, feeling does not come in aid of feeling, as for Wordsworth; Tennyson does not recognize "in nature and the language of the sense/ The anchor of my purest thoughts, the nurse,/ The guide, the guardian of my heart, and soul/ Of all my moral being."[21] The act of perception is fully realized in the present, but it lacks meaning. Tennyson's sight of happy autumn fields cannot, in itself, lead even to the kind of tragic meditation to which the sound of a happy nightingale prompted Keats:

> 'Tis not through envy of thy happy lot,
> But being too happy in thine happiness. . . .

From this excruciating and transitory empathy Keats goes on to make of the nightingale a symbol of the heart's desire before the bird vanishes and his poem ends. But Tennyson's autumn fields can neither tease the mind into or out of thought; they merely drop from view as the poet pursues his feelings about the days that are no more. And this act of reflection, though a testimony to the inadequacy of the present, cannot quite attain the immediacy of sensation and so fails as an attempt to recover the past.

The increasing poignancy of this failure is what the last three stanzas so effectively describe. Each of these stanzas offers a separate image for the paradoxical presence/absence of the past. As Cleanth Brooks has insisted, the days that are no more are not merely the conventional "dear, dead days beyond recall"; they are also tantalizingly vivid and near.[22] Yet the more tantalizing this past is made to seem, by the increasing concreteness and vividness of the imagery, the more its unrecapturability is emphasized. The remembered kisses after death and those by hopeless fancy feigned on lips that are for others bring the dichotomy to its intensest point. A kiss, the

---

[21]"Tintern Abbey," ll. 108-111. On the question, "Is an intelligible First Cause deducible from the phenomena of the Universe?" discussed by the Apostles, Tennyson voted "No" (*Memoir,* I, 44 n.). "Strange that these wonders should draw some men to God and repel others," he is reported as saying on looking through a microscope. "No more reason in one than in the other" (*Memoir,* I, 102). See also *In Memoriam,* CXXIV.

[22]*The Well Wrought Urn,* p. 157.

quintessence of palpability, is the most tenuous memory or, if only imaginary, the cruelest dream. This awareness that the past, like a restless ghost, can neither sink into oblivion nor take on real substance underlies the appellation "Death in Life." It seems a richer, less histrionic variation of the "O dark of bright! O foul of fair!" exclamation in the early poem "Memory" (*UEP*, p. 34).

The complexity of Tennyson's attitude toward the past informs virtually every detail of the poem. There is, for example, an added twist to the paradox of presence/absence suggested by the application of the term *fresh* to the days that are no more. They are fresh not only in the sense that youth and all first things are fresh, but also because they are not part of the dreary present. In *In Memoriam* Tennyson ponders the possibility that "the past will always win/ A glory from its being far" (**XXIV**), and hence it would seem that the very quality that makes these lost days sad also accounts for their sweetness. The strangeness of the past, however, is in delicate balance with its familiarity; the past, as Tennyson says elsewhere, "is like a travell'd land now sunk/ Below the horizon" (*The Cup*, II, 134-135). Thus in "Tears" the ship returning from the underworld and the one sinking below the verge are associated with unknown realms, but they bear with them "friends" and "all we love."

Finally, the epithet *wild*, applied to the days that are no more but seemingly transferred from the persona himself, deserves some comment. Brooks has given an excellent account of this detail in the poem, but for our purposes it should be added that a "wildness" attributable to both the mourner and his memories is particularly appropriate to Tennyson's conception of the past as we have been tracing it. Just as the tears themselves originate, as it were, in some supra-personal source, there is a passion, a vitality, that inheres as much in the past itself as in him who longs for it. Tennyson's own phrase, "The Passion of the Past," expresses in its very ambiguity (albeit unintentionally) not only his desire *for* the days that are no more, but also the almost autonomous life these days assume within his memory.[23]

[23]Thomas J. Assad, "Tennyson's 'Tears, Idle Tears,'" *Tulane Studies in English*, XVIII (1963), 71-83, comments on this ambiguity. Professor Assad's explication of the poem came to my attention after the present essay was scheduled for publication. See also his reading of "Break, Break, Break" (*TSE*, XII [1962], 71-80).

III

In Memoriam stands as Tennyson's most elaborate descant on the subject of loss and weaves together virtually all of the thoughts and feelings regarding the past and the passing of time that pervade his work, especially that of the pre-laureate period. With Hallam's death, as Arthur Carr puts it, "the melancholic temperament upon which Tennyson had boldly erected the structure of his art was now baptized in the experience of real grief."[24] And in the elegy that commemorates it, the loss of his friend becomes the "one pure image of regret" (CII) embodying those various longings and deprivations which constitute Tennyson's passion of the past. The character of this loss is such, and the range of response to it is such, that all those guises in which Tennyson was wont to express this passion—guises of abandonment, disinheritance, and guilty exile—are encompassed by it. Thus, though other grim aspects of death are confronted in the poem, it is the separation of the living from the dead that moves Tennyson most deeply. Hallam is, beyond all else, "My Arthur, whom I shall not see" (IX, XVII). It is the living, not the dead, who are to be pitied, for to live is to bear the death-in-life of bereavement. Amid Tennyson's myriad doubts concerning the meaning of death, the fact of separation stands as a certainty.[25]

> My paths are in the fields I know,
> And thine in undiscover'd lands. (XL)

So predominant is this note that the common assumption that the poem's chief concern is the reconciliation to death[26] should be somewhat modified. It is true that *In Memoriam* reveals great waverings in this as in other matters, but Canto LXXXII ("I wage not any feud

[24]*University of Toronto Quarterly,* XIX (1950), 372.

[25]I am not forgetting those lyrics in which Tennyson speaks of communion with the dead, most notably in Canto XCV, but also in XCI, XCIII, XCIV, and CXXX. Not only are moments of communion fleeting, but Tennyson also seems to regard them as experiences of a quite different order from human contact, having their chief value as a presentiment of a future state rather than as, in themselves, a substitute for earthly fellowship.

[26]See, for example, Baum, *Tennyson Sixty Years After,* p. 125.

with Death") must be taken seriously as a central statement of the case:

> Nor blame I Death, because he bare
>   The use of virtue out of earth;
>   I know transplanted human worth
> Will bloom to profit, otherwhere.
>
> For this alone on Death I wreak
>   The wrath that garners in my heart:
>   He put our lives so far apart
> We cannot hear each other speak.

At least it is fair to insist that the poem is not merely concerned abstractly with the question of immortality; what death must mean to the living, and not what it might mean for the dead, is the vital question. What Tennyson primarily feels, as Canto LXXXII indicates, is the curse of time, the inevitable severance from "all we love" in the past. Blighted by this curse, life becomes a desolate and lonely path, with "prospect and horizon gone" (XXXVII), "changed from where it ran/Thro' lands where not a leaf was dumb,...and all was good that Time could bring" (XXIII). In the abandonment of the present, the future can only seem a "secular abyss" (LXXVI).

This sense of abandonment brings with it, as in so many of Tennyson's poems, a concern with memory. Indeed, the elegy is not only *in memoriam,* it is essentially *de memoria;* nothing in the poem, I think, comes closer to being a unifying theme. Consider Canto I, more truly than the Prologue the real beginning. In this lyric the poet, challenging the assumption "that men may rise on stepping stones/ of their dead selves to higher things," asks how one may be sure so forward-looking an attitude will be justified by subsequent events. This goes beyond an uncertainty as to whether suffering will be rewarded; it is as if Tennyson, with his characteristic sense of discontinuity, were questioning the very ontology of "the future." What does one have, then, except his recollections of the past? More particularly, how can love—that ultimate reality, that essential value —survive, save through that remembrance which is grief?

> Let Love clasp Grief lest both be drown'd,
>   Let darkness keep her raven gloss.
>   Ah, sweeter to be drunk with loss,
> To dance with Death, to beat the ground,

> Than that the victor Hours should scorn
> The long result of love, and boast,
> "Behold the man that loved and lost,
> But all he was is overworn."

It is an implicit irony of *In Memoriam* that the attainment of consolation would itself be a deeper sorrow. While the poet can grieve for his friend, while his memory remains fresh enough to be painful, love must be real, must indeed transcend the material dimensions of time and space. "I long to prove," writes Tennyson in Canto XXVI, "No lapse of moons can canker love"; and to that end sorrow must be claimed as "No casual mistress, but a wife" (LIX).

I grieve, therefore love is might be a fair statement of the proposition that in one way or another underlies much of *In Memoriam*. Nor can there be much doubt that this is a crucial affirmation. As an earthly counterpart of that "Immortal Love" Tennyson invokes in the Prologue, his love for Hallam testifies in a world of sense to the reality of spirit. For if such "human love and truth" is not "as dying Nature's earth and lime" (XCVIII) there are grounds for men to consider themselves "not only cunning casts in clay" (CXX), but something more.

Thus in those lyrics where the poet feels his memories of the dead friend fading and his sorrow subsiding, a note of anxiety occurs "(O last regret, regret can die!" [LXXVIII]). This anxiety is expressed through an interesting reversal in several poems that take up the notion that Hallam in death will forget the bereaved poet or that the living friends is no longer worthy of the dead one (LX-LXIV, XCVII). These, I feel, seem much less affected and sentimental when it is recognized that they are simply inversions of a more serious, "actual" fear that the poet will forget Hallam. Similarly, the way the poet's sense of guilt becomes involved in his sorrowings (VII, LXVIII) reveals his anxiousness lest he break faith with his friend by ceasing to mourn him. In other lyrics, however, Tennyson voices confidence that love can survive the curse of time. In LXXXI, using the image of an ear of grain brought to sudden maturity by the touch of frost, he appears to feel that death has in some way perfected or purified his love. Again, in LXXXV Tennyson speaks of his friendship as one

> Which masters Time indeed, and is
> Eternal, separate from fears.

> The all-assuming months and years
> Can take no part away from this.

If the immediate concern is to enunciate, in suitably elegiac terms, the proposition *I grieve, therefore love is,* the elegiac situation — wherein Tennyson from the emptiness of the present casts his mind back upon his friend, "to whom a thousand memories call" (CXI) — draws the poet toward a more fundamental assertion: *I remember, therefore I am.* For memory is sought not only in substantiation of love, but also as a means of being.[27] His friend lives *in* memory, but the poet himself would establish his own existence *through* memory. The grounds of this assertion may be found in Canto XLV, concerned with speculations of an almost Freudian kind upon the development of self-consciousness in the child.[28] The infant, Tennyson supposes, makes no distinction between his environment and himself; he "has never thought that 'this is I.'" But as the child grows he develops a sense of self and, along with this "separate mind," what Tennyson calls "clear memory." By this he may be referring to the point from which our earliest recollections begin — prior existence being obliterated in the ordinary consciousness by what is technically known as childhood amnesia. In any case, memory is taken to be an essential part of human identity. The poem goes on to conclude that a growing isolation is the price of this developing self-consciousness; but if existence implies isolation within the self, isolation from one's past self is oblivion. Thus the family removal from Somersby treated in sections C-CIV, by weakening the poet's

---

[27] A passage in "The Lover's Tale" (ll. 112-131), one of the most suggestive statements on memory in all of Tennyson's works, is more explicit on this point than anything in *In Memoriam,* and it provides an illuminating perspective on the latter poem:

> Yet is my life nor in the present time,
> Nor in the present place. To me alone,
> Push'd from his chair of regal heritage,
> The Present is the vassal of the Past:
> So that, in that I *have* lived, do I live,
> And cannot die, and am, in having been —
> A portion of the pleasant yesterday,
> Thrust forward on to-day and out of place.

> (ll. 112-119)

[Sigmund Freud,] *Civilization and Its Discontents* (Doubleday Anchor New York, 1958), pp. 4-6.

bonds with the past, seems like a second death of his friend. Both his boyhood and the years of his friendship with Hallam have made this the scene of those memories wherein existence is contained. Life will go on there, but Tennyson will not be a part of it:

> As year by year the laborer tills
> His wonted glebe, or lops the glades,
> And year by year our memory fades
> From all the circle of the hills.   (CI)

The ambiguity in these lines, if allowable, is particularly expressive. The primary meaning must be that the family will be forgotten by the neighborhood it is leaving; but as they are forgotten, they will also forget. Both senses in which "our memory fades/ From all the circle of the hills" aptly suggest a drawing away from the life of the past; and indeed, in the poetic context, to be forgotten and to forget come to the same thing.[29] In Canto CIV, which seems a part of this "removal group" as well as a prelude to the third Christmas, even the sacred festival seems meaningless, because the strangeness of the setting holds it apart from the sanctifying power of the past:

> Like strangers' voices here they [i. e., the bells] sound
> In lands where not a memory strays,
> Nor landmark breathes of other days,
> But all is new unhallow'd ground.

Ultimately, "place" is not of decisive importance to Tennyson—a physical return to Locksley Hall, to Mablethorpe, or to "The Dell of E—" does not result in a renewed existence—but the removal cantos do suggest in a negative way how memory is related, in *In Memoriam,* to the fullest sense of being.

This relationship, as might be expected, plays a significant part in Tennyson's speculations on the hereafter. Though acknowledging the traditional conception of death as a Lethean draught (LXIV), he is drawn to a contrary idea of eternal bliss as the recovery of the past:

> So then were nothing lost to men;
> So that still garden of the souls

[29]A similarity to the motif, mentioned earlier, of Tennyson's fear lest the dead Hallam forget him should be noted.

> In many a figured leaf enrolls
> The total world since life began.   (XLIII)

This is the Tennysonian equivalent of the soul's attainment of essential knowledge; the watchtower from which John Donne hoped to "see all things despoyl'd of fallacies" promised, for Tennyson, a vista of "The eternal landscape of the past" (XLVI). The perfection of memory is an inherent aspect of that realization of complete being which constitutes the "spiritual prime" (XLIII) beyond the grave.

Yet to the earth-bound poet memory remains not only imperfect but painful. And the shape Tennyson finally gave his collection of elegies stresses a desire to escape from an inert nostalgia and somehow still be faithful to his lost friend. Consequently, in the course of the poem Hallam becomes less a shadow of the past and more of a beacon from the future—as a type of human earthly perfection (CXXVII, Epilogue) and, one might say, as Tennyson's Beatrice, a link from this world to the next. Like the protagonist of "Locksley Hall," Tennyson's persona in *In Memoriam* seeks to "mix with action" and looks again toward the "wondrous Mother-Age"; his "old affection of the tomb" admonishes him to "Arise, and get thee forth and seek/ A friendship for the years to come" (LXXXV), and he may even without dread "contemplate all this work of Time,/ The giant laboring in his youth" (CXIII). Unlike the hero of the former poem, however, he does not renounce his symbol of the past in the process, but reinterprets it to incorporate a promise of future reunion:

> Dear friend, far off, my lost desire,
>   So far, so near in woe and weal,
>   O loved the most when most I feel
> There is a lower and a higher;
>
> Known and unknown, human, divine;
>   Sweet human hand and lips and eye;
>   Dear heavenly friend that canst not die,
> Mine, mine, for ever, ever mine;
>
> Strange friend, past, present, and to be;
>   Loved deeplier, darklier understood;
>   Behold, I dream a dream of good,
> And mingle all the world with thee.   (CXXIX)

In the concluding sections of *In Memoriam* it is as if Tennyson wished to challenge his characteristic sense of discontinuous existence with a radically different view. Georges Poulet has observed that "the nineteenth century had in the highest degree what Renan calls the *intuition of becoming*,"[30] and it is precisely from this intuition that Tennyson attempts finally to wrest consolation in *In Memoriam*. At Canto CVI ("Ring out wild bells") there is a crucial turn toward the "to be," and this emphasis culminates in the Epilogue with its celebration of a wedding and the anticipated engendering of a new soul—"a closer link/ Betwixt us and the crowning race." A poem beginning in death and alienation thus ends in an emphatic tribute to generation. What Poulet terms "the discontinuity of inward duration" (p. 30) is supplanted by an organic involvement in human process:

> For all we thought and loved and did,
> And hoped, and suffer'd, is but seed
> Of what in them is flower and fruit.

(ll. 134-136)

Being, then, is identified not with memory and with isolated self-consciousness, as was the case in Canto XLV, but with one's awareness of his part in this process. Poulet's description of "nineteenth-century time" furnishes the ideal gloss, and I cannot refrain from quoting him once more:

> It is a becoming which is always future.... I exist and I participate in the existence of things only insofar as I experience their generation.[31]

Unfortunately, this consolation is not assimilated into the poem with complete success. For one thing, the vision of futurity does not attain a clear focus; it has, one might say, both eschatological and Utopian aspects, and these, as Professor Baum contends, are connected only by the loosest kind of analogy.[32] The "one far-off divine event" (Epilogue) and "the secular to-be" (XLI) remain essentially unrelated concepts. In the second place, Tennyson is unable to evoke future bliss with anything like the power with which he renders the loss of past joy. The closest he is able to come is to imagine eternity as a reunion with the past. Eliot's observation that "his

[30]*Studies in Human Time*, p. 31.
[31]*Studies in Human Time*, p. 32.
[32]*Tennyson Sixty Years After*, p. 125.

concern is for the loss of man rather than for the gain of God"³³ is not only true, it also diagnoses Tennyson's failure to make a real poetic climax of his elegy's *consolatio.*

IV

Although Tennyson's vision of eternity may be no substitute, aesthetically speaking, for "the tender grace of a day that is dead," there were at least two other directions in which his imagination turned that offered it a more promising escape from the barren present. These were the worlds of dream and of legend or myth.³⁴ Neither involves rejection of his passion of the past; both, in fact, appealed to him as atemporal realms in which the felicity of the past could be felt as present.

In *In Memoriam,* sleep may, like its "kinsman" death, release the soul from its temporal bonds and bring a reunion with the past:

> Sleep, Death's twin-brother knows not Death,
> Nor can I dream of thee as dead.
> I walk as ere I walk'd forlorn,
> When all our path was fresh with dew.   (LXVIII)

As Tennyson acknowledges in the same lyric, dreams may be troubled; but when they are free from anxiety there is nothing like that painful consciousness of the present that accompanies memory. Or, to put it another way, the temporal dimension is totally absent when sleep forges, in Tennyson's phrase, "A night-long present of the past" (LXXI). Nor is this renewal mere illusion, for as the poet insists, "Dreams are true while they last, and do we not live in dreams?" ("The Higher Pantheism").

Of course, though we may live in dreams, we do so only sporadically and unpremeditatively, and as a link to the past they are therefore obviously limited. "In Deep and Solemn Dreams" *(UEP),* one of Tennyson's first dream poems, is concerned with both the value and the ultimate inadequacy of the dream state. It describes the

---

³³*Essays Ancient and Modern* (New York, 1936), p. 197.

³⁴E. D. H. Johnson, *The Alien Vision of Victorian Poetry* (Princeton, 1952), pp. 22-29, discusses dreams in Tennyson's poetry as "a way of sublimating his concern with the life of the imagination." See also Carr, [*University of Toronto Quarterly,* XIX (1950),] 368-371, on Tennyson's "regression" into dream and "the liberating power of legend."

dream world as a City of the Blest, "Brooded o'er by dovelike rest" whose perfect stasis brings a recovery of the past:

> All adown the busy ways
> Come sunny faces of lost days,
> Long to mouldering dust consign'd,
> Forms which live but in the mind.

It is significant that these faces look upon the poet "With tearless ageless eyes" and that the poem later refers to "The sacred charm of tearless sleep," for it is thus clear that such dreams are free from the "idle tears" which inevitably attend temporal memory. The dream, however, cannot last; it fades away, leaving the poet "Hopeless, heartless, and forlorn." This evanescence is the theme of another early poem, "And Ask Ye Why These Sad Tears Stream," in which the poet dreams of his beloved "as t'was yesterday"; but the vision vanishes, and he awakens "double weary." Thus the dreamer may re-experience the past, but because the dream is independent of his will he can neither retain nor recall it. In "A Dream of Fair Women" (ll. 273-284) Tennyson expressly likens the futile attempt to recover a dream to the vain efforts of memory. As their appeal to the nostalgic imagination is similar, so memory and dream — though different in the degree and nature of their success — are alike in their ultimate failure.

It was the realm of myths and legends that came closest to constituting an idealized past that could solace Tennyson's imagination as a kind of eternal presence. Memory, "dealing but with time," cannot enable the soul to "climb beyond her own material prime" ("The Two Voices," ll. 376, 378); dreams are only "true while they last." But myths are like King Arthur's city: "built/ To music, therefore never built at all,/ And therefore built forever" ("Gareth and Lynette," ll. 272-274). The timelessness of myth was one of its greatest attractions to the Victorians; George Grote, perhaps the age's most influential authority on mythology as well as its greatest classical historian, regarded the world of myths as "a world completely distinct from historical fact."[35] It was, he insisted, "a past which never was present,"[36] not merely in the sense that its happen-

---

[35]*The Minor Works of George Grote* (London, 1873), p. 117. This is from an essay originally published in 1843. I have attempted to characterize the Victorian interest in myth in "Victorian Mythology," *Victorian Studies,* VI (Sept., 1962), 5-28.

[36]*History of Greece* (New York, 1875 [1st ed., 1846]), I, 44.

ings were historically untrue but also in the sense that the mythic past was different in kind from the historical past, from such a past as the present is always becoming. What this kind of perception about myths could mean to poetry William Morris explained in *The Earthly Paradise:*

> So let me sing of names remembered,
> Because they, living not, can ne'er be dead,
> Or long time take their memory quite away
> From us poor singers of an empty day.
>
> ("An Apology," ll. 18-21)

Tennyson was never so outspoken, but there can be no doubt of his deep affinity for "that new world which is the old" ("The Day-Dream," l. 168) or of his feeling that it embodied a "present past" more accessible yet scarcely less appealing than the "past present" of personal memory. "The Lotos-Eaters," one of the crucial poems of his early maturity, provides a particularly useful illustration of that appeal. A mythological poem having to do with the contrast between two antithetical kinds of existence, it is itself the representation of one of these antitheses. The poem is not only *about* lotos-land, it is a product of the lotos-land of Tennyson's mythological imagination.

The most notable feature of this land of the lotos-eaters is its time-lessness. It is "a land/ In which it seemed always afternoon" (ll. 3-4), "A land where all things always seem'd the same" (l. 24). Time stands still and change and transience are unknown. This static existence is carefully set in sharp contrast to the ceaseless motion of the sea —"the wandering fields of barren foam" (l. 42)—on which Odysseus and his men have been wearisomely journeying. The sea thus represents, as it does in "Break, Break, Break," a temporal existence from which the lotos fruit offers escape into "dreamful ease." To one who has tasted the fruit, the breaking waves sound distant and meaningless:

> whoso did receive of them
> And taste, to him the gushing of the wave
> Far far away did seem to mourn and rave
> On alien shores.   (ll. 30-33)

However, this flight from time and toil is not, as it is in the Homeric original, mere oblivion but rather the attainment of a transcendent awareness. The enchanted branches of the lotos enable one to penetrate beyond the barrier of death itself,

> To muse and brood and live again in memory,
> With those old faces of our infancy.
>
> ("Choric Song," ll. 65-66)

Clearly, then, this is not only an existence exempt from time, it is also one in which the past can somehow be recovered. Tennyson uses the word *memory*, but the memories of these lotos-eaters are quite distinct from those ordinary temporal recollections which, though dear, have not the power to compel because they belong to the mutable:

> Dear is the memory of our wedded lives,
> And dear the last embraces of our wives
> And their warm tears; but all hath suffered change.
>
> ("Choric Song," ll. 69-71)

Whereas the one kind of "memory" can negate time, the other actually intensifies the sense of transience so painful to the mariners:

> Time driveth onward fast,
> And in a little while our lips are dumb.
> Let us alone. What is it that will last?
> All things are taken from us, and become
> Portions and parcels of the dreadful past.
>
> ("Choric Song," ll. 43-47)

As a realm beyond the reach of time, where the tender grace of the past is eternally present, the land of the lotos-eaters depicts an imaginative ideal which myth and legend could in their way realize. Arthur Hallam is mythicized into the dying king of "Morte d'Arthur"; Tennyson's own grief and his resolution not to yield to it find their mythic translation in "Tithonus" and "Ulysses." The treatment Tennyson gave these subjects makes the poems in question seem to us something of "period pieces," but his attraction to them need hardly strain the modern comprehension. In an essay titled "The Heritage of Myth in Literature," Hermann Broch writes:

> Myth and logos attest to the unity of the human race as it stretches across the centuries, to the timelessness of each achievement, and man is thus enabled to divine also the timelessness of the self. ... Only through the union of past and future is that continuous present created for which the soul longs and into which it desires to enter. This pres-

ent, a continuum of past, present, and future, is timeless and there-fore the soul finds rest in it.

Chimera, IV [Spring, 1946], 33-34, 36[37]

Tennyson's "Passion of the Past" is just such a longing for the con-tinuous present; and in the way such mythic figures as Oenone, Tiresias, Bedivere, and Demeter could dramatically embody his own lyric moods he discovered a means by which the self might in some measure elude the isolation and flux of temporal existence.

However, no one could read "The Lotos-Eaters" and feel that this dreamful ease was being offered as an unqualified ideal. The positive values of timelessness and a reunion with the past involve the forsaking of responsibility and an indifference to humanity; and although this poem lacks the high moral tone Tennyson would all too often take, it is clear that irresponsibility and inhumanity are not condoned. The poem itself leaves the dilemma unresolved, but as Tennyson went on to explore the lotos-land of myth and legend he tried conscientiously to relate it to actual human con-cerns. "It is no use," he told his son, "giving a mere réchauffé of old legends."[38] Consequently, it became his customary technique to cast the legendary material in what he considered a modern "frame." The resulting marriage of ancient matter with modern meaning was not necessarily unfortunate, though often—especially in *Idylls of the King*—it proved to be so. And even when the frame seems most obtrusive, the poem usually retains some of the saving grace of Tennyson's nostalgic impulse. For the old legends, as I have tried to indicate, remained one important source of that "far and far away" to which Tennyson was always responsive. The Laureate became in-creasingly involved with maintaining a place in the march of mind suited to his image, but as an Ancient Sage he could still ask the question to which, early and late, he sought reply:

Today? but what of yesterday?   ("The Ancient Sage," L. 216)

[37] *Chimera*, IV [Spring, 1946], 33-34, 36.
[38] Memoir, II, 364.

In Memoriam

by T. S. Eliot

Tennyson is a great poet, for reasons that are perfectly clear. He has three qualities which are seldom found together except in the greatest poets: abundance, variety, and complete competence. We therefore cannot appreciate his work unless we read a good deal of it. We may not admire his aims: but whatever he sets out to do, he succeeds in doing, with a mastery which gives us the sense of confidence that is one of the major pleasures of poetry.

It is, in my opinion, in *In Memoriam,* that Tennyson finds full expression. Its technical merit alone is enough to ensure its perpetuity. While Tennyson's technical competence is everywhere masterly and satisfying, *In Memoriam* is the less unapproachable of all his poems. Here are one hundred and thirty-two passages, each of several quatrains in the same form, and never monotony or repetition. And the poem has to be comprehended as a whole. We may not memorize a few passages, we cannot find a "fair sample"; we have to comprehend the whole of a poem which is essentially the length that it is. We may choose to remember:

> Dark house, by which once more I stand
> Here in the long unlovely street,
> Doors, where my heart was used to beat
> So quickly, waiting for a hand,
>
> A hand that can be clasp'd no more—
> Behold me, for I cannot sleep,
> And like a guilty thing I creep
> At earliest morning to the door.

"In Memoriam." From T. S. Eliot, *Selected Essays* (London: Faber and Faber Ltd., 1932), pp. 175 and 182-90. Reprinted by permission of Faber and Faber Ltd. and Harcount Brace Jovanovich, Inc.

> He is not here: but far away
>   The noise of life begins again,
>   And ghastly thro' the drizzling rain
> On the bald street breaks the blank day.

This is great poetry, economical of words, a universal emotion in what could only be an English town: and it gives me the shudder that I fail to get from anything in *Maud*. But such a passage, by itself, is not *In Memoriam: In Memoriam* is the whole poem. It is unique: it is a long poem made by putting together lyrics, which have only the unity and continuity of a diary, the concentrated diary of a man confessing himself. It is a diary of which we have to read every word.

Apparently Tennyson's contemporaries, once they had accepted *In Memoriam,* regarded it as a message of hope and reassurance to their rather fading Christian faith. It happens now and then that a poet by some strange accident expresses the mood of his generation, at the same time that he is expressing a mood of his own which is quite remote from that of his generation. This is not a question of insincerity: there is an amalgam of yielding and opposition below the level of consciousness. Tennyson himself, on the conscious level of the man who talks to reporters and poses for photographers, to judge from remarks made in conversation and recorded in his son's Memoir, consistently asserted a convinced, if somewhat sketchy, Christian belief. And he was a friend of Frederick Denison Maurice —nothing seems odder about that age than the respect which its eminent people felt for each other. Nevertheless, I get a very different impression from *In Memoriam* from that which Tennyson's contemporaries seem to have got. It is of a very much more interesting and tragic Tennyson. His biographers have not failed to remark that he had a good deal of the temperament of the mystic—certainly not at all the mind of the theologian. He was desperately anxious to hold the faith of the believer, without being very clear about what he wanted to believe: he was capable of illumination which he was incapable of understanding. The "Strong Son of God, immortal Love," with an invocation of whom the poem opens, has only a hazy connexion with the Logos, or the Incarnate God. Tennyson is distressed by the idea of a mechanical universe; he is naturally, in lamenting his friend, teased by the hope of immortality and reunion beyond death. Yet the renewal craved for seems at best but a continuance, or a substitute for the joys of friendship upon earth. His desire for immortality never is quite the desire for Eternal Life; his concern is for the loss of man rather than for the gain of God.

> shall he,
> Man, her last work, who seem'd so fair,
>   Such splendid purpose in his eyes,
>   Who roll'd the psalm to wintry skies,
> Who built him fanes of fruitless prayer,
>
> Who trusted God was love indeed,
>   And love Creation's final law—
>   Though Nature, red in tooth and claw
> With ravine shriek'd against his creed—
>
> Who loved, who suffer'd countless ills.
>   Who battled for the True, the Just,
>   Be blown about the desert dust,
> Or seal'd within the iron hills?

That strange abstraction, "Nature," becomes a real god or goddess, perhaps more real, at moments, to Tennyson than God *("Are God and Nature then at strife?")*. The hope of immortality is confused (typically of the period) with the hope of the gradual and steady improvement of this world. Much has been said of Tennyson's interest in contemporary science, and of the impression of Darwin. *In Memoriam,* in any case, antedates *The Origin of Species* by several years, and the belief in social progress by democracy antedates it by many more; and I suspect that the faith of Tennyson's age in human progress would have been quite as strong even had the discoveries of Darwin been postponed by fifty years. And after all, there is no logical connexion: the belief in progress being current already, the discoveries of Darwin were harnessed to it:

> No longer half-akin to brute,
>   For all we thought, and loved and did
>   And hoped, and suffer'd, is but seed
> Of what in them is flower and fruit;
>
> Whereof the man, that with me trod
>   This planet, was a noble type
>   Appearing ere the times were ripe,
> That friend of mine who lives in God,
>
> That God, which ever lives and loves,
>   One God, one law, one element,

            And one far-off divine event,
        To which the whole creation moves.

These lines show an interesting compromise between the religious
attitude and, what is quite a different thing, the belief in human per-
fectibility; but the contrast was not so apparent to Tennyson's contemporaries. They may have been taken in by it, but I don't think
that Tennyson himself was, quite: his feelings were more honest
than his mind. There is evidence elsewhere — even in an early poem,
Locksley Hall, for example — that Tennyson by no means regarded
with complacency all the changes that were going on about him in
the progress of industrialism and the rise of the mercantile and
manufacturing and banking classes; and he may have contemplated
the future of England, as his years drew out, with increasing gloom.
Temperamentally, he was opposed to the doctrine that he was moved
to accept and to praise.[1]

Tennyson's feelings, I have said, were honest; but they were
usually a good way below the surface. *In Memoriam* can, I think,
justly be called a religious poem, but for another reason than that
which made it seem religious to his contemporaries. It is not religious because of the quality of its faith, but because of the quality of
its doubt. Its faith is a poor thing, but its doubt is a very intense
experience. *In Memoriam* is a poem of despair, but of despair of a
religious kind. And to qualify its despair with the adjective "religious" is to elevate it above most of its derivatives. For *The City of
Dreadful Night,* and the *Shropshire Lad,* and the poems of Thomas
Hardy, are small work in comparison with *In Memoriam:* it is greater than they and comprehends them.[2]

In ending we must go back to the beginning and remember that
In Memoriam would not be a great poem, or Tennyson a great poet,
without the technical accomplishment. Tennyson is the great master
of metric as well as of melancholia; I do not think any poet in English has ever had a finer ear for vowel sound, as well as a subtler
feeling for some moods of anguish:

[1]See, in Harold Nicolson's admirable [*Tennyson: Aspects of His Life, Character,
and Poetry* (London, 1923)], pp. 252 ff.

[2]There are other kinds of despair. Davidson's great poem, *Thirty Bob a Week,* is
not derivative from Tennyson. On the other hand, there are other things derivative
from Tennyson besides *Atalanta in Calydon.* Compare the poems of William Morris
with *The Voyage of Maeldune,* and *Barrack Room Ballads* with several of Tennyson's later poems.

> Dear as remember'd kisses after death,
> And sweet as those by hopeless fancy feign'd
> On lips that are for others; deep as love,
> Deep as first love, and wild with all regret.

And this technical gift of Tennyson's is no slight thing. Tennyson lived in a time which was already acutely time-conscious: a great many things seemed to be happening, railways were being built, discoveries were being made, the face of the world was changing. That was a time busy in keeping up to date. It had, for the most part, no hold on permanent things, on permanent truths about man and god and life and death. The surface of Tennyson stirred about with his time; and he had nothing to which to hold fast except his unique and unerring feeling for the sounds of words. But in this he had something that no one else had. Tennyson's surface, his technical accomplishment, is intimate with his depths: what we most quickly see about Tennyson is that which moves between the surface and the depths, that which is of slight importance. By looking innocently at the surface we are most likely to come to the depths, to the abyss of sorrow. Tennyson is not only a minor Virgil, he is also with Virgil as Dante saw him, a Virgil among the Shades, the saddest of all English poets, among the Great in Limbo, the most instinctive rebel against the society in which he was the most perfect conformist.

Tennyson seems to have reached the end of his spiritual development with *In Memoriam;* there followed no reconciliation, no resolution.

> And now no sacred staff shall break in blossom,
> No choral salutation lure to light
> A spirit sick with perfume and sweet night,

or rather with twilight, for Tennyson faced neither the darkness nor the light, in his later years. The genius, the technical power, persisted to the end, but the spirit had surrendered. A gloomier end than that of Baudelaire: Tennyson had no *singulier avertissement.* And having turned aside from the journey through the dark night, to become the surface flatterer of his own time, he has been rewarded with the despite of an age that succeeds his own in shallowness.

In Memoriam:
The Linnet and the Artifact

by Alan Sinfield

> All, as in some piece of art,
>   Is toil cooperant to an end.   (CXXVIII)
> I do but sing because I must,
>   And pipe but as the linnets sing.   (XXI)

These two comments on the nature of poetry from *In Memoriam* illustrate the twin attitudes behind the poem. The first suggests that a work of this art is an artifact, finished and perfected with all its parts carefully designed so as to contribute to a meaningful whole, perhaps with a moral purpose. The second shows the poet as writing because he cannot help himself, because he has to express his feelings. In this account the poet has little conscious control: his emotional state governs his mind, and he can write only what he feels. There is no thought of an end to be achieved, no suggestion of a pre-arranged scheme to which every part must contribute.

These quotations pick out precisely the duality in *In Memoriam* and in its language. Like most of Tennyson's work, it does not fit easily into pre-existing categories of literary criticism. In particular, it is a mixture of attributes generally associated with the neo-classical writers of the eighteenth-century Enlightenment and with the early nineteenth-century Romantic movement. Thus on the one hand we have the familiar picture of Tennyson as the black-blooded melancholic, brooding over the Lincolnshire Wolds, writing "Byron is

"In Memoriam": The Linnet and the Artifact." From Alan Sinfield, *The Language of Tennyson's* "In Memoriam" (Oxford: Basil Blackwell, Publisher, 1971). Reprinted by permission of Basil Blackwell Publisher.

dead" in the chalk and presenting in *In Memoriam* the intimate diary of a man confessing himself.[1] On the other hand we find the Poet Laureate, associated by F. L. Lucas with Theocritus and Callimachus, Virgil and Horace, Pope and Gray in "their mellowed learning, their chiselled style, their pleasure in remoulding the brave tales of older days into a more perfectly polished form."[2] One view of Tennyson's poetry finds him personal, subjective and impressionistic, the other sees him as a public writer, the mouthpiece of his age, using a highly stylized mode of poetic language to give classical form and order to his utterances. The duality is observed by a recent critic, who remarks, "He is a romantic and an idealist and a sentimentalist; but he is also a realist, a Classicist and a satirist."[3]

I am well aware of the dangers involved in describing Tennyson in these terms. A. O. Lovejoy has claimed that one cannot meaningfully speak of "Romanticism," but only of several "Romanticisms,"[4] and Geoffrey Clive has declared that "The ruptures and divisions in modern consciousness which often continue to be associated with nineteenth-century Romanticism were just as characteristic of the eighteenth century, although differently expressed."[5]

However, the majority of students of the history of ideas accept that there are two distinct clusters of attributes which can be labelled "Enlightenment" and "Romanticism." Whether they were successively or simultaneously present, and whether or not they can be seen as self-conscious movements where we can meaningfully enrol all the writers who have been marshalled under their banners, does not matter for my purposes. Perhaps the most important aspect of these terms for a study of Tennyson is that they exist in critics' minds, where they provide neat pigeon-holes into which he can be tidily fitted. Tennyson cannot be fully comprehended without some understanding of the modes of thought which characterized his

---

[1]See Sir Harold G. Nicolson, *Tennyson: Aspects of his Life, Character and Poetry* (London, 1923), pp. 9-10; and T. S. Eliot, *Selected Prose* (paperback, London, 1963), p. 170.

[2]F. L. Lucas, ed., *Tennyson: Poetry and Prose* (London, 1947), p. ix.

[3]Edward Elton Smith, *The Two Voices: A Tennysonian Study* (Lincoln, Nebraska, 1964), p. 55.

[4]Arthur O. Lovejoy, "On the Discrimination of Romanticisms," in *Essays in the History of Ideas* (Baltimore, 1948). For a reply see René Wellek, "The Concept of "Romanticism" in Literary History," *Comparative Literature,* I (1949), 1-23 and 147-72.

[5]Geoffrey Clive, *The Romantic Enlightenment* (paperback, New York, 1960), p. 20.

immediate predecessors, the Romantics; but, at the same time, there
are elements in his art which derive from impulses more often
associated with the eighteenth century. The attempt to [interpret]
Tennyson in terms solely of the one or the other results in a devalu-
ing of his achievement: he becomes a victim of literary history. . . .

In Memoriam displays the extremes of both attitudes. On the one
hand the poet pipes but as the linnets sing, on the other we find that
all is toil coöperant to a carefully devised and executed end. Tennyson's approach to the problems of love and death, morality and faith
created by the death of Arthur Hallam is in many ways subjective,
personal, individualistic. The poet is shown creating his own values
from his own imaginative resources in the Romantic manner.
Though *In Memoriam* has been widely thought of as propounding
a philosophy for its times, this view will not account for the greater
part of the poem, which is devoted to presenting the poet's developing *experience*. The poet himself says that this is so:

> If these brief lays, of Sorrow born,
>   Were taken to be such as closed
>   Grave doubts and answers here proposed,
> Then these were such as men might scorn.   (xlviii)

In Memoriam presents us with the successive thoughts and feelings
of a person; it is not, until the end, the ideas put forward that count,
but the attitudes which the poet adopts towards those ideas. We do
not find an argument, but something much more like the growth of
the poet's mind (the subtitle of *The Prelude*). We do not watch the
expounding of a philosophy, but the changes in the poet's outlook.

The crucial section in the poet's development is xcv, for it is here
that he experiences a vision which puts him in touch with a supra-
rational reality. As the poet reads Hallam's letters,

> So word by word, and line by line,
>   The dead man touch'd me from the past,
>   And all at once it seem'd at last
> The living soul was flash'd on mine,
>
> And mine in this was wound, and whirl'd
>   About empyreal heights of thought,
>   And came on that which is, and caught
> And deep pulsations of the world.

In the second line quoted Hallam is "The dead man," but by the fourth he has become "The living soul." Most of *In Memoriam* has been taken up with the poet's various thoughts, but none of them has more authority than another. The vision of section xcv (which alludes plainly to Dante's Paradise) has a unique significance because it provides the poet with a sanction for belief other than mere speculation or wishful thinking. Throughout the poem his main desire has been for renewed contact with Hallam; the vision supplies this. The poet is encouraged to believe that there is something more than physical life and final death, and his other problems disappear. As a result of this experience he knows that there is something other than impotent mankind and indifferent nature, that Hallam does still exist, that they will be reunited one day and that Hallam can still be with him in his present life. The poet had considered all these possibilities and many others, but only the supra-rational experience could give him authority for believing in what his fantasies and dreams had always represented to him as desirable. At the beginning the poet lost touch with Hallam: in section xcv he regains it, and the optimistic conclusion of the poem becomes possible.[6]

All this shows a strong dependence on subjective experience as a way of reaching truth, and is fully consonant with Romantic ways of thinking. It is impossible for the poet's claims to be verified: the experience was in his mind and he believes it. Tennyson's son tells us that he exclaimed:

> Yet God *is* love, transcendent, all pervading! We do not get *this* faith from Nature or the world. If we look at Nature alone, full of perfection and imperfection, she tells us that God is disease, murder and rapine. We get this faith from ourselves, from what is highest within us, which recognizes that there is not one fruitless pang, just as there is not one lost good.[7]

[6]For a detailed discussion of section xcv see my article in *The Major Victorian Poets: Reconsiderations,* ed. Isobel Armstrong (London, 1969). It is seen as the turning point also by J. L. Kendall, "A Neglected Theme in Tennyson's *In Memoriam,*" *Modern Language Notes,* LXXVI (1961), 414-20; M. J. Svaglic, "A Framework for Tennyson's *In Memoriam,*" *Journal of English and Germanic Philology,* LXI (1962), 810-25; and Carlisle Moore, "Faith, Doubt and Mystical Experience in *In Memoriam,*" *Victorian Studies,* VII (1963), 155-69.

[7]*Works, The Eversley Edition,* ed. Hallam Lord Tennyson (London, 1908), III, 214.

This is just what happens in *In Memoriam*: the poet gets his faith
from within himself, and the poem is a record of his experience. He
began by speaking of the *loss* of a philosophy: "I held it truth"

> That men may rise on stepping-stones
> Of their dead selves to higher things.

By the end of the poem he has at last arrived at a settled way of
looking at life. Because he is sure that "I shall not lose thee tho' I
die" (cxxx) he can also believe that man can be "The herald of a
higher race" (cxviii). Human existence is not purposeless for, whatever setbacks there may be, man is seen as striving ever upwards to
God. This evolutionary theory of the universe is already apparent
in the lines I have just quoted from section i; the point is whether
the poet can accept it. Hallam's apparently meaningless death
shattered his faith, but the vision of section xcv gives him the authority he needs for an optimistic outlook.

Tennyson is very explicit in his dependence upon personal experience, and exhibits just that distrust of scientific method and
reasonable arguments for a mechanistic universe which I have
described as characteristic of the reaction against the Enlightenment.

> Let Science prove we are, and then
> What matters Science unto men,
> At least to me? I would not stay.   (cxx)

He tells us in section cxxiv that he has his faith because "the heart/
Stood up and answer'd "I have felt'"; he almost despises attempts
to reason out a belief based on the argument from design:

> I found Him not in world or sun,
>   Or eagle's wing, or insect's eye;
>   Nor thro' the questions men may try,
> The petty cobwebs we have spun.   (cxxiv)

Hume had long ago pointed out that the mechanistic universe pre-
supposes only the kind of God who would make that mechanism.[8]
For Tennyson, a mechanic God was not good enough, for He could
not guarantee that love would endure, that there was a point to
Hallam's death and the poet's deprivation, that the two men might
meet again at some time. Only a vision where "The living soul was

---

[8]Alfred North Whitehead, *Science and The Modern World* [(New York, 1925)],
pp. 432-3.

flash'd on mine" could underwrite these desires. Thus he declares that Knowledge is "earthly of the mind," whereas Wisdom is "heavenly of the soul" (cxiv). Science, for Tennyson, deals with the material world and tries to understand it by rational processes, but for him the most important truths are to be discovered through a personal experience in which the mind is freed by a vision from the restraints of both matter and reason. And this attitude Tennyson held to the end of his life—"Nothing worthy proving can be proven," he is still writing in "The Ancient Sage."

When critics charge Tennyson with stupidity or romantic vagueness they may well have these aspects of *In Memoriam* in mind. It should be clear, however, that his subjective mode of arriving at beliefs is not his alone, but is entirely in accord with the reaction against the Enlightenment. For Robert Langbaum, "The essential idea of romanticism" is:

> the doctrine that the imaginative apprehension gained through immediate experience is primary and certain, whereas the analytic reflection that follows it is secondary and problematical. The poetry of the nineteenth and twentieth centuries can thus be seen in connection as a poetry of experience—a poetry constructed upon the deliberate disequilibrium between experience and idea, a poetry which makes its statement not as an idea but as an experience from which one or more ideas can be abstracted as problematical rationalisations.[9]

Milton and Pope set out to explain the ways of God to men: they are secure in the case they wish to make from the start, and their concern is to present it clearly and convincingly. Tennyson starts by saying how he has lost his faith, and it is only after describing the experience of three years that he can state a coherent set of beliefs. Jung declared that this is the only procedure which seems viable in the twentieth century: "The modern man abhors dogmatic postulates taken on faith and the religions based upon them. He holds them valid only in so far as their knowledge-content seems to accord with his own experience of the deeps of psychic life."[10] As for certain of the Romantic poets, this operation pivots for Tennyson upon a moment of mystical awareness. Seen from this point of view, the familiar charge that the Victorians always constructed a dream world into which they could escape becomes quite untenable. In *In Mem-*

---

[9]Robert Langbaum, *The Poetry of Experience* (paperback, New York, 1963), p. 35.
[10]C. G. Jung, *Modern Man in Search of a Soul* (paperback, London, 1961), p. 239.

oriam at least it is nearer the truth to claim that Tennyson is tapping psychic depths in order to frame a world view that is in harmony with his profoundest experience of reality. The implications of this process for a study of the poem's language must not be ignored. ...

A principal corollary of the Romantic side of *In Memoriam* is that the poem should *look like* the poet's experience. This is the function of the realistic background detail—both the scenic description and the poet's family setting. The character of the poem as an evolving experience is also evident in the sequence of short sections, each relatively self-contained, which makes up the totality. Each section encapsulates a moment in the poet's development, a thought or an incident, and the flexibility of length allows just the amount of elaboration the subject requires. A more rigid form would falsify the experience. In some ways, in fact, we can think of *In Memoriam* as rather like a novel. It opens with the central character musing to himself about his loss, then he strolls down to the graveyard (as an impressionable young man might). More of his meditations follow (iii); he goes to bed, and the reader sees how his loss affects his sleep (iv). Later on he thinks about his art (v), and then he receives a letter from a friend, which sets off a further train of thought (vi). Very early in the morning he goes for a walk to the dead man's house (vii). These events are such as might appear in a novel, but there is no novel like this in the nineteenth century. The poem lacks all the linking passages we expect in a novel. We are not told how or why the poet visits the graveyard in section ii or Hallam's house in vii: we are given no information that is not immediately relevant to his inner emotions. All extraneous matter is excluded so that we are made to concentrate on the poet's most personal thoughts and feelings. The focus is on his internal development, but there is sufficient background to give the sequence credibility.

The short sections make this economy and intensity possible. Each is a moment in the continuum of the poet's changing attitudes, with other parts of his life cut neatly away. T. S. Eliot had the point precisely when he declared that *In Memoriam* has "the unity and continuity of a diary, the concentrated diary of a man confessing himself."[11] It has been objected that the sections are not presented in the order in which they were composed. Study of the manuscripts shows that this is certainly true, but we are concerned with the poem, not Tennyson's life. It may well be that *In Memoriam* consists large-

[11]*Selected Prose*, p. 170.

ly of things that happened to Tennyson and it may be that it does not; it is mostly impossible to decide, and in my view fairly unimportant. In order to keep clear the distinction between biography and poem I propose always in this study to use "Tennyson" of the man who historically wrote *In Memoriam,* and "the poet" of the "I" in the poem. The facts of composition do not affect the diary-like appearance of the poem, which is a major cause of the reader's impression that what he has before him has the validity of an actual experience.

The section-sequence structure, so faithful to Romantic modes of thought, has troubled critics by its lack of obvious overall form. Almost all have tried to divide the poem up into fairly self-contained parts—what Nicolson called "its three arbitrary divisions of Despair, Regret and Hope, ticked off symmetrically by the successive Christmas Odes."[12] These divisions are indeed arbitrary, but not, I believe to be found in the poem. It will be objected that Tennyson mentioned parts, but he suggested two quite different schemes and it seems likely that it was pressure of questioning that elicited the "parts" rather than anything inherent in the poem.[13] There is no need of divisions; the movement from grief to acceptance is not smooth and regular, but then, neither is life. Like the Romantics, Tennyson avoids predetermined forms which would cramp the expression of an individual experience. The poet tends to take three steps forward and two back, and it is this process of gradual, moment by moment development, visible only if we stand off a little from the text, which creates a sense of the reality of the poet's experience.

The typical movement of the poem does not follow a pattern of logic, or even of simple thought association. The governing factor is the rise and fall in the poet's feelings; the poem moves in waves from one high point of emotional intensity to the next, with the passages in between building up to and leading away from these points. At the first Christmas, for instance, we have two sections of anxiety and mundane preparations before the climax of section xxx, where the family hopefully sings "They do not die." The moment of deep feeling is the crest of a relatively mundane wave, even as

[12]Nicolson, *Tennyson,* p. 297; cf. J. C. C. Mays, *"In Memoriam:* An Aspect of Form," *University of Toronto Quarterly,* XXXV (1965-6), pp. 22-46.

[13]See Hallam Lord Tennyson, *Alfred Lord Tennyson, A Memoir* (London, 1897) (cited hereafter as *Memoir),* I, 305, and James Knowles, "Aspects of Tennyson II," *Nineteenth Century,* XXXIII (1893), 182.

the family's excitement arose out of their commonplace preparations for Christmas. Leading away from section xxx is a series
taking up on a more prosaic level the question of the continuing
existence of Hallam. Can the family's optimism be justified, the
poet asks: the wave falls back again after the moment of intensity.

The poet on several occasions uses this very metaphor for his
changing emotions—in section xix, for example, he compares the
movement of his grief to the tide of the river Wye. *In Memoriam*
proceeds in waves: a subject is taken up, gathers to a head, breaks
in a climax, and then sinks back again, though occasionally a heavy
swell comes unexpectedly. The section-sequence structure embodies
a kind of rhythm of experience which it is difficult to define further.
The form of *In Memoriam* recreates the shapes of the life of the
emotions.

The final aspect of the Romantic side of *In Memoriam* which I
wish to bring forward here is again related to the practice of relying
upon imaginative experience as the primary means of arriving at
basic and enduring truths. Since rational analysis is seen as inade-
quate to grasp the essential significance of the poet's various moods,
he uses repeatedly a process of "redefinition." By this I mean that
he does not dissect an event to reveal its meaning, but restates it in
other terms, approaches it from another angle to see how it looks
from there. The experience is redefined so that the totality of its
significance can be gathered from the different accounts of it.

There are two distinct forms of this redefinition process. The first
is its local use, where its function is to make clear the nature of a
current emotional state. This is apparent in the tendency to follow
a section describing an experience with another trying to place it in
the poet's continuing development or evoking a related situation to
which it can be compared. Section vii, for instance, describes how
the poet goes to Hallam's door but finds no one there. In section viii
this event is considered from the point of view of an imaginary
happy lover who discovers that his fiancee is not at home when he
calls; he is analogous to the poet in section vii and provides another
way of looking at the same situation. The differences are also important, however: the lady will presumably be at home tomorrow,
but Hallam can never return. This mode of operating is invaluable
to a writer like Tennyson who is concerned to express the nature of
an elusive emotion—Shelley's "To a Skylark" is a splendid example

of its extended use. The experience is redefined in other terms so that its essential qualities can be distilled.

The second form taken by this process is vital to the large-scale structure of *In Memoriam*. The poet repeatedly alludes after a period of time to an earlier event so that the intervening change of attitude can be immediately seen. The development of his experience is charted primarily by these reminders of earlier scenes which bring out the difference in the poet's outlook. This is most evident in the sections which refer back explicitly across the poem—Christmas, spring, the anniversaries of Hallam's death and the visits to the yew tree all show the poet's attitude measured against recurring external events. In section ii, for example, the yew tree is seen as a figure of deathly constancy, but when he returns in the spring he finds that the yew does experience "the golden hour/ When flower is feeling after" (xxxix). There can be such a thing as love and happiness in the face of death, he now realizes, but sorrow still controls his mind: "Thy gloom is kindled at the tips,/ And passes into gloom again." His state of mind is progressively redefined in terms of his altered attitudes to the same object.

The importance of this same process in the work and thought of Wordsworth and Coleridge has been expounded by Stephen Prickett.[14] He stresses that to them growth was only possible through the realization of the inadequacy of previously adopted patterns of perception, through the reaction of new experiences on what had gone before. This theory of mental development which is explicit in "Tintern Abbey" or "Frost at Midnight" is the implicit structural basis of *In Memoriam*. The earlier poets show how thinking over former attitudes brings them to a new formulation; in *In Memoriam* the reader must perceive for himself how the poet's emotional response is progressively redefined, but the signs are all there in the writing. This process, like the other aspects of the poem discussed in this chapter, will appear again and again in the detailed discussion of language which is to follow.

I have suggested that Tennyson's way of finding values by which to live is related to Romantic modes of thought and that it affects various aspects of the structure of *In Memoriam*. The section-sequence is a superb form for embodying moment by moment the poet's changing moods and ideas without forcing them into a rigid

[14]*Coleridge and Wordsworth: The Poetry of Growth* (London, 1970).

frame; the redefinition process is necessary to capture the poet's states of mind and to chart his attitude as it evolves. These facets of the poem have perplexed and alienated critics, but the full story is even more complicated. There are aspects of the poem—of meaning and language—which do not allow us simply to say, it is a Romantic poem and we must treat it as such. It is also objective, impersonal and general; in other words, it exhibits characteristics usually associated with the Enlightenment.

Of course, this dichotomy between Romantic and neo-classical attributes is relative and is not meant to imply that one group of qualities is completely absent in a writer normally connected with the other. The distinctive factor in Tennyson's approach is the strong presence of both extremes. Consider these remarks he made:

> This is a poem, *not* an actual autobiography. ... "I" is not always the author speaking of himself, but the voice of the human race speaking thro' him.
>
> It is rather the cry of the whole human race than mine. In the poem altogether private grief swells out into thought of, and hope for the whole world. ... It is a very impersonal poem as well as personal.[15]

These comments are the antithesis of the Romantic reliance upon subjective experience, but they too indicate one side of *In Memoriam*. Here we see Tennyson not simply singing like the linnet, but writing to the end of expressing the voice of the human race; he has almost adopted the Enlightenment stance of universal intelligibility, acceptability and familiarity. The poem is conceived of as stating a common human position which will be recognized as true and relevant by the whole of mankind. Though I have asserted that the rearrangement of the sections during the poem's composition does not affect its appearance as a diary, it does show the dichotomy in Tennyson's approach. *In Memoriam* is a record of his experience, but at the same time it is designed to be the voice of the human race. Wordsworth, we know, quite often modified his experience when he used it in his poems, but his alterations were of a completely different kind. He is characteristically to be found concealing the fact that another person was present who also found the event important; he emphasizes the uniqueness of the experience to him. Tennyson, on the other hand, typically generalizes his feelings in *In Memoriam*,

---

[15]*Memoir*, I, 304-5; Knowles, "Aspects of Tennyson," p. 182.

stressing that they are common to many people. He insists at the same time on both individuality and generality.

The poem was accepted by its Victorian readers as being of relevance to them, and it is most significant that *The Prelude,* published in the same year, achieved nowhere near the success at the time despite Wordsworth's reputation and the uncertain reviews of Tennyson's earlier work. The repeated references to other people in related situations (often, it may seem to us, rather Victorian situations) contributes powerfully to this generalizing effect. The poet is like young men and girls who have lost their lovers, mothers and fathers who have lost their sons, widows and widowers. He may well say in section xcix that the myriads who have memories of births, bridals and deaths "count as kindred souls;/ They know me not, but mourn with me." The poet's expression of his own loss comes to stand for the feelings of all bereaved people; to his readers *In Memoriam* represented in part at least what oft was thought.

Certain Romantic poets would perhaps have claimed that what they wrote was in some sense the cry of the whole human race, but Tennyson is distinctive in the deliberate way he sets about generalizing his experience and making it relevant to public issues. The whole process is very carefully managed. At the beginning of the poem the poet has lost the values he had lived by, his whole view of life has been shaken. For the most part, however, he is too absorbed in his immediate grief to think of that. Nevertheless, the question of Hallam's immortality leads back to larger issues, and the problems of life after death, contact between the dead and the living, the future of mankind and God's attitude to His creation feature strongly in sections xxxiv-lvii. Before, the world looked good to the poet and he assumed it was good; now it looks bad, and to prove it good is not easy. He finds himself completely unable to resolve the difficulties he has raised. So after section lvii he drops these problems, leaves them on one side, and turns instead, in a series of less intense sections, to consider the relative positions of Hallam and himself. He thus acts out the reliance upon experience which I have described as basic to *In Memoriam.* Unable to resolve his doubts by dogma or reasoning, he falls back on the personal. It is only as a result of the private vision of section xcv that he can return to public issues: reassurance in his personal life gives him the authority to speak with confidence on the general subjects he had been forced to abandon.

He has not proved the world good, but he has had a personal experience which makes him believe that it is, and Hallam becomes an advance guard in the onward march of mankind.

The poet's confidence in speaking of public subjects at the end of the poem is, therefore, completely justified dramatically: the standards which were lost when Hallam died have been found again, and now have a far more secure basis. The poet has discovered his values in his own experience in Romantic fashion, but the resulting affirmation goes beyond the problematic rationalisations which the Romantic might achieve. It is very general in its scope and very specific in its details. At the end of *In Memoriam* the poet takes up a position on "the feud of rich and poor," "ancient forms of party strife," "false pride in place and blood,/ The civic slander and the spite" (cvi). All this is quite different from the linnet compelled to sing, from the black-blooded melancholic. In the Romantic period, according to Graham Hough, "The emphasis shifts from social man to the individual man, when he is alone with his own heart or alone with nature." We find both these emphases in *In Memoriam*.

The prime factor in the poem which encourages us to view it in the Enlightenment way as a carefully wrought artifact is the high degree of stylization which we usually find in the details of the language. Some element of stylization is perhaps always present in poetry, but such writing as,

> Sweet after showers, ambrosial air,
> > That rollest from the gorgeous gloom
> > Of evening over brake and bloom
> And meadow,   (lxxxvi)

is as self-consciously ordered as the sequence of sections is (apparently at least) casual. In the details of Tennyson's language we find all the artificiality and the concentration upon making an object to be admired for its beauty which is usually associated with the eighteenth century. There is no shortage of examples—

> Fair ship, that from the Italian shore
> > Sailest the placid ocean-plains
> > With my lost Arthur's loved remains,
> Spread thy full wings, and waft him o'er.   (ix)
> One whispers, "Here thy boyhood sung

> Long since its matin song, and heard
> The low love-language of the bird
> In native hazels tassel-hung."   (cii)

We feel that every word is picked individually and polished before use. At no time does Tennyson seem to want us to feel that he is using the language of men, that he is writing things down as they come to him. As we read *In Memoriam* we are always fully conscious that it is a work of art; it is not just the linnet singing because he must express his unruly emotions, but also toil cooperant to a carefully designed end.

This is not to say, however, that the language of the poem is the same throughout. Indeed, it has been accused by Baum of having "too much variety, both of style and of content."[16] Here we see the Tennysonian paradox in its full glory. The variety of content is the result of the need to show the poet's experience: Tennyson's Romantic approach to the problems of human existence demands that he include the fullness of life, for general reflections can result only from the felt reality of experience. The variety of style, on the other hand, results from a determined matching of language to content whereby ornate diction and syntax are used for lofty subject matter and a more prosaic mode for the commonplace; in other words, we have here the Enlightenment notion of *decorum*. When Baum compares sections lix and cxxii he is taking a considered declaration of intent—

> My centred passion cannot move,
> Nor will it lessen from to-day—

and placing it beside an ecstatic celebration of the possibility of communion with the dead—

> The wizard lightnings deeply glow,
> And every thought breaks out a rose.

The language is appropriate to the thought of each section.

This eighteenth-century principle of decorum, which was based ultimately on the belief that everything was put in its proper place by God and that the artist's task was respectfully to display this order, is fundamental to Tennyson's language—despite the subjectivity and irrationality of his outlook. Bernard Groom brings

---

[16]Paull F. Baum, *Tennyson Sixty Years After* (Chapel Hill, 1948), pp. 124-5; cf. Geoffrey Tillotson, *Augustan Poetic Diction* (London, 1964), p. 60.

out this tendency by remarking how Tennyson admired Swinburne's *Atalanta in Calydon*, but "asked whether it was *"fair"* to use the language of the Bible in poems so antagonistic to the spirit of Christianity. For Tennyson, it was a matter of poetic decorum and intellectual integrity to respect the historical associations of words and their religious implications."[17] The rise and fall of emotion which is the basis of *In Memoriam* is matched with a variation in the degree of elaboration in language, but the two nevertheless stem from what have traditionally been opposed views of the nature of poetry.

The language of *In Memoriam* is adjusted according to the demands of decorum whilst maintaining a continual artificiality which defies the Romantic canon of spontaneity. Tennyson's avoidance of startling effects and his cultivation of the nuance produces an air of delicate restraint which contributes further to the neo-classical tone of the poem. He rarely jerks us violently by strange juxtapositions of words or jarring rhythms; thus we see the preponderance of images drawn from nature and the lack, for instance, of twin compasses (though Tennyson admired Donne's poem for its "wonderful ingenuity"[18]). This delicate shading of detail will be seen in all aspects of Tennyson's language. The reader must attend closely if, for example, he is to appreciate solely from the repetition of the words "true and tried" that the Epilogue is written to the same man as section lxxxv and thus completes a smooth movement from isolation in grief to involvement with other people; or if he is to notice how the attribution of the story of the raising of Lazarus to *"that* Evangelist" (xxxi) reminds the reader that the incident is reported in only the one Gospel and is thereby the more uncertain. Rather than dislocating language to force it into his meaning, Tennyson is to be found gently modifying it to suit his requirements.

Over against the record of a man who broods upon his loss until a personal vision brings reassurance, then, is the delicate and elaborate stylization of language in *In Memoriam*. Even section lix, which has been mentioned as an example of relatively straightforward language, employs rhetorical exclamation and inversion, personification and archaism — "O Sorrow, wilt thou rule my blood." There is a Romantic and a classical impulse in Tennyson's poem.

---

[17]Bernard Groom, *The Diction of Poetry from Spenser to Bridges* (Toronto, 1955), pp. 252-3.

[18]*Memoir*, II, 503.

Study of the manuscripts makes it clear that both these tendencies were present throughout its composition; it is not true, as critics have guessed, that the earliest written sections were spontaneous overflows of feeling in simple language whilst the later ones reveal the falsity of their emotional stimulus by their artificial manner. Section ix ("Fair ship, that from the Italian shore/ Sailest the placid ocean-plains"), for instance, was one of the first, whereas section vii ("Dark house by which once more I stand/ Here in the long unlovely street") is not in the Trial Edition of 1850, though Nicolson surmised that it was "obviously an actual experience."[19]

The result of this consistent stylization is an affirmation through language of an order and design of which Tennyson was personally only precariously assured. His language habits are in many ways those of the Enlightenment: they often irradiate the sense of a harmonious system which we find in Pope. Several critics have noted the likeness of the two writers, and Tennyson remarked how the perfection of some lines by Pope brought tears to his eyes.[20] In both cases the self-conscious creation of a beautifully made object implies a desire to aver an ultimate order in the universe. ...

In *In Memoriam* the reliance upon intense personal experience as a way to truth suggests the Romantic linnet who has to express his unruly feelings. Yet, at the same time, the stylized language, like the attempt to represent the feelings of all mankind, implies a desire to regain Enlightenment values of order and design through toil cooperant to an end. Of course, neither pole was ever more than a matter of emphasis. Romantic poets in fact fashioned their poems into works of art, they could make general declarations about the nature of human existence, and they sometimes wrote in ornate language (one thinks especially of Keats). Nevertheless, in *In Memoriam* we find a strong movement out towards *both* poles. Tennyson's mode of finding value in life is exceptionally subjective and the shaping of his poem shows it in many ways, but at the same time he makes a large claim for the general applicability of his experience and preserves decorum in diction within a consistently high degree of stylization. [Meyer] Abrams sums up the change the Romantics introduced:

[19]Nicolson, *Tennyson*, p. 297; and see Baum, *Tennyson Sixty Years After*, p. 116.
[20]Quoted by Sir Charles Tennyson, *Alfred Tennyson* (London, 1949), p. 452; see also Edmund Wilson, *Axel's Castle* [(New York, 1931)] , p. 14, and William Paton Ker, *Collected Essays* (London, 1925), I, 268.

The first test any poem must pass is no longer, "Is it true to nature?" or "Is it appropriate to the requirements either of the best judges or the generality of mankind?" but a criterion looking in a different direction; namely, "Is it sincere? Is it genuine? Does it match the intention, the feeling, and the actual state of mind of the poet while composing?"[21]

None of these questions by itself will serve for *In Memoriam*. A far more complex response is demanded.

We may speculate briefly on the reasons for this duality in Tennyson's writing. They may lie, as Auden suggested, in his character, and the "tidiness" may be "a *defense,* as if he hoped that through his control of the means of expressing his emotions, the emotions themselves, which he cannot master directly, might be brought to order."[22] Other writers, however, have seen a general trend back towards classical qualities in the mid-nineteenth century. Edmund Wilson finds a reaction, specially prominent in France, against the looseness and sentimentality to which Romanticism was open, and Walter E. Houghton produces a lot of evidence of English disenchantment with introspective poetry.[23] In the Victorian period thought turned inexorably towards the problem of faith, but people were tired of being depressed by morbid personal doubts. Hence the liking for the heroic leader and narrative verse where one could see people coping with life, rather than the laments of the individual who could not see his way through the intellectual mist left by the loss of confidence in religious faith.

Obviously a return to the effortless security of the Enlightenment was impossible, and hence *In Memoriam* shows values being derived from personal experience in the Romantic manner. Nevertheless, the poet could exert himself to relate his work to the feelings of ordinary people, and this Tennyson does, as well as stating through the stylization of his language his ultimate orientation towards stable values. His determination to make in his poems something as perfect and highly wrought as possible is less a sign of a confident belief in an existing order than of a need to create a small piece of sanity and design within a general chaos. Several of his remarks about poetry in *In Memoriam* are concerned with the question "What

[21]Abrams, *The Mirror and the Lamp,* [(New York, 1953)] p. 23.

[22]W. H. Auden, *Tennyson: An Introduction and Selection* (London, 1946), p. xviii.

[23]Edmund Wilson, *Axel's Castle,* pp. 12-14; Walter E. Houghton, *The Victorian Frame of Mind,* [1830-1870 (New Haven, 1957)] , pp. 334-6.

hope is here for modern rhyme" (lxxvii), and his desire for perfection may be seen as an attempt to raise a monument in the shifting sands of modern life. The vision described in section xcv gave hope for the eventual triumph of good, but only through his art could Tennyson recapture immediately the harmony and beauty which the Enlightenment had observed in the functioning of the whole universe.

In the last analysis there may be no contradiction at all. D. G. James notices just the same dichotomy in Arnold, but argues that the impulse towards the classical is in fact another kind of Romantic yearning:

> the classical becomes only a symbol for the inviolable thing, the other, the unattainable, the transcendent; and it is erected into such a symbol only by a certain play of self-deception, and by a refusal to face historic realities. Because this is so, the hunger for the classical in the modern spirit is a useless form of escape from its own nature and destiny; and this is what is in Arnold's [1853] Preface.[24]

James is severe, but it is doubtful whether this form of Romantic aspiration is more suspect than any other, or than the Enlightenment certainty (in the face of all the facts, it must seem to us) that all is well. The more difficult it is to account for the vicissitudes of human life, the more desperate will be any positive assertion, until the point when it is recognized that no assertion at all is possible. Tennyson did not reach this point but it was only through a very personal mystical experience that he was able to arrive at a secure position. His eagerness to move from his vision to general issues shows the same desire for a system in the universe that we find in his language. The structure and language of *In Memoriam,* then, are the product of a desperate need for order in the absence of any clear and agreed means of establishing it. In these conditions it is perhaps not suprising that Tennyson's poetry contains elements which seem to be contradictory when viewed in the light of what was possible in the eighteenth and early nineteenth centuries. ...

[24]D. G. James, *Matthew Arnold [and The Decline of English Romanticism* (Oxford, 1961)] , pp. 59, 65.

Maud

by Jerome H. Buckley

Tennyson's distaste for all false convention determines the themes and penetrates the very texture of *Maud,* which is at once the most dissonant of all his major works and the most varied in its rich operatic harmonies. Dante Gabriel Rossetti, who attended a memorable reading of the "monodrama," was impressed by the intensity of the lyrics but rather shocked by the violence of the plot and astonished by the alternation of tenderness and ferocity. All in all, he told William Allingham, it is "an odd De Balzacish sort of story for an Englishman at Tennyson's age."[1] Though very few of the reviewers shared Rossetti's admiration, most agreed that *Maud* was indeed odd and un-English and most obscure; and one summed up the common reaction by suggesting that the title had one vowel too many, no matter which. But the friends of independent mind, whose opinion Tennyson should have valued, Jowett, Ruskin, the Brownings, all felt the bold strength and originality of the experiment; and at least one loyal Tennysonian, William Johnson Cory, declared that now more than ever Tennyson belonged only to those free spirits beyond the reach of a stodgy respectability:

> Leave him to us, ye good and sage,
> Who stiffen in your middle age.
> Ye loved him once, but now forbear;
> Yield him to those who hope and dare,
> And have not yet to forms consign'd
> A rigid ossifying mind.[2]

"Maud." From Jerome H. Buckley, *Tennyson: The Growth of a Poet* (Cambridge, Mass.: Harvard University Press, 1960), pp. 140-46. Copyright © 1960 by the President and Fellows of Harvard College. Reprinted by permission of the author and publishers.

[1] Quoted from a suppressed letter by M. L. Howe, "Dante Gabriel Rossetti's Comments on *Maud*," *Modern Language Notes,* XLIX (1934), 291.

[2] Quoted in *Memoir,* I, 393, from Cory's *Ionica* [(London, 1858-1877)] . Cf. Cory's

Whether the hero of *Maud* commands or repels the reader's sympathy, he at least suffers no rigidity of mind. Created to bear the burden of manifold uneasiness and turbulent emotion, he remains amorphous and unstable, less distinct than his own moods, less vivid than his melodramatic history. "The peculiarity of this poem," as Tennyson explained (though there are other and more striking peculiarities), "is that different phases of passion in one person take the place of different characters."[3] But, unlike the speakers of Browning's best monologues, the person, from whose single and often singular point of view the whole plot must unfold, is a sensibility rather than an individual. He is—according to the poet—"a morbid poetic soul" and thus a Byronic antihero, a little like Heathcliff of *Wuthering Heights,* much like the narrator of "Locksley Hall," a kinsman of the "Spasmodic" protagonist like Alexander Smith's Walter or Sydney Dobell's Balder, a dispossessed, disconsolate young man who exists for us only in his own self-appraisals. He is, in short, the epitome of the self-conscious, sensitive, but unproductive post-Romantic, "at war with [himself] and a wretched race."

War in all its ambiguity supplies the frame of *Maud,* the point of departure and the source of resolution. The hero begins by musing on the death-stained "blood-red heath" and the fate of his father, who has been, he believes, a victim of the undeclared private war of greedy speculation. For the apparent tradesman's peace, he has decided, is in reality a "Civil war,...and that of a kind/ The viler, as underhand, not openly bearing the sword." Deceit has reached down to the local village where "Jack on his alehouse bench has as many lies as a Czar," and perfidy has invaded his own impoverished household, where the manservant and the maid are "ever ready to slander and steal." On a higher level, "the man of science" is sedulously vain in his quest for personal glory, and even "The passionate heart of the poet is whirl'd into folly and vice." The sanction for a universal selfishness seems to be the endless war of nature, the fierce struggle for survival,

> For nature is one with rapine, a harm no preacher can heal;
> The Mayfly is torn by the swallow, the sparrow spear'd by
>   the shrike,

acknowledgment that Tennyson was "the light and joy of my poor life"; see A. C. Benson, ed., *Ionica* (London, 1905), p. xviii.

[3]*Memoir,* I, 396.

> And the whole little wood where I sit is a world of plunder
>   and prey.

Yet Maud, yearning no doubt for a true knight of her own, sings a ballad of battles long ago when men could rise above selfish desire; and the hero, hearing, dreams of a good society in which each man no longer "is at war with mankind." But he himself implicitly accepts the rule of selfish warfare by seeking satisfaction under "the Christless code" of the duel. Then only at the depth of the madness which ensues does he recognize the horror of his guilt, "the red life spilt for a private blow," and the difference between "lawful and lawless war." The grim agent of his recovery is the "lawful" war in the Crimea, of which, as he embarks, he knows nothing except that military demand has for the moment imposed upon a dissident society the need of full cooperation. Though the war will bring its own tragedies, in it the "land…has lost for a little her lust of gold"; and the ending of the false peace seems essential to the establishment of any true peace. Convinced that the nation has found a worthy cause, the hero, at least temporarily, may feel one with his kind and so persuade himself, "it is better to fight for the good than to rail at the ill." Thus the war without provides a "moral equivalent" for the immoral war within.

Throughout *Maud* war in some sort is the expression of unreason in the self or the society, a restless passion which may be turned to good or evil purpose. The original alternative title of *Maud* was *The Madness,* and madness in many variations remains its central theme. From the outset the hero, even as he denounces "the vitriol madness" of the age, fears for his own sanity, since his father, he remembers, was subject to moods of insane wrath. The roaring sea and "the scream of a madden'd beach" become correlatives of the social war and his own anguish; and he resolves to find "a passionless peace" in "the quiet woodland ways"—that is, in full and deliberate retreat from all social obligation and "most of all," he insists, "from the cruel madness of love." But he senses almost immediately that his misanthropy is itself the result of an absurd and morbid ignorance of the real world. When the love of Maud overwhelms him, he yields to a complete physical and emotional intoxication, despite his awareness of love's fatality:

> What matter if I go mad, I shall have had my day.

Maud's beauty, however, may yet save him "Perhaps from madness," and his passion, lifting him "out of lonely hell," may seem a total good. The act of love transports him to an earthly paradise symbolized by the beloved's garden, where the cedar-tree sheltering Maud must—he imagines—know the same delight as its "Forefathers of the thornless garden, there/ Shadowing the snow-limb'd Eve from whom she came." In this little Eden the rose and the lily, each imaging attributes of Maud herself,[4] commingle in passionate purity; and the hero tells the lily of Maud's faithfulness as "the soul of the rose" enters into his blood. If he is now mad, it is with the enraptured madness of pure devotion. But the murderous encounter with Maud's brother arouses once more the selfish passions of pride and rage which drive him forever from the garden and abandon him to the horror of a far different madness. The madhouse to which he is eventually confined is another hell, worse than the loneliness, peopled with dead men gabbling of their selfish obsessions in an eternal chatter "enough to drive one mad." In his delusion he has been persistently haunted by the "ghastly Wraith" of Maud, "a hard mechanic ghost," the avenging conscience, an image which his own troubled mind has distorted and desecrated. Recovery comes only when in a dream he beholds the true spirit of Maud descending "from a band of the blest" and pointing toward the cooperative war that will bring him mental peace. Then at last he may exorcise "the dreary phantom" and so escape all madness in the firm resolution that

> It is time, O passionate heart and morbid eye,
> That old hysterical mock-disease should die.

The Crimean War was, of course, a major international mistake, in which the "blunder" at Balaklava was only a characteristic incident. But if we can for the moment accept the fiction that it was a righteous social enterprise such as might effect the hero's regeneration, we may begin to appreciate the pattern of *Maud* as a poetic whole, the complex relation between the themes of war and madness and the deliberate ironic reversals. Despite the frenzy of its content, *Maud* is the most carefully constructed of Tennyson's longer poems; and the verse throughout, for all its onrush of senti-

---

[4]Cf. E. D. H. Johnson, "The Lily and the Rose: Symbolic Meaning in Tennyson's *Maud*," *PMLA*, LXIV (1949), 1222-1227.

ment, is calculated and controlled with great discretion. The rhetoric and even bombast of the first four sections, elaborately interweaving natural description, social comment, and self-analysis, is carried by a breathless speed of movement, largely trochaic and anapaestic, and an excited abruptness of imagery. The more colloquial recitatives that follow and later recur at frequent intervals, sometimes on the dead level of iambic prose, sometimes heightened a little by a sudden sharp thrust of satire, relax the tension and provide transitions to the great arias of the monodrama: "Go not, happy day," where the image of the rose is repeated like a full note in music and the sound conquers all sense; "I have led her home" with its rich reflective sensuality; the ecstatic aubade, "Come into the garden, Maud"; and the troubled nostalgic "O that 'twere possible." In each of these lyrics all is aesthetically ordained; no effect is accidental. The concentration of language, we may be sure, was achieved by studious revision no less than an instinctive sense of verbal rightness. The apostrophe to the stars, for instance, in "I have led her home" originally described modern astronomical knowledge as "some cheerless fragment of the boundless plan/ Which is the despot of your iron skies...";[5] recast slightly, the passage gains almost beyond measure—the hero is

> brought to understand
> A sad astrology, the boundless plan
> That makes you tyrants in your iron skies,
> Innumerable, pitiless, passionless eyes,
> Cold fires, yet with power to burn and brand
> His nothingness into man.

With a similar deliberation "Come into the garden, Maud" exploits to an extreme the pathetic fallacy,[6] a device normally very rare in Tennyson's work:

> She is coming, my dove, my dear;
>   She is coming, my life, my fate;
> The red rose cries, "She is near, she is near;"
>   And the white rose weeps, "She is late;"
> The larkspur listens, "I hear, I hear;"
>   And the lily whispers, "I wait."

[5]Unpublished, "Harvard Notebook 30".

[6]Ruskin's well-known essay, "On the Pathetic Fallacy," approvingly cites this lyric as an example of the justified use of the "fallacy"; see *Modern Painters,* Part IV, ch. 12.

> She is coming, my own, my sweet;
> Were it ever so airy a tread. ...

Appraised rationally, the conversation of the flowers invites the parodic treatment it receives in *Alice Through the Looking Glass:*

> "She's coming!" cried the Larkspur. "I hear her footstep, thump, thump, thump, along the gravel-walk!"

But the lyric on its own operatic terms is indestructible and as far removed from the English common sense of *Alice* as are the verses of the Persian Hafiz, which may have suggested its imagery.[7] For the whole monodrama at its most intense moves beyond reason altogether into realms of immediate sensuous apprehension.

Maud, then, is to be judged not as a realistic case history but as a kind of "symbolist" poem, in which Mallarmé could properly find the materials and emphases of a later literature— *"romantique, moderne, et songes et passion."*[8] Tennyson, however, did strive to present dream, reverie, and even madness with a close precision of detail. He attempted a clinical accuracy in his depiction of the mad-house, and he grounded his hero's delirium on the best available knowledge of abnormal psychology. His understanding of mental unbalance dictated his invention of Maud's antitype as the per-version by a distraught mind of its real object of desire:

> 'Tis the blot upon the brain
> That *will* show itself without.

And his awareness of the quality of perception at moments of crisis, when the self must find release from agonizing subjectivity, prompted his hero's meditation on the shell thrown ashore by the Breton storm:

> Strange, that the mind, when fraught
> With a passion so intense
> One would think that it well
> Might drown all life in the eye,—
> That it should, by being so overwrought,

---

[7] See J. D. Yohannan, "Tennyson and Persian Poetry," *Modern Language Notes,* LVII (1942), 89-90, and cf. W. D. Paden's reply, *MLN,* LVIII (1943), 652-656.

[8] Stéphane Mallarmé, *Divigations* (Paris, 1897), p. 112, from his obituary, "Tennyson vu d'ici," contributed to Henley s *National Observer,* VIII (1892), 611-612.

> Suddenly strike on a sharper sense
> For a shell, or a flower, little things
> Which else would have been past by!

The concern in *Maud* with the social forces that condition human behavior may have led Rossetti to consider the plot oddly "De Balzacish." But the psychological "realism" of the shall passage, as Rossetti should best have known, is more Pre-Raphaelite than Balzacian. It recurs poetically in "The Woodspurge" of Rossetti himself, and its effect may be traced in a great many Victorian genre paintings all more or less Pre-Raphaelite, where the distress of the subject is rendered by "an hallucinatory vividness in the natural objects around him."[9] Tennyson's practice of such realism was influenced no doubt by a common contemporary regard for detail. Yet the immediate source of the whole psychology of *Maud* was assuredly his own observation and experience, his personal melancholia and his familiarity from childhood with the darker neuroses of his father and his brothers.

[9]Graham Reynolds, *Painters of the Victorian Scene* (London, 1953), p. 23.

Lucretius

by Douglas Bush

Lucretius (1868) may be considered from two points of view, that of classical scholars and that of critics of English poetry. It is, all scholars have agreed, a masterly condensation of, and commentary on, one of the world's greatest philosophical poems, and it is an intensely vivid portrait of the man its author may have been.[1] There is no need, and no space, to show here the astonishingly close Lucretian texture of Tennyson's lines, or the accuracy and imaginative spaciousness of his rendering of Lucretian ideas. He was evidently as steeped in Lucretius as Aristophanes was in Euripides, though the modern poet's fear of modernism did not include humor among its weapons. As a piece of English poetry, however, *Lucretius* has been both vehemently praised and vehemently damned. To mention only recent opinions, I prefer the critical eulogy of Mr. Lascelles Abercrombie, who is a poet, to the uncritical condemnation of Mr. Harold Nicolson, who is not;[2] and I should like to quote Mr. Abercrombie because his essay, read after this chapter was done, seemed to support one of its main (and of course not novel) theses. In showing that Tennyson lacks "structural inspiration," that in the main he gives us, not poems, but a "continual succession of splendid moments," the critic excepts *Maud* and *Lucretius:*

"Lucretius." From Douglas Bush, *Mythology* (Cambridge, Mass.: Harvard University Press, 1937), pp. 213-16. Copyright 1937 by the President and Fellows of Harvard College; Copyright © 1965 by Douglas Bush. Reprinted by permission of the publisher.

[1][In addition to W. P. Mustard, *Classical Echoes in Tennyson* (New York, 1904), see John Churton Collins, *Illustrations of Tennyson* (London, 1891); Katharine Allen, "Lucretius the Poet, and Tennyson's Poem 'Lucretius,'" *Poet Lore,* 11 (1899), 529-48; Sir Richard Jebb, "On Mr. Tennyson's 'Lucretius,'" *Macmillan's Magazine,* 18 (1868), 97-103; and Ortha Wilner, "Tennyson and Lucretius," *Classical Journal,* 25 (1930), 347-66. — Ed.]

[2]Harold Nicolson, *Tennyson* ([London,] 1923), p. 14; *Revaluations,* by Lascelles Abercrombie, Lord David Cecil, *et al.* (Oxford University Press, 1931), pp. 68, 72.

Both of these are splendid pieces of great imaginative structure, and in
both the structure is given, not indeed by the intellectual life, but by
the passion of a consistently objectified character. And in both we have
those unique moments of sense, thought, and feeling all compounded
together which are Tennyson's peculiar property; and these enchant
us not merely in themselves, but in the pregnant imaginative purpose
with which they are charged.

Lucretius is of course very different from Tennyson's other poems
of antique inspiration. The subject is "historical" and not mythological, it is Roman and not Greek. The poem lacks the classical
poise of *Ulysses,* for the writer, like his hero—and not quite like the
real Lucretius at the time he composed the *De Rerum Natura*—
seems to be still engulfed in the swirling currents of immediate
experience. As a mental thunderstorm with lurid flashes of lightning,
Lucretius out-Brownings Browning. How much of the feverish intensity of Tennyson's manner is to be attributed to his conception of
the subject, and how much to "spasmodic" and Swinburnian fashions
in verse,[3] one cannot be sure. At any rate the poem is a very powerful picture of a noble Roman patriot who feels himself breaking
along with the old republic; a Roman conscience which in its torments is more Hebraic and puritan than Greek; a Roman intellect
which has sought with passionate honesty for the truth that delivers
from evil and fear; a prophet and preacher of serenity whose creed
has failed him; a poet and philosopher whose joy in nature has
turned to ashes.[4]

Lucretius springs directly out of Victorian religious and ethical
problems, and reminds us of numerous other poems, such as
Arnold's *Empedocles,* and many of Tennyson's own. *In Memoriam*

---

[3] *Maud,* says Mr. Nicolson, had signalized Tennyson's consciousness of the spasmodics, and in *Lucretius* he thinks the poet had decided to mix a little Swinburnian
wine with the limpid waters of Camelot (*Tennyson,* pp. 207, 230). But the Swinburnian element is confined to the two weakest passages in the poem, that is, the two
which attempt to be boldest, the lines about the breasts of Helen and the naked
Oread, and these might be justified in motive if not in manner by the last part of
Lucretius' fourth book; see also i. 133 ff., iv. 33 ff.

[4] The Lucretius who only with the knife can woo the "Passionless bride, divine
Tranquility," carries us back to Tennyson's juvenile play *The Devil and the Lady,*
where he had written of "Boyhood's passionless Tranquillity" (p. 65).

is full of similar questionings, though Hallam had "faced the spectres of the mind" and laid them, and had come at length "To find a stronger faith his own."[5] In 1866 Tennyson declared that he would commit suicide if he thought there was no future life,[6] and he treated that theme, in a modern setting, in *Despair* (1881), a poem which has not, I think, provoked any contradictory critical estimates. Further, if God and immortality are delusions, there is no armor against the lusts of the flesh. Tennyson's Lucretius had believed himself secure, but an abhorrent unseen monster laid "vast and filthy hands" upon his will. "Divine Philosophy" has pushed beyond her mark and become "Procuress to the Lords of Hell"; Lucretius (because of the love-philter, of course) has not fled "The reeling Faun, the sensual feast."[7] With these phrases from *In Memoriam* one might link the crude moralizing of *By an Evolutionist,* or that unfortunate drama *The Promise of May,* which gave the impression that Tennyson believed immorality the inevitable consequence of religious skepticism. I mention these various poems only to illustrate again the immense advantages, both positive and negative, which Tennyson derived from confining himself within a classical frame.

Such poems also help to make clear the modern implications of *Lucretius,* in which the nature of the treatment forbids any Christian answer to the despair of the materialist. To say that the modern moral does not come home to us, that the reading of *Lucretius* never settled a doubt, is not of course a damaging statement, though the poem would lack most of its force if Tennyson had not been dealing with what was to him and his age a living issue. He started from the Victorian predicament, but he surrendered himself with such imaginative passion to the presentation of Lucretius that the result was a great poem and not a harangue. Unlike *The Lotos-Eaters,* it is not a mosaic of beautiful lines but a whole, a serious and impressive picture of spiritual disintegration. And once more Tennyson reproduces that favorite vision of his, of the Homeric and Lucretian

[5]*In Memoriam,* xcvi.

[6]*Memoir,* II, 35. The dramatic use of storm and calm in *Lucretius* reminds one of Palgrave's account of the overwhelming effect of the reading of the *De Rerum Natura* late one night at Tennyson's house (*ibid.,* II, 500). Cf. Lucretius, i. 271 ff., vi. 281 ff.

[7]*In Memoriam,* liii, cxviii.

gods in their "sacred everlasting calm";[8] here it is not so much a symbol of divine indifference to the world as of a divine lotos-land where all human doubts and fears are at rest.

[8]*Odyssey*, iv. 566, vi. 43; *De Rerum Natura*, iii. 18. When Rawnsley said of the passage, "Of course that is Homer," Tennyson replied, with that strange scientific naïveté of his, "Yes, but I improved on Homer, because I knew that snow crystallises in stars." See W. F. Rawnsley, "Personal Recollections of Tennyson," *Nineteenth Century*, XCVII (1925), 7.

Idylls of the King: Evolving the Form

by John Rosenberg

"Perfection in art," Tennyson remarked, "is perhaps more sudden sometimes than we think; but then the long preparation for it, that unseen germination, *that* is what we ignore and forget."[1] The unseen germination of the *Idylls of the King* goes back at least to that moment in Tennyson's early youth when he first read Malory and "the vision of Arthur as I have drawn him...had come upon me."[2] The vision remained with him until his death, within a few months of which he made the last of the innumerable revisions of the *Idylls*. As Kathleen Tillotson observes, the poem, which is so richly concerned with time and change, was itself subject in the long course of its composition to the pressures of time and change.[3]

Yet despite its tortuous evolution, the *Idylls* displays a remarkable unity. The germ of the whole, the fragmentary "Morte d'Arthur," drafted in 1833, revised in 1835, and published in 1842, was so instinctually right in tone and design that over a quarter of a century after its first publication Tennyson could incorporate it without change into the still-unfinished *Idylls* of 1869. During the next two decades he continually altered and expanded the design of the larger poem without violating the verbatim integrity of this first-composed but last-in-sequence of the idylls. With the hindsight the completed poem grants us, we can see that this last of the idylls had to come first, or at least that no other segment of the Arthurian cycle

"Idylls of the King: Evolving the Form." From John Rosenberg, *The Fall of Camelot* (Cambridge, Mass.: Harvard University Press, The Belknap Press, 1973), pp. 13-33. Copyright © 1973 by the President and Fellows of Harvard College. Reprinted by permission of the author and publishers.

[1] H. Tennyson, *Memoir,* I, 453n.

[2] Ibid., II, 128.

[3] Kathleen Tillotson, "Tennyson's Serial Poem," *Mid-Victorian Studies* (London, University of London, Athlone Press, 1965), p. 109.

could have fit with fewer complications into Tennyson's ultimate
design. At this stage in the decline of the Round Table, the cast of
characters has dwindled to Arthur and the sole surviving knight
who witnesses his passing, and the overriding theme of the poem—
the wasting away of human aspiration in the face of time—is felt at
its keenest. Drawn to that part of the Arthurian myth which most
compelled his imagination, Tennyson begins abruptly upon a
conjunction—*"So* all day long the noise of battle rolled"—which
implies everything that comes before it yet leaves him the maxi-
mum freedom in later developing the full story.[4]

In 1833 the coincidence of a personal catastrophe with what can
only be described as a lifelong obsession led Tennyson to begin his
two "Arthur" poems, the "Morte d'Arthur" and *In Memoriam*. The
obsession concerned some apocalyptic upheaval—of a city, a civilization, of the earth itself—and is present in Tennyson's earliest
writing. The catastrophe was the sudden death of Arthur Hallam,
the news of which reached Tennyson on October 1, 1833, and his
response to which he made public seventeen years later in *In
Memoriam*. The "Morte d'Arthur" was as much a reaction to the
actual Arthur's death as was *In Memoriam*. The earliest manuscript
fragments of the two poems appear in the same notebook, and
Tennyson himself strongly hints at their common origin in the
autobiographical "Merlin and the Gleam" (1889):

> Clouds and darkness
> Closed upon Camelot;
> Arthur had vanished
> I knew not whither,
> The king who loved me,
> And cannot die...   (st. VII)

The king who "loved *me*" and cannot die is clearly Arthur Hallam,
yet he is also the Arthur of the *Idylls*.[5] The two are virtually indis-
tinguishable: "Thou art the highest and most human too," Guin-

[4]See ibid., pp. 86-88.

[5]Hallam Tennyson's gloss on the stanza, which he gives as the poet "gave it to me,"
lifts this interpretation out of the realm of speculation: "Here my father united the
two Arthurs, the Arthur of the Idylls and the Arthur 'the man he held as half
divine.'" (H. Tennyson, *Memoir*, I, xiv-xv.) Fifty years before writing in "Merlin
and the Gleam" of the adored friend who "cannot die," Tennyson had used exactly
the same phrase to describe the mythical king in the "Morte d'Arthur." The poet
has a dream-vision in which the king returns "thrice as fair" from Avilion and is

evere says of her king (G, 644); and Tennyson addresses the king of *In Memoriam* as "Known and unknown; human, divine" (sec. CXXIX). Given the internal and external evidence, Sir Charles Tennyson's comment on the connection between Hallam's death and the "Morte d'Arthur" strikes me as indisputable: Tennyson in part "sublimate[d] in *Morte d'Arthur* his own passionate grief at the death of Arthur Hallam."[6] Beneath the measured cadences of Bedivere's lament for Arthur's passing, one senses the urgency of personal statement, as if Tennyson himself were forced to "go forth companionless" into an alien world. His profoundly personal quest for reunion with Hallam in *In Memoriam* — "Descend, and touch, and enter" (sec. XCIII) — becomes in the *Idylls* a profoundly impersonal despair for the passing not only of a hero but of civilization.

Haunted all his life by the ghosts of such passings, Tennyson was understandably drawn to the story of the doomed king who falls with the death of his kingdom. In his boyhood, before he had read Malory, Tennyson had written a whole series of poems whose titles alone betray his preoccupation with the subject: "The Fall of Jerusalem," "The Vale of Bones," "Babylon," "Lamentation of the Peruvians."[7] The Library of Trinity College, Cambridge, contains the manuscript of a poem far more ambitious than these which is remarkably premonitory of the apocalyptic close of the *Idylls*. Written when Tennyson was probably not more than fifteen, "Armageddon" draws in its climactic passage upon the chapter in Revelation (16) in which the angels of the Lord pour out His wrath upon mankind on the Day of Judgment. The confused shoutings and "dark terrific

---

greeted with the words, "Arthur is come again: he cannot die." Still another variant (unpublished) of this line — "...*our* Arthur cannot die" (italics added) — appears in the Trinity College Library, Tennyson MS. 0.15.39.

[6]"*The Idylls of the King,*" *The Twentieth Century,* 161 (1957), 279. In this connection, Tennyson's comment on the date at which he resolved to write a long poem on King Arthur takes on a special significance: "When I was twenty-four I meant to write a whole great poem on it, and began it in the 'Morte d'Arthur.'" Tennyson turned twenty-four in the year of Hallam's death. (See W. J. Rolfe, ed., *The Poetic and Dramatic Works of Alfred, Lord Tennyson* [Boston and New York, Houghton Mifflin, 1898], p. 849.)

[7]Composed when Tennyson was between fifteen and seventeen and published in *Poems by Two Brothers* (1827). Dating from the same period, the recently published "Napoleon's Retreat from Moscow" belongs with this series. Cf. the lines which describe the deserted city as "wan/ And pale and tenantless and void of Man." (Christopher Ricks, "The Tennyson Manuscripts," *Times Literary Supplement,* August 21, 1969, 919.)

pall" that obscure the battle of the Last Day in "Armageddon" also mark Arthur's last dim battle in the West. And the "dim cries/ ...As of some lonely city sacked by night" that accompany Arthur's passing echo the passage in "Armageddon" in which is heard.

> the long low moaning
> Of inarticulate thunder like the wail
> Of some lost City in it's [*sic*] evil day.[8]

The pervasiveness of the apocalyptic mode of vision throughout Tennyson's works has never been sufficiently appreciated. Previsions of some fiery fall—of Troy in "Oenone," of Camelot throughout the *Idylls,* of the earth itself in the early and astonishing "Kraken"[9] —are among the most striking motifs in his verse. The "annihilating anarchy" of "Armageddon" reappears near the end of *In Memoriam,* where the ice-capped mountains topple,

> And molten up, and roar in flood;
> The fortress crashes from on high,

[8]Trinity College Library, unpublished Tennyson MS, 0.15.18. Quoted by permission of the Master and Fellows of Trinity College, Cambridge. Cf. the identical simile in *The Princess:* "There rose a shriek as of a city sacked" (sec. IV, 147). Although the prohibition on publication of the Trinity manuscripts has recently been lifted, the full text of "Armageddon" has yet to be published. The most sustained passage in the poem anticipatory of "The Passing of Arthur" describes "the annihilating anarchy" of war,

> ...a thick day,
> Palled with dun wreaths of dusky fight, a day
> Of many thunders and confused noise,
> Of bloody grapplings in the interval
> Of the opposed Battle...   (sec. III, 14-18)

[9]See the closing lines of "Oenone"; Leodogran's dream in "The Coming of Arthur" (432-438); Pelleas' dream in "Pelleas and Ettarre" (504-509); Guinevere's dream of burning cities in "Guinevere" (75-82); the close of "The Kraken," in which the sea-monster

> ...will lie
> Battening upon huge seaworms in his sleep,
> Until the latter fire shall heat the deep;
> Then once by man and angels to be seen,
> In roaring he shall rise and on the surface die.

Cf. Revelation 8:8-9: "And the second angel sounded, and as it were a great mountain burning with fire was cast into the sea: and the third part of the sea became blood; And the third part of the creatures which were in the sea, and had life, died."

> The brute earth lightens to the sky,
> And the great Aeon sinks in blood.[10]   (sec. CXXVII)

This same apocalyptic landscape reappears in the great close of the *Idylls,* where Arthur moves his host by night

> Back to the sunset bound of Lyonnesse—
> A land of old upheaven from the abyss
> By fire, to sink into the abyss again;
> Where fragments of forgotten peoples dwelt,
> And the long mountains ended in a coast
> Of ever-shifting sand, and far away
> The phantom circle of a moaning sea.[11]   (PA, 81-87)

The image of some catastrophic upheaval figures crucially in Tennyson's earliest outline of an Arthurian poem. The sketch is remarkable in that it contains no narrative action whatsoever, yet its very stasis foreshadows one of the central symbols of the *Idylls,* the towering, illusory city poised on the brink of the abyss:

> On the latest limit of the West in the land of Lyonnesse, where...all is now wild sea, rose the sacred Mount of Camelot. It rose from the deeps with gardens and bowers and palaces, and at the top of the Mount was King Arthur's hall, and the holy Minster with the Cross of gold. Here dwelt the King in glory apart, while the Saxons whom he had overthrown in twelve battles ravaged the land, and ever came nearer and nearer.

[10]Cf. Revelation 16:18-20: "And there were voices, and thunders, and lightnings: and there was a great earthquake, such as was not since men were upon the earth.... And the cities of the nations fell. ...And every island fled away, and the mountains were not found." In *In Memoriam,* Hallam, the imagined witness to the holocaust in sec. CXXVII, "smilest, knowing all is well." The apparently pyromaniacal smile is intended to shock the reader into the realization that Hallam is no longer merely human and comprehends the earth's going up in flames as part of God's larger design. Hence he *smilest,* exactly as the Angel in "Armageddon" looks on the Apocalypse he describes with an "ineffable smile" (sec. II, 55).

[11]Christopher Ricks points out that this line, so apt in its context of moaning warriors and ghostly king, was in fact composed some thirty-five years before its first publication in "The Passing of Arthur." The line was originally part of a canceled stanza of "How often, when a child, I lay reclined" (1833), was then printed in a trial edition of *The Lover's Tale,* suppressed a second time, and finally published in the 1869 edition of the *Idylls.* Again one is struck by the consistency of Tennyson's preoccupations, which impelled him to brood for half a lifetime until he had created a fitting context for an image that haunted him. See Christopher Ricks, "Tennyson's Methods of Composition," *Proceedings of the British Academy,* 52 (1966), 218-219.

The Mount was the most beautiful in the world, sometimes green and fresh in the beam of morning, sometimes all one splendour, folded in the golden mists of the West. But all underneath it was hollow, and the mountain trembled, when the seas rushed bellowing through the porphyry caves; and there ran a prophecy that the mountain and the city on some wild morning would topple into the abyss and be no more. ...[12]

The hollowness of the mountain figures in the finished *Idylls* as the mists which enshroud the sacred Mount and symbolizes the whole series of interlocking illusions and betrayals that finally bring Camelot down in flames. Tennyson remains true to this earliest image of a fair appearance succumbing to a fatal reality, but his conception of Arthur "dwelling in glory apart" undergoes a significant change. The isolated Arthur of the prose sketch recalls one aspect of Tennyson himself in the 1830's, torn between his attraction to the "golden mists" of the imagination and the claims of social responsibility (the ever-encroaching Saxons). The Arthur of the *Idylls,* however, must abandon the "Palace of Art" in order to do the work of this world. Yet the "many-corridored complexities" of Camelot (MV, 730) also enshrine the aesthetic imagination, which Tennyson felt was threatened by the rationalist-materialist bias of his age. In reanimating the myth of Arthur he was deliberately trying to conserve ancient modes of thought and feeling that he knew to be vital not only to his private activity as a poet but to the continuity of our culture. This conviction informs the close of the very early "Timbuctoo,"[13] in which the Spirit of Fable praises

> The permeating life which courseth through
> All the intricate and labyrinthine veins

[12]Hallam Tennyson reprints the prose sketch in *Memoir,* II, 122-123, and dates it as "about 1833," but it seems probable that the fragment is somewhat earlier and predates the "Morte d'Arthur." The image of the hollow mountain may have been suggested by a passage in Malory in which Arthur "dreamed a wonderful dream... that him seemed he sat upon a chaflet in a chair, and the chair was fast to a wheel [of Fortune] ...and the king thought there was under him, far from him, an hideous deep black water, and therein were all manner of serpents...foul and horrible; and suddenly the king thought the wheel turned up so down, and he fell among the serpents, and every beast took him by a limb." (Bk. XXI, ch. 3.)

[13]The poem gained for Tennyson the Chancellor's Gold Medal at Cambridge in 1829. The prize cost him little effort since, in his own words, he won it by "the turning of an old poem on *'Armageddon'* into *'Timbuctoo'* by a little alteration of the beginning and the end." (H. Tennyson, *Memoir,* II, 355.)

> Of the great vine of *Fable,* which, outspread
> With growth of shadowing leaf and clusters rare,
> Reacheth to every corner under Heaven,
> Deep-rooted in the living soil of truth.   (216-221)

The Spirit surveys the splendid domes and gardens of a city that symbolizes the poetic imagination, and laments that they must all soon fall victim

> To keen *Discovery:* soon yon brilliant towers
> Shall darken with the waving of her wand;
> Darken, and shrink and shiver into huts,
> Black specks amid a waste of dreary sand,
> Low-built, mud-walled, Barbarian settlements.
> How changed from this fair City!   (240-245)

The fall of this fair city of the imagination is one of the most striking anticipations in Tennyson's early verse of the fall of Camelot; in both "Timbuctoo" and the *Idylls* the "brilliant towers" of the mind's own building give way to a desolate, post-civilized landscape of forgotten peoples and waste sands.

I have tried to suggest why Tennyson's imagination was so strongly predisposed to the story of Arthur, and why in the year of Hallam's death he was moved to begin his first major poem on what he called "the greatest of all poetical subjects."[14] It remains for us to see how, having found his subject, he reshaped it in the light of his own genius.

A clue to Tennyson's earliest intentions appears in the introductory verses to the "Morte d'Arthur," where we learn that the poet has burnt his epic on "King Arthur, some twelve books," for they

---

[14] H. Tennyson, *Memoir,* II, 125. Of Tennyson's three Arthurian poems roughly contemporary with the "Morte d'Arthur"—"The Lady of Shalott," "Sir Launcelot and Queen Guinevere," and "Sir Galahad"—only the first has any intrinsic interest, and it is far closer to Tennyson's private concerns as a poet than it is to Arthurian romance. "I met the story first in some Italian *novelle,*" he told F. J. Furnival; "but the web, mirror, island, etc., were my own. Indeed, I doubt whether I should ever have put it in that shape if I had been then aware of the Maid of Astolat in *Mort Arthur*" (Christopher Ricks, ed., *The Poems of Tennyson* [London, Longmans, 1969], p. 354). It would be of interest to know precisely when the poem was begun (Ricks's "written by *c.* May 1832" slips out of one's hands) since that would establish a firm *earliest* date for Tennyson's reading of Malory, or at least of bk. XVIII, in which the lily-maid's story appears. Kathleen Tillotson *(Studies,* p. 85) suggests that all three poems belong to Tennyson's Cambridge period; at any rate, they quite evidently predate the "Morte d'Arthur."

were mere "faint Homeric echoes, nothing-worth." Only the "Morte" was plucked from the flames in the conviction that "its use will come." The imaginary burning of the books is more than a device for introducing, in medias res, the isolated fragment on Arthur's passing.[15] It symbolizes Tennyson's rejection, sometime between the drafting of the "Morte" in 1833 and its publication nine years later, of an epic model for the *Idylls.* "At twenty-four I meant to write an epic or drama of King Arthur," he remarked after the *Idylls* was nearly completed: "I said I should do it in twenty years; but the Reviews stopped me." Hypersensitive to criticism, Tennyson was doubtless distressed by the mixed reviews of the "Morte";[16] if they in fact stopped him, one can only be grateful. Eleven more books in the ostensibly epic form of the "Morte" might indeed have produced "Homeric echoes, nothing-worth."[17] As is, he began with that part of the Arthurian cycle which, together with "The Coming of Arthur," most lends itself to epic treatment: the national hero who creates a kingdom and dies in single combat in its defense. Tennyson himself pointed out that the form and style of these two frame poems are "purposely more archaic" than the ten Round Table

[15]Tennyson had additional motives for so diffidently introducing the "Morte." He was understandably cautious about introducing the reader to the then unfamiliar subject of Arthur. (Tillotson, *Studies,* p. 82.) He was also attempting, ineffectually as it turned out, to disarm his critics by anticipating their charge that he was escaping into the past:

> Why take the style of those heroic times?
> For nature brings not back the Mastodon,
> Nor we those times; and why should any man
> Remodel models?

[16]H. Tennyson, *Memoir,* II, 89-90; W. J. Rolfe, ed., *The Poetic and Dramatic Works of Alfred, Lord Tennyson* (Boston and New York, Houghton Mifflin, 1898), p. 849. The most important of the reviews that stopped Tennyson was John Sterling's in the *Quarterly Review* of September 1842. But the review scarcely gave grounds for so drastic a result "The miraculous legend of 'Excalibur,' " Sterling wrote, "does not come very near to us, and as reproduced by any modern writer must be a mere ingenious exercise of fancy. The poem, however, is full of distinct and striking description, perfectly expressed."

[17]That Tennyson describes the "Morte" as the *eleventh* book of the burned epic suggests that he may have originally intended to follow it, as Malory does, with Lancelot and Guinevere's renunciation of earthly love, their final interview at Almesbury, and their deaths. In the *Idylls,* Tennyson merely alludes earlier in the poem to these events, thus reserving "The Passing of Arthur" for the climactic position and closing the circle begun with "The Coming of Arthur."

idylls which they enclose.[18] Once the final design completed itself in his mind, he turned the initial disparity to aesthetic advantage. He added to the original epic fragment the great opening lines of "The Passing" (1-169) that draw together all the dominant symbols of the *Idylls,* thereby binding the "Morte" to all that precedes it. And by setting off from the Round Table idylls the paired poems which mark Arthur's coming into the mutable world and passing into another, Tennyson incorporates into the very structure of the *Idylls* its cyclic themes of change and permanence, of time and eternity.

Despite its evident excellence, one detects a certain unevenness in the "Morte." Its most moving moments are elegiac rather than epic, pictorial rather than narrative, such as Arthur's eulogy to his fallen knights or Bedivere's lament as he watches the barge vanish, knowing that he must

> ...go forth companionless,
> And the days darken round me, and the years,
> Among new men, strange faces, other minds.   (PA, 404-406)

One suspects that Tennyson's abandoned prose sketch, in which absolutely nothing happens but everything is seen with fixed intensity, was in fact closer to his essential genius than the more conventionally epic portions of the "Morte." Yet the Arthurian story to which he had committed himself was crowded with actions of all kinds, some suited to epic treatment, such as Arthur's last battle, some to the highly mannered conventions of romance, such as the tale of Lancelot and Elaine, some to a more allegorical handling, such as the story of Merlin and Vivien, which Tennyson recast as a medieval debate of body and soul. The reviewers doubtless slowed his progress, but the seventeen-year hiatus between the publication of the "Morte" and that of the first four idylls of 1859 was due far more to Tennyson's uncertain quest for a form that would encompass the inherent diversity of his subject.[19]

In addition to the prose sketch for an Arthurian work, Tennyson

[18]H. Tennyson, *Memoir,* II, 133; cf. I, 483.
[19]Between 1833 and 1859 Tennyson was also deeply engaged in writing his elegy to the *other* Arthur, in substantially revising the *Poems* of 1832, composing new poems for the 1842 volume, and writing *The Princess* (1847) and *Maud, and Other Poems* (1855).

considered two other schemes, both fortunately abandoned. One was for a drama or masque in five acts; the scenario, with its projected "Chorus of Ladies of the Lake," disastrously suggests a sort of Christmas pantomime set to music. The second, more fragmentary outline calls for an allegorical rendering in which Arthur is to stand for "Religious Faith," Merlin for "Science," and the Round Table for "liberal institutions."[20]

Although Tennyson very soon gave up the idea of structuring the *Idylls* as a strict allegory, his commentators persisted in interpreting the poem as such, provoking him to remark: "They have taken my hobby, and ridden it too hard, and have explained some things too allegorically, although there is an allegorical or perhaps rather a parabolic drift in the poem."[21] Tennyson appears to have been both flattered by the finding of allegorical significances in the *Idylls* and deeply apprehensive that such readings were reductive of his whole intention. Hence his revealingly ambiguous reply to those who asked whether or not the Three Queens who appear at Arthur's coronation stand for Faith, Hope, and Charity: "They are right, and they are not right. They mean that and they do not. They are three of the noblest of women. They are also those three Graces, but they are much more. I hate to be tied down to say, '*This* means *that,*' because the thought within the image is much more than any one interpretation."[22] By "parabolic drift" and "thought within the image," Tennyson means precisely what we mean by *symbol,* the antithesis of the reductive, this-for-that equivalence which his commentators have found in the *Idylls*. The point is not that allegory is simplistic—a patent absurdity—but that the *Idylls* is not an allegory and that those who so read it are forced into simplistic conclusions.

Yet in a curiously conspiratorial way Tennyson encouraged such misreadings: "By King Arthur I always meant the soul, and by the Round Table the passions and capacities of a man."[23] But if, as Tennyson writes in the Epilogue, the *Idylls* is about "Sense at war with Soul," why is the "sinful" Lancelot, usurper of the Soul's bed, the secular hero of the poem? The answer lies in a confusion of in-

[20]H. Tennyson, *Memoir,* II, 123-125.

[21]Ibid., pp. 126-127. In a less familiar and stronger version of this passage, Tennyson complains that the commentators "have explained many things too allegorically." (H. Tennyson, *Materials for a Life of A. T.* [privately printed, 1895], II, 259.)

[22]H. Tennyson, *Memoir,* II. 127.

[23]Ricks, *Poems,* p. 1464.

tention in Tennyson and of perception in his critics. An allegorical residue remains embedded in the overall symbolic structure of the poem, although only once—when Arthur ("Soul") denounces Guinevere ("Sense")—does the mixture of modes jar on the reader. Elsewhere, this residue results in a certain deficiency of realization, as with the Lady of the Lake or those

> three fair queens,
> Who stood in silence near his throne, the friends
> Of Arthur, gazing on him, tall, with bright
> Sweet faces, who will help him at his need.   (CA, 275-278)

The difficulty with the trio is that they have no narrative function and no real connection with the poem's central characters or symbols, and so they stand in idle silence. They are simply part of the magical donné of Arthurian legend, to which Tennyson remains perhaps too diffidently faithful. His awareness of this dilemma always shows itself in a failure in his craft as a poet: the verse either becomes portentous or, as in the cited passage, lapses into the *contrivedly* prosaic (unlike Wordsworth, Tennyson is incapable of being unwittingly prosaic).

At the other extreme from an abstraction such as the Lady of the Lake ("The Church") are those characters who so richly embody the poem's moral and psychological complexities that any attempt to tag them with allegorical labels at once breaks down. Lancelot, for example, is larger than any didactic formula we might devise to contain him, and it is his greatness as a character that...compels us, in our attempts at explanation, to enlarge our terms of moral definition. His love for his king is as absolute as his love for his queen, and it is his tragedy that loyalty to one must be disloyalty to the other:

> The great and guilty love he bare the Queen,
> In battle with the love he bare his lord,
> Had marred his face, and marked it ere his time.
>
> (LE, 244-246)

The whole force of this passage lies in the juxtaposed "great *and* guilty": the guilt of the love is indisputable, but so too is its greatness, by which Tennyson means not only intensity but nobility. Indeed, the guilt is a function of the nobility; were it not for Lancelot's nobility, he would feel no guilt, and without the guilt, there would be less greatness. The paradox of the adultery of Lancelot and

Guinevere is that it not only "mars" them (and the kingdom) but ultimately ennobles them (and the kingdom), as Tennyson emphasizes by contrast with another adulterous triangle—the guiltless, peculiarly modern and joyless affair of Tristram and Isolt.

Yet in a recent book on the *Idylls* we read that Lancelot's guilty love of Guinevere "has coarsened not only his moral sensibilities but also his appearance."[24] Nothing could more starkly illustrate the pitfalls consequent upon reading the *Idylls* as a war of Sense versus Soul, in which certain characters represent the vices of the first and others the virtues of the second. The warfare, as James D. Merriman has brilliantly shown, "is not between individuals, but rather within individuals, and the various characters in the *Idylls* illustrate at any given time some stage of victory or defeat in that inner struggle."[25] Gawain's losing inner battle exactly parallels the outer struggle of the kingdom. His progressive degeneration from idyll to idyll is so beautifully integrated with that of the realm, from its founding in the spring to its barren end in the winter, that we scarcely notice him, for the changes in the character's moral foliation all but merge with those of the kingdom. Lancelot's far more tempestuous struggle moves in the opposite direction, toward salvation, and even those characters at the moral extremes of humanity—the harlot Vivien, for example—have an energy and solidity that elude any reductive personification such as "The Flesh." Only Galahad stands outside the arena of moral combat, and his victory over the flesh, as Merriman points out, "comes at the expense of simply abandoning the world, the real battleground of the war between Sense and Soul."[26]

The *Idylls* dramatizes on all levels the only conflict that can engage the mature moral imagination—the clash not of right versus wrong but of right versus right. Allegorical interpretations of the *Idylls* obscure this distinction and substitute didactic solutions for the moral dilemmas it poses. Thus one critic assures us that the *Idylls* represents the triumph of "the high soul of man" over the passions, while another describes the poem as an allegory of the

---

[24]Claude de L. Ryals, *From the Great Deep: [Essays on "Idylls of the King"* (Athens, Ohio, 1969),] p. 121. I must in fairness add that this excerpt is not at all representative of the quality of insight elsewhere in the book.

[25]James D. Merriman, "The Faultless King: Tennyson and the Matter of Britain," unpub. ms., no pagination.

[26]Ibid.

collapse which "must follow the rejection of spiritual values."[27] Yet the moral of the *Idylls* is not that men must abide by spiritual values, any more than the moral of *Othello* is that wives should look to their linen. In this sense, the poem is totally without a moral but explores instead the ambiguous results of man's quest for such values, and the disastrous effects of abandoning them. In "Lancelot and Elaine" *denial* of the flesh proves fatal, and as "The Holy Grail" makes clear, spiritual values can drive men as mad as sexual obsession. Tennyson suggests a possible connection between the two: the color red, which throughout the *Idylls* symbolizes sexuality, is also associated with the Grail itself, first seen as "rose-red" by a nun in a condition of erotic ecstasy, then as "blood-red" by Galahad—as is fitting for the vessel that bore Christ's blood.

Even of this simplest of the poem's thematic antitheses—white as purity, red as passion—we cannot say *"this* means *that."* The lily maid of Astolat, white in purity, is at first glance a personification of Virgin Innocence; but her dreams are insistently sexual and the sleeve she gives Lancelot is scarlet, for her purity, like the nun's, is profoundly passionate. Because the lily maid is not a conventional figure in an allegory, our impulse is to distort her into a modern simplism of our own: seeming purity masking a libidinous reality. Yet like the symbols associated with her, she is neither this nor that, but both pure *and* passionate, sexual *and* innocent, embodying the same intense conjunction of contrary elements that draws her instantly—and fatally—to Lancelot.

In 1859, when "Lancelot and Elaine" was published, Tennyson for the first time grouped his new series of Arthurian poems under the general title *Idylls of the King*.[28] An idyll is a "little picture" of a character or mood colored by a single, dominant emotion. Tenny-

[27]Henry Alford, in an article on the *Idylls* that Tennyson praised *(Contemporary Review*, 13 [1870], 107); F. E. L. Priestley, "Tennyson's *Idylls," Critical Essays on the Poetry of Tennyson*, ed. John Killham (London, Routledge & Kegan Paul, 1960), p. 242. Although I believe that Priestley errs in describing the *Idylls* as "primarily allegorical" (Killham, *Critical Essays*, p. 240), his essay remains most illuminating. The best case against reading the *Idylls* as allegory has been made by S. C. Burchell, "Tennyson's 'Allegory in the Distance,'" *PMLA*, 68 (1953), 418-424. Burchell takes his title from a letter of Jowett to Tennyson: "The allegory in the distance *greatly strengthens, also elevates, the meaning of the poem."* (H. Tennyson, *Memoir*, I, 449.)

[28]"Lancelot and Elaine" was published together with the Geraint idylls, "Merlin and Vivien," and "Guinevere." The reader, if he recalled the earlier "Morte

son's choice of the plural *idylls* stresses his intention, as Jerome Buckley points out, to portray "not a single unified narrative but a group of chivalric tableaux selected from a great mass of available legend. ...Each of the Idylls moves through a series of sharply visualized vignettes toward its pictured climax, its moment of revelation."[29] Yet true as this is, one's experience of the *Idylls* is less static than it suggests. The sharply visualized vignettes which characterize so much of the poem—Lancelot kneeling before Guinevere in the vine-clad oriel window, Balin and Balan "sitting statue-like" by the fountain—are not simply pictures but *actions,* or rather their pictorial intensity is so great that we experience them as actions. The very early "Mariana" consists entirely of this hypercharged description. Imprisoned in her moated grange, Mariana is an animate extension of the setting, the setting a symbolic embodiment of her mental entrapment. The *Idylls* is filled with such moments of fixed intensity in which the energy of outward action turns in upon itself and narration becomes a kind of dramatized vision. The first critic to perceive this quality in Tennyson's verse was Arthur Hallam, and there is a certain ghostly aptness in summoning Hallam to illuminate the poetry in which he later figures so largely. Reviewing the volume in which "Mariana" first appeared, Hallam remarks on Tennyson's

---

d'Arthur" at all, was not encouraged to make comparisons, for in entitling the new collection *Idylls,* Tennyson clearly distinguished it from the "Morte," which had borne the prefatory title "The Epic." The four new poems are all loosely linked by the theme of true and false love. A rejected title for the 1859 idylls underscores their thematic connection: "The True and the False: Four Idylls of the King." The connections are real but at this stage of the poem's evolution one feels them to be more fortuitous than intrinsic. Enid, the true wife who appears false to the suspicious Geraint, contrasts with Guinevere, the false wife who appears true to the unsuspicious Arthur. The harlot Vivien, who deceives and destroys her lover Merlin, contrasts with the virgin Elaine, who destroys herself for love. Tennyson's deletion of "Four" from the provisional title suggests his reluctance to commit himself to further poems in the series, the neutral *Idylls of the King* leaving it to the reader to surmise if more were to come. The four idylls were composed between 1856 and 1859, and in the 1859 edition were entitled "Enid," "Vivien," "Elaine," and "Guinevere." "Enid" was divided into two parts in 1873 and given the final titles of "The Marriage of Geraint" and "Geraint and Enid" in 1886. (See Ricks, *Poems,* p. 1525.)

[29]Jerome Hamilton Buckley, *Tennyson: The Growth of a Poet* (Cambridge, Mass., 1960), pp. 172-173.

power of embodying himself in...moods of character, with such extreme accuracy of adjustment, that the circumstances of the narration
seem to have a natural correspondence with the predominant feeling,
and, as it were, to be evolved from it by assimilative force. ...These
expressions of character are brief and coherent: nothing extraneous
to the dominant fact is admitted, nothing illustrative of it, and, as it
were, growing out of it, is rejected. They are like summaries of mighty
dramas. ...We contend that it is a new species of poetry, a graft of the
lyric on the dramatic.[30]

Although the phrase was not in Hallam's vocabulary, he comes
astonishingly close to saying in 1831 what we are only now recog-
nizing in the 1970's: Tennyson is essentially a symbolist poet. Donald
Smalley has noted the anomalous fact that while on one side of the
Channel middle-class Victorians were finding the *Idylls* congenial
to their taste, on the opposite shore the poem was being appreciated
by an audience that "the Laureate would scarcely have anticipated
or been likely to welcome—the French Symbolists." The influence
of Tennyson on Poe ("I regard him as the noblest poet who ever
lived") and, through Poe, on Baudelaire and Mallarmé constitutes
one of the vital currents flowing into the poetry of our century.
Mallarmé translated "Mariana," Baudelaire borrowed from Tennyson, and Yeats, who read Hallam's essay in the 1890's, found it indispensable to an understanding of the French Symbolists.[31]

The symbolist technique that Hallam recognized in "Mariana"

[30]Hallam's review of *Poems, Chiefly Lyrical* (1830) appeared in the *Englishman's Magazine* of August 1831, when he was not yet twenty, and is reprinted in
Jump, *Tennyson*, pp. 34-49.

[31]For the quotation from Donald Smalley, see "A New Look at Tennyson—and
Especially the *Idylls,*" *Journal of English and Germanic Philology*, 51 (1962), 356.
For Tennyson's influence on the Symbolists, see Marjorie Bowden, *Tennyson in
France* (Manchester, Eng., Manchester University Press, 1930), pp. 56-57, 100-101,
112, 134; Valerie Pitt, *Tennyson Laureate* (London, Barrie and Rockliff, 1962),
p. 6; H. M. McLuhan, "Tennyson and Picturesque Poetry," reprinted in Killham,
Critical Essays, pp. 67-70. Mallarmé's translation of "Mariana" appeared in the
October 18, 1874, issue of *La Derniere Mode,* the review which he founded. See
also his obituary appreciation of Tennyson entitled "Tennyson vu d'ici," *The
National Observer*, October 24, 1892, pp. 611-612. For Baudelaire's borrowing from
"The Lotus-Eeaters," see *Le Voyage,* VII, strophes 5 and 6. For Poe's praise of Tenny-
son, see "The Poetic Principle," *The Complete Works of Edgar Allan Poe*, vol.
XIV, ed. James A. Harrison (New York, Fred De Fou, 1902), p. 289.

reaches its furthest development in the *Idylls*. The solitary Elaine in her tower, dreaming of Lancelot and stripping the silken case from his naked shield, is a more complex version of Mariana in her moated grange. Tennyson's whole problem in structuring the *Idylls* consisted in getting Elaine, as it were, down from her tower and onto the poem's field of action. A long narrative poem made up of separate vignettes, however sharply visualized, would collapse of its own static weight. Tennyson solved the problem by incorporating individual characters into the larger landscape of the *Idylls;* as in "Mariana," he obliterates the gap between self and scene and frees himself from bondage to conventional narrative. Building on the techniques of the classical idyll, with its intensification of mood, its highly allusive texture, its startling juxtapositions, flashbacks, and deliberate discontinuities, Tennyson creates an inclusive psychological landscape in which all the separate consciousnesses in the poem participate and in which each action is bound to all others through symbol, prophecy, or retrospect.[32]

Seen from this perspective, the first lines Tennyson composed for the *Idylls* take on a singular significance. The "Morte" begins with the simplest and apparently slightest of alterations from Malory:

> So all day long the noise of battle rolled
> Among the mountains by the *winter* sea...

Tennyson's shift in the setting of Arthur's death from summer to winter suggests that from the start he had in mind the symbolic season in whose cycle of florescence and decline every scene and character in the *Idylls* is enmeshed. It is impossible to exaggerate the fullness of consequence this single alteration bears. Throughout Malory, with the exception of the closing chapters, one feels the suspension of time characteristic of romance. In such a world everything is possible, coincidence abounds, and spring is eternal. Only in "Gareth and Lynette," the first of the Round Table idylls, does Tennyson allow his reader this primal fantasy of romance. By linking the separate idylls to the cycle of seasons, Tennyson transposes the dominant mode of Arthurian myth from romance to tragedy, in which the only release from time is death.

[32]For further speculation on the classical idyll in relation to Tennyson and modern poetry, see H. M. McLuhan's lively "Introduction" to *Alfred Lord Tennyson: Selected Poetry* (New York, Rinehart, 1956), pp. xiv-xv, xxi. See also J. M. Gray, "A Study in Idyl: Tennyson's 'The Coming of Arthur,'" *Renaissance and Modern Studies,* 14 (1970), 111-150.

The symbolic season, then, enabled Tennyson to control the random, timeless sequence of events in Malory.[33] In the *Morte d'Arthur,* for example, the tragedy of Balin and Balan precedes the romance of Gareth and Lynette. Tennyson reverses the order of the two tales, as elsewhere he compresses the more diffuse episodes in Malory or cuts them altogether.[34] What remains of this distillation from the

[33]In comparing Tennyson and Malory I am aware of the difficulty of avoiding invidiousness. Perhaps the most nearly neutral formulation would be that Malory is a great story-teller and Tennyson a great poet, and that Tennyson's departures from the *Morte d'Arthur* are largely a consequence of this difference. Tennyson selects and compresses where Malory can afford to be diffuse; Malory is rapid and encyclopedic where Tennyson is elaborate, yet intense. Malory's characters are in constant motion, camping and decamping, love-making, marching and jousting. Tennyson's characters do all of these things but also reflect upon them. They seem less like anonymous figures rushing headlong through a landscape than extensions of the landscape itself, which they in turn animate with their own natures. Malory's characters inhabit a simpler world of heroic action. Tennyson's characters inhabit the more familiar world of divided wills and anguished introspection; they are ourselves, veiled in mist.

Where Malory has most mastered his materials, Tennyson follows him most closely, as in "The Passing of Arthur" and the finely-wrought tale of Lancelot and Elaine. Where Malory appears lost in the prolixity of his own sources, as in the wearisome account of Arthur's Roman wars, Tennyson drastically compresses him. In certain idylls, most notably "Guinevere," he freely invents, and for the two Geraint idylls he uses Lady Charlotte Guest's translation of the *Mabinogion,* his only major source other than Malory. Throughout the *Morte d'Arthur* one senses a certain unsureness of control, with the central story of King Arthur and his Round Table slipping in and out of focus. Too often the hundreds of encounters of knights in combat—first on horseback, then unhorsed, then hand to hand, each contest ever so slightly varied from the last—take on the peculiar unreality of multiple copulations in a modern best-seller, endless variations in erotic posture currently gratifying a taste akin to that for the never-ending joust in medieval romance. Tennyson's genius in giving coherence to the inherent diffuseness of Arthurian romance can only be appreciated by going back to his sources and seeing, retrospectively, how he has breathed life and depth into the mass of intransigent matter on which he drew. Guilty neither of slavish imitation nor of mindless license, he perceived the "fine things" in Malory but also saw that they were "loosely strung together without art."

[34]In addition to reversing the order of certain tales, Tennyson transposes characters and settings in others. In Malory's version of "Lancelot and Elaine," as the barge bearing the dead Elaine appears, "by fortune King Arthur and Queen Guenever were speaking together at a window" (bk. XVIII, ch. 20). Tennyson retains Malory's setting but replaces the narratively irrelevant Arthur with Lancelot, who pays tribute to Guinevere at the moment Elaine's barge passes by. The shift is slight but crucial, for the scene now symbolizes the larger narrative of which it is a part: Lancelot at the apex of a tragic triangle, torn between his dying love for the guilty Guinevere and his innocent love for the dead Elaine.

Morte d'Arthur Tennyson orders along a strict narrative sequence
in which the clock of Arthur's fall ticks at a steadily accelerating rate.
Yet this *linear* movement through time, while it lends a propulsive
thrust to the narrative, tends to make of each idyll a separate episode spaced out along the temporal chain. And so Tennyson super-
imposes upon this strict chronological sequence a much more fluid
temporal movement in which events that are narratively sequential
appear to take place simultaneously in the reader's mind. Thus
although "Balin and Balan" comes quite early in the chronological
sequence and is set in the time of the lady-fern and the lily, we are
made to feel a sudden acceleration of the symbolic season, in con-
sonance with this first of the idylls that ends tragically. By implying
early in "Balin and Balan" that Arthur's youth has passed, Tennyson
ages his hero and the kingdom in a single line:

> Early, one fair dawn,
> The light-winged spirit of his youth *returned*...
>
> (18-19, italics added)

The very brevity and symmetry of "Balin and Balan"—it is less than
half as long as "Gareth and Lynette," one third as long as the Geraint
idylls that precede it—reinforce this sense of propulsive doom.

Tennyson's manipulation of time in the *Idylls* produces an effect
akin to that of syncopation in music or, closer to his medium, to
departures from regular meter in a line of verse. When the stress
falls unexpectedly, it falls with twice the weight. The annual Tournament of Diamonds, spaced over nine years, establishes the normal
temporal rhythm of the poem. But in *"The Holy Grail,"* when the
knights seek violent escape from the diurnal world to the world of
eternity, Tennyson causes time to run amok: the narrative is deliberately discontinuous and kaleidoscopic; lightning and darkness,
droughts and floods, replace any recognizable moment of day or
year; apocalyptic time—in which all times are simultaneously present—displaces chronological time.

Throughout the *Idylls* leitmotifs of all kinds cut across the linear
narrative and connect past and future. "Merlin and Vivien" opens
with an impending storm that finally bursts in the closing lines;
recurrent images of tempests and waves gather to a climax the storm
of warring passions internalized in Merlin and externalized in nature. Before Vivien seduces him, indeed before the "present" in
which the idyll is narrated, Merlin has

> walked with dreams and darkness, and he found
> A doom that ever poised itself to fall,
> An ever-moaning battle in the mist,
> World-war of dying flesh against the life.   (188-191)

The wave poised to break symbolizes the seer's prevision of his own doom, but his fall is both a cause and prophecy of the larger fall of the kingdom. And so the dreams and darkness through which he walked later become the clouds of self-doubt that enshroud Arthur at the end; the moaning struggle in the mist foreshadows the last dim battle in the West, when the "wave" of heathen at last engulfs the kingdom, and it reverberates back to the founding, when Arthur pushed back the heathen wave and "made a realm and reigned" (CA, 518).

Like each of the idylls, "Merlin and Vivien" tells a self-contained story that is also interwoven into the central story of Arthur's coming and passing. Through dreams, prophecy, and retrospect, through recurrent symbols, characters, settings, and verbal echoes, any part of the poem implies all other parts. Guinevere's marriage vow to Arthur, itself ironic—"King and my lord, I love thee to the death!" (CA, 469)—is ironically echoed much later by the vow of Tristram to Isolt:

> Come, I am hungered and half-angered—meat,
> Wine, wine—and I will love thee to the death—
>
> (LT, 713-714)

a lie made true by Tristram's murder the instant after it is sworn, as Guinevere's lie is finally proven true by her repentance in the convent of Almesbury.

The major characters reappear from idyll to idyll, forming a "human chain of kinship"[35] whose linkages serve the same unifying function as the poem's clusters of symbols. Minor characters who appear only once, or rarely, are in turn incorporated into the larger story by a kind of analogical patterning through which one character reenacts the role previously played by another. The early idylls present special problems of narrative continuity, for happy endings are by definition self-contained, as the tag-phrase "they lived happily ever after" makes clear.[36] "Gareth and Lynette" has just such an

---

[35]The phrase is from an unpublished essay by Pearl Chesler on "Men and Women in the *Idylls of the King.*"

[36]See Kathleen Tillotson's discussion of this point in *Studies,* pp. 91, 106-107.

ending: Gareth's fearsome adversaries prove to be mock-monsters in disguise, and the novice knight wins the scornful lady. "Pelleas and Ettarre" tells the same story in reverse,[37] the later idyll retrospectively enriching the earlier. Fair appearance conceals a hideous reality, and the sadistic Ettarre drives the young Pelleas impotent and mad. Gareth tests and finds himself at a time when the integrity of the kingdom and his own naive idealism are in perfect accord.

[37]Although "Gareth and Lynette" and "Pelleas and Ettarre" are widely separated in the published order of the idylls, Tennyson began work on one immediately after finishing the other, which perhaps accounts for their closeness in theme and characterization. He wrote most of "Pelleas and Ettarre" in the summer of 1869, completed it by September, and turned to "Gareth and Lynette" later that month or very early in October. Unlike "Pelleas and Ettarre," however, "Gareth and Lynette" gave him great difficulty and he did not complete it until 1872, when it was published together with "The Last Tournament" (which had first appeared separately the previous year). The difficulty, one suspects, arose from Tennyson's going back to the bright beginnings of the realm and working in a deliberately light vein, just after completing the somber "Pelleas and Ettarre" and before starting the later, darker idylls of "The Last Tournament" and "Balin and Balan."

The tangled history of the composition and publication of the *Idylls* is unraveled in Sir Charles Tennyson's *Alfred Tennyson,* in his "The Idylls of the King" *(Twentieth Century* 51 [1957] , 277-286), and in Kathleen Tillotson's *Studies,* pp. 80-109. Less detailed but more accessible accounts appear in the headnotes to the separate idylls in Rick's *Poems.* I have collated these and other sources (not always in agreement) in the following list:

Idyll	Date of Composition	Date of Publication
"Morte d'Arthur" (lines 170-440 of "The Passing of Arthur")	1833-1834	1842
"Merlin and Vivien"	1856	1859
"The Marriage of Geraint"	1856	1859
"Geraint and Enid"	1856	1859
"Guinevere"	1857-1858	1859
"Lancelot and Elaine"	1858-1859	1859
"Dedication"	1861	1862
"The Holy Grail"	1868	1869
"The Coming of Arthur"	1869	1869
"Pelleas and Ettarre"	1869	1869
"Gareth and Lynette"	1869-1872	1872
"The Passing of Arthur"	1869	1869
"The Last Tournament"	1870-1871	1871
"To the Queen"	1872	1873
"Balin and Balan"	1872-1874	1885

Pelleas is Gareth reborn in decadent times; the clash between his idealism and the corruption of the kingdom destroys him, for he can find no supporting matrix for his fledgling identity. "What name hast thou?" Lancelot asks as Pelleas bears down upon him in blind rage. "No name, no name," he shouts, "I am wrath and shame and hate and evil fame" (551-556).

As certain characters seem to exchange identities, so certain settings recur throughout the *Idylls*. Early in "Balin and Balan," for example, Balin observes a meeting between Lancelot and Guinevere in a garden of roses and lilies. The queen walks down the path of roses toward Lancelot but he pauses in his greeting, for he has dreamed the previous night of "That maiden Saint who stands with lily in hand/ In yonder shrine" (256-257), and the dream restrains him, just as his praise of the perfect purity of the lilies chills Guinevere:

> "Sweeter to me," she said, "this garden rose
> Deep-hued and many-folded! sweeter still
> The wild-wood hyacinth and the bloom of May.
> Prince, we have ridden before among the flowers
> In those fair days—not as cool as these,
> Though season-earlier."   (264-268)

Guinevere nowhere more richly expresses the sensuousness which first drew Lancelot to her than in these lines, "deep-hued and many-

---

From the list it will be seen that, after the initial impetus that produced the "Morte d'Arthur," Tennyson's work on the *Idylls* was concentrated into two periods, roughly a decade apart. The first, from 1856 (or late in 1855) to 1859, resulted in the *1859 Idylls of the King* (the Geraint idylls, "Merlin and Vivien," "Lancelot and Elaine," and "Guinevere"). The second, from 1868 to 1874, produced all the remaining idylls, with "Balin and Balan" a kind of tailpiece. "The Coming of Arthur," "The Holy Grail," "Pelleas and Ettarre," and "The Passing of Arthur" were published in the 1869 *The Holy Grail and Other Poems*. "Gareth and Lynette" and "The Last Tournament" appeared in the 1872-1873 Imperial Library Edition of Tennyson's *Works*, together with the eight previously published idylls. At this stage Tennyson believed that he required additional idylls "to make Vivien come later into the Poem" (Ricks, *Poems*, p. 1465), and the long-delayed appearance of "Balin and Balan" may have reflected his desire to publish it with an as-yet-unwritten companion, also to precede "Merlin and Vivien." If I am correct, the abandoning of this intention was signaled by Tennyson's publication of "Balin and Balan" in 1885, followed by the division of "Geraint and Enid" into two independently entitled idylls in 1886 (thus completing the "twelve books" mentioned in the "Morte"). In 1888—fifty-five years after its inception—Tennyson published the collected *Idylls* in their final form.

folded." The consequences of that first, fatally joyous meeting reverberate throughout the poem, as here, when the sight of the lovers shocks Balin into his former "violences," and he rides off from the orderly garden into the wilderness where he meets his death. The garden scene works perfectly within the narrative of "Balin and Balan" at the same time that it takes us back, through Guinevere's reminiscence, to the time before the founding of the Round Table and forward to "Lancelot and Elaine." The scene opens out to become the entire setting of the later idyll, in which Lancelot again must walk the same divided path and choose between the rose of Guinevere and the lily-maid of Astolat.

In the light of such subtle architectonics one is at a loss to understand much of the twentieth-century criticism of the *Idylls:* "Utterly wanting in unity and coherence of structure...strikingly uneven... a collection of episodes. ...Tennyson could not tell a story at all... he failed signally to bring out the underlying, archetypical significance of the ancient mythological symbols he was employing."[38] Tennyson could of course tell a story perfectly well. He handles the conventional narrative devices with virtuosity, ranging from the first-person monologue of Percivale in "The Holy Grail" to the omniscient narrator in "Lancelot and Elaine," from the simple plot of "Merlin and Vivien" to the complex interweavings of the two adulterous triangles in "The Last Tournament." Yet however skillfully he might retell the tales in Malory or the *Mabinogion,* he would end where he began, with "a collection of episodes." And so he developed, in Hallam's phrase, "a new species of poetry" in order to convey his vision of Arthurian myth to the contemporary world. Like every great long poem, the *Idylls* draws on traditional forms and is itself a new genre. Shakespeare had Seneca and Marlowe; Milton had Homer; but tragedy and epic radically redefine themselves in their works. Tennyson bears this same innovative relation to tradition, but we have yet to assimilate into our literature this poem which is at once epic and lyric, narrative and drama, tragedy and romance. Our difficulty with Tennyson's "medieval charade" is not its derivativeness but its novelty.

[38]Paull F. Baum, *Tennyson Sixty Years After* (Chapel Hill, 1948), p. 213; Ricks, *Tennyson* (New York, Macmillan, 1972), p. 264; Arthur Christopher Benson, *Alfred Tennyson* (1907; reprint ed., New York, Greenwood Press, 1969), p. 198; T. S. Eliot, *Essays Ancient and Modern* (London, 1936); John Heath-Stubbs, *The Darkling Plain* (London, Eyre and Spottiswoode, 1950), p. xiv.

Late Poems

by E. A. Francis

I

Frater Ave Atque Vale distinguishes itself against the prevailing tenor of violence and sentimentality in Tennyson's verse c. 1880, and together with *The Ancient Sage* anticipates the later achievement of *Demeter and Other Poems* (1889). Written for his brother Charles, who died in 1879, the little poem is at once memorial, greeting, and farewell. It is a celebration of the brother made in Catullus' words, words altered by the poet's experience and vision. Tennyson writes of real places, and tradition experienced in them. It is by now well known that by combining the joyous language of Catullus xxxi with the bitter pathos of ci Tennyson reachieves a balance of emotion comparable with the balance of *Tears, Idle Tears*. But what is not so clear is that Catullus ci and xxxi combine in the poem without achieving a perfect blend.

Multas per gentes et multa per aequora vectus ("wandering through many countries and over many seas," ci)[1] is bitterly sorrowful, the griever speaking in vain to the silent ashes of his dead brother. His words are a ritual of death offered with offerings *prisco quae more parentum/ tradita sum tristi munere ad inferias* ("which by the custom of our fathers have been handed down—a sorrowful tribute—for a funeral sacrifice," vv. 7-8). Such tribute expects no answer or renewal. The ever-repeated rituals for the repetition of death echo hopelessly into the poem's final cry, *frater ave atque vale* ("O my brother, hail and farewell!" v. 10). These words are the portal by which we enter Tennyson's poem and dis-

---

"Late Poems" by E. A. Francis. This article appears for the first time in this volume.

[1] Texts and translations quoted from *Catullus, Tibullus and Pervigilium Veneris*, trans. F. W. Cornish (London, 1924).

cover, at its heart, a living tradition given in the joyous language of Catullus xxxi.

Beyond the title's portals of hail and farewell, the poet journeys out to a place shared with Charles, in the language of Catullus's return to his house at Sirmio. Catullus revisits it with joy, scarce believing he has left Bithynia and come safely home:

> o quid solutis est beatius curis,
> sum mens onus reponit, ac peregrino
> labore fessi venimus larem ad nostrum
> desideratoque acquiescimus lecto?   (vv. 7-10)

> Ah, what is more blessed than to put cares away, when the mind lays by its burden, and tired with labour of far travel we have come to our own home and rest on the couch we longed for?

The mind "lays by its burden." I think we should read with emphasis the fact that far travel is a hard labor, and that Catullus rests now from wandering, his mind at last at ease: *Hoc est quod unumst prolaboribus tantis* ("this it is which alone is worth all these toils," v. 11). This release may also be true of the poet Tennyson, for whom the poem, though written as memorial for Charles, is a "homecoming" to a simple mode of verse and to simple clear speech.[2]

Catullus is Master at Sirmio, and in greeting the place he asks that *he* be greeted as well:

> salve, o venusta Sirmio, atque ero gaude:
> gaudete vosque, o Lydiae lacus undae:
> ridete, quicquid est domi cachinnorum.   (vv. 12-14)

> Welcome, lovely Sirmio, and rejoice in your master, and rejoice ye too, waters of the Lydian lake, and laugh out aloud all the laughter you have in your home.

Let Sirmio and the lake about it laugh out, deliberately release the laughter that is within. This is the reward of toil, the nature of mastering, the reality and ease of "home." Here "salve" is the greeting of the everyday Roman, and "venusta," for Catullus, the adjective associated with Venus, holding the emotion of the lover.[3]

Thus when Catullus comes home at last, asking to be greeted by the

---

[2] Compare *The Daisy* (written August 1853) and *To the Rev. F. D. Maurice* (dated January 1854).

[3] C. J. Fordyce, *Catullus: A Commentary* (Oxford, 1961), p. 169, l. 12n.

lake's laughter and Sirmio's beauty, he asks to be greeted by one who loves. He suggests too that it is not only he who comes home, but, with him, the tradition of Greek poetry which he has made his own through his practice. Stylistically, he has gone east to Bithynia and consciously remade Greek forms for his own work.[4] And he has learned from Alexandria, as Virgil learned, the associative value of the proper name: *"Lydiae"* is not pedantry, but the sign of a living poetic tradition. Thus the laughter he asks for is Lydian.

The emphasis upon "living" tradition is as important for Tennyson as for Catullus. There is laughter in a homecoming to place and tradition that provides break from labor and grief. Catullus had made two kinds of greeting in the source poems for Tennyson's simple lyric, one a formal greeting to the dead, the other a familiar greeting to home. Tennyson saw their relation and, what is more, saw their relation to his own artistic history:

> Row us out from Dezenzano, to your Sirmione row!
> So they rowed, and there we landed—'O venusta Sirmio!'
> There to me through all the groves of olive in the summer glow,
> There beneath the Roman ruin where the purple flowers grow,
> Came that 'Ave atque Vale' of the Poet's hopeless woe,
> Tenderest of Roman poets nineteen-hundred years ago,
> 'Frater ave atque Vale'—as he wandered to and fro
> Gazing on the Lydian laughter of the Garda Lake below
> Sweet Catullus' all-but-island, olive-silvery Sirmio!

Portal to the verse, the hail and farewell of ci echoes again in the embrace of xxxi, where the laughter of Garda holds joy and eros, and where the Roman ruins Tennyson presumed to be those of Catullus' house show in the colors Tennyson used of death and elegiac renewal in *In Memoriam*. The very colors of the island in summer are an interchange of gray, violet, and green. In the recollection of such beauty with its associated recollection of Charles, the "hopeless woe" of Catullus can echo in the memory and in the present without destruction or severe pain. Tennyson knows the shape of loss, yet knows that loss is not a resting place. He had spoken the "Ave" of Catullus ci at *In Memoriam* LVIII, taking leave of his first wild grief for Hallam. There the beloved was "richly shrined" in verse, but the farewell was, as in Catullus ci, hopeless, eternal, and one of unremitting pain. Tennyson left that section of

[4]*Ibid,* pp. 169-70, 1. 13n.

the elegy with a promise given by an external voice: "abide a little longer here,/ And thou shalt take a nobler leave." That promise, interpreted in poetic terms as a rise to heroic speech and fatherhood in time, had issued ultimately in the passion of *Maud* and the formally designed historicity of *Idylls of the King.* Now the "Ave" is spoken again, but in familiar and nonheroic form. Thus *Frater ave atque vale* moves beyond the wild pain of loss implied by the Catullan reference in *In Memoriam* to the strength of a poetic tradition fully assimilated and to the simplicity of the "middle voice." Tennyson's grief for Charles is not separable into "phases" of passion, and heroic acts are not needed to resolve it.[5] The middle voice of *Frater ave atque vale* marks the best poems written at the end of Tennyson's life. It governs the rhetoric and order of *Demeter and Other Poems,* a volume which depends upon the recovery and revision of attitudes from *In Memoriam.*

II

Demeter and Other Poems (1889) moves, as it were, among the ways of death, searching for the form of a completed elegy, and for an accommodation with the necessity of endings. The book's design, though imperfect and in the central sections inconsistent, moves purposefully from the quiet address *To the Marquis of Dufferin and Ava* (memorial for Tennyson's son Lionel), to the equally quiet resolution of *Crossing the Bar,* the poem Tennyson wanted to represent the sense of an ending in each volume of his works published after 1889.

Tennyson's son Lionel died en route to England from India during April of 1886 and his body was buried at sea. Two and a half years later Tennyson made a poem on the occasion in the meter of *In Memoriam.* Grief and memorial are only portions of the whole, for the memorial to Lionel is reached through an address to the man who had cared for the poet's dying son, the Governor-General of India, Lord Dufferin:

> At times our Britain cannot rest,
> At times her steps are swift and rash;

[5]Contrast *Maud* and *In Memoriam,* the latter of which Tennyson described to Knowles as divisible into nine "phases" of grief.

> She moving, at her girdle clash
> The golden keys of East and West.   (ll. 1-4)

Dufferin's rule and Lionel's death play themselves out across the body of the Empire, where Britain *in propria persona* is the meeting of East and West so often desired and so often unachieved in Tennyson's early and middle verse.[6] Ruling wisely and well, Dufferin overcomes the need for force, and hence for the passionate and violent feeling still evident in *The Defense of Lucknow*[7] and *The Charge of the Heavy Brigade.* His is the beaten "gold" of achieved power, "gold" that is to give way in the recurrent image patterns of the volume to the "gold" of Victoria's jubilee, to the power of her gold to hold distant thunder in check, and at last to the poet's "gold" that precedes the satisfying twilight and sunset of *Crossing the Bar.* Dufferin permits England's rule to be quiet:

> Not swift or rash, when late she lent
> The sceptres of her West, her East,
> To one, that ruling has increased
> Her greatness and her self-content.   (ll. 5-8)

Dufferin brings peace to the geographical domain with which Tennyson's political poetry and early conquest verse had concerned itself; the meter of *In Memoriam,* so useful as an expression of unending circularity, is now used to signify unity and calm, and the old geography becomes the context for the new memorial:

> But since your name will grow with Time,
> Not all, as honouring your fair fame
> Of Statesman, have I made the name
> A golden portal to my rhyme:
>
> But more, that you and yours may know
> From me and mine, how dear a debt
> We owed you, and are owing yet
> To you and yours, and still would owe.

[6]The history of Tennyson's use of the contrast between East and West is complex. In *Armageddon* the tents of Satan, set against the sunset, face the "silver tents beside the moon" which are part of the lovely East. In *The Hesperides* the conqueror from the East sails west to a vision of apples reddening and ripening in the western sun. In Tennyson's early historical poems from *Poems by Two Brothers* the forces of the East are in conflict with the armies of the "Western" Mediterranean world.

[7]*The Defense of Lucknow* uses the images of tempest and storm for battle in India which Tennyson first used in *The Expedition of Nadir Shah into Hindostan.*

> For he—your India was his Fate,
>   And drew him over sea to you—
>   He fain had ranged her through and through,
> To serve her myriads and the State. ...

>   (ll. 13-24)

Lionel had physically traveled the poet's old world, with a young soul as pure as Arthur Hallam's had been:

> A soul that, watched from earliest youth,
>   And on through many a brightening year,
>   Had never swerved for craft or fear,
> By one side-path, from simple truth.   (ll. 25-28)

Lionel, like Hallam, "Might have chased and claspt Renown/ And caught her chaplet" (ll. 29-30),[8] yet he sickened in foreign lands as Hallam did, taking his journey homeward on a vessel which was to become a funeral ship. The recovery of detail is striking. The geography of legend, early dreams, and battles, breached by the son and now unraveled backward toward England, reflects upon the poet. India's shore becomes the fatal "bar" that so many of the poet's speakers have attempted. This time the poet cannot waft the ship home upon holy words. The tragedy he most deeply feared in the second phase of *In Memoriam*—that Hallam's body should "toss with tangle and with shells" (X, 20)—is Lionel's fate. The sensual, cruel sea, so often viewed as both rich and destructive, holds the child that resulted from the poet's choice of fatherhood in time, the view that dominates the Epilogue of *In Memoriam*. Thus the poem rises to the muted terror of stanzas IX-XII, a passage which represents the moment of burial in dreams that will not be still:

> But ere he left your fatal shore,
>   And lay on that funereal boat,
>   Dying, "Unspeakable" he wrote
> "Their kindness," and he wrote no more.

> And sacred is the latest word;
>   And now the Was, the Might-have-been,
>   And those lone rites I have not seen,
> And one drear sound I have not heard,

> And dreams that scarce will let me be,
>   Not there to bid my boy farewell,

[8]Cf. *In Memoriam* LXIV.

> When That within the coffin fell,
>   Fell—and flashed into the Red Sea,
>   Beneath a hard Arabian moon
>   And alien stars.... (ll. 33-46)

The significance of the lines cannot be missed. The one drear sound, the poet's inability to be present at the event, the recall of those early romantic and imaginative views of the East, are brought now to "a hard Arabian moon" beneath "alien stars." Lionel's death places Tennyson back at the core of an old vision, and once again he is not present at its crisis.[9] The sound of the falling coffin becomes a bad dream which haunts the poet as bad dreams haunted Lucretius.

At the end of *In Memoriam* Tennyson represents himself as a surrogate father to his time, finding exodus for private dreams and private sorrows in social endeavor and epic forms. To have become father in fact immediately thereafter, in the early years of his marriage, suggested that the poet had accepted the lesson he preached to others in *The Princess* and the elegy, and that his commitment to life was personal and unvicarious. These facts could have elicited despair in the face of Lionel's death, but they do not. In the address to Dufferin Tennyson does not falter. Quietly and naturally the poem turns away from pain to the resolution of grief in something which is equally personal and real:

> But while my life's late eve endures,
>   Nor settles into hueless gray,
>   My memories of his briefer day
> Will mix with love for you and yours. (ll. 49-52)

At the center of the poem's emotion the speaker knows the ancient terror of loss, set this time in a social and geographic frame. Dufferin's rule is good though the son dies; the old land of Tennyson's early poetry is calm even as it produces another death. This sense of balance is brilliantly imaged in the verse form of the poem. Tennyson uses the elegiac stanza he had made for Hallam to speak an address to the friend, in the familiar tone that had characterized

---

[9]In his introductory chapter Christopher Ricks, *Tennyson* (New York, 1972), writes of Tennyson's characteristic refusal to complete poems and plots, his insistence upon remaining at the threshold of dramatic experience. So in *Armageddon* the speaker does not see the last battle; *Timbuctoo* ends without conclusion; and *Maud* concludes on the eve of the war in the Crimea.

The Daisy earlier. Here the stanza is transparent, rarely end-stopped. Though quatrains are distinct, they move easily from one to the next, without the agonies of pause and recapitulation so familiar from *In Memoriam*. We hear the poet speaking not to himself, but outward from self to the living friend. The father of the form is not bound by it; elegy seeks epistle.

III

The poems which succeed *To the Marquis of Dufferin and Ava* in *Demeter and Other Poems* move from acceptance and a confirming celebration of Victoria's "gold" to darker and more pathetic ways of death. Together with *To Ulysses,* placed later in the volume, *Jubilee* and *Dufferin* accomplish the goal of *The Poet* stated so many years before: the conversion of sword and fire to peace. Both Victoria and her agent are wise, both permit "harvest." Yet the poems that follow these alter the peace with which the volume begins. The emotional descent of the volume from *Dufferin* to *The Ring, Forlorn,* and *The Leper's Bride* is dizzying, but the attributes of this descent light up the significance of the volume's last poems, and the relation of the volume to Tennyson's final verse. The initial joy of the volume, stated in its earliest poems, has now to be won again.

Demeter and Persephone presents this situation clearly. We can read *Dufferin* as the gateway to a recapitulation. Where *Dufferin* recovers the land of *Poems by Two Brothers* in a memorial framed by Horatian address, *Demeter and Persephone* recovers the mythological preoccupations of 1832-1842, as *The Death of Oenone* was also to do. Dedicating the poem to Jebb, Tennyson begins:

> Fair things are slow to fade away,
> Bear witness you, that yesterday
>   From out the Ghost of Pindar in you
> Rolled an Olympian. ...

(ll. 1-4)

Demeter and Persephone exists as a ghost within the poet, a good and bad dream struggling to be brought to light.[10] Dead in its own

---

[10]Tennyson wrote a number of poems concerning "bad dreams" in his later career, among them *Lucretius* (1868), *The Voyage of Maeldune* (1880—a series of nightmares), and *Rizpah* (1880).

land, "Trinacrian Enna," the tale blossoms "again on a colder isle" (ll. 11-12). The retelling of the tale is worth reading in its own terms, but what especially strikes me about the poem is its handling of death, of Pluto, and of Demeter's special knowledge. Persephone comes back to earth out of darkness and at dawn, as if from a land of dreams, indeed "led upward by the God of ghosts and dreams" (l. 5). She is dazed "with passing thro' at once from state to state" (l. 7). This is one version of Tennyson's image of recovery, the primary act of the last poems. Lazarus came back, but only with difficulty could be brought to recognition of himself (*In Memoriam* XXXI). Demeter brings Persephone back to unity of place, so that day "might break through clouded memories once again/ Of thy lost self" (ll. 9-10). The similarity of these lines to Oenone's experience in the later poem (1889-1890) should be obvious. The tale of Demeter blossoms again in a late, gray time. Old legends, old dreams recur. Both notions express Tennyson's reapprehension of the early forms of his verse in his last years, and his wish to evaluate them fully before his death. We cannot emphasize enough the centrality of dream in the late poems. Here it is the God of Dreams who tells Demeter the Truth of her loss by sending the form of Persephone to her in sleep. Through her he tells of the bitter unity of things:

> The Bright one in the highest
> Is brother of the Dark one in the lowest
> And Bright and Dark have sworn that I, the child
> Of thee, the great Earth-Mother, thee, the Power
> That lifts her buried life from gloom to bloom,
> Should be for ever and for evermore
> The Bride of Darkness.   (ll. 93-99)

Faced with the poet's repeated assertion that dark and bright are kin, and that the child is a lost child, Demeter manages a solution impossible for the poet: she shares her child with time. Despite the obvious differences, there is kinship, I think, between the poet's act in *Dufferin* and Demeter's act. Demeter returns Persephone to middle space and the simplicities of the middle earth. She undergoes a passion of grief, then finds quiet. She recovers the child, via dreams, from the fiery dark world of Pluto (ll. 23-28). She manages to do this by truth drawn out from within, by what she knows, through dream, as a portion of her buried life. The legend of Demeter is a version of the poet's own artistic process, as legends had often been for Tennyson.

It is easy to discount the last lines of the poem as merely "Christian," yet another example of a pagan voice lifting itself like those of Cleon, Karshish, Empedocles, or the Ancient Sage toward Christian truth but half-revealed. I think these lines should be read, rather, as a poet's prayer for release, bound to a mother's prayer for her child. Demeter's wish for her daughter's safe return, her prayer against fire, is synonymous with the poet's desire for tranquility in this volume, his conscious exclusions of battle, fire, and heroic modes. And it repeats the mourner's desire in *In Memoriam* for spring. In *Demeter and Persephone* the lift towards spring begins with images of harvest, and proceeds to Persephone's rebirth. The volume is likewise based on a metaphor of returning spring.

IV

I would claim, then, that *Demeter and Other Poems* struggles toward the quiet of the middle voice, and toward a sense of harvest or full tide that expresses the poet's late wish to make a quiet end to "bad dreams," those manifestations of violence which recur as late as *The Voyage of Maeldune*. The central sections of the volume seem to question this wish, for they turn to the hidden doubt of *Vastness* and to the melodrama of *The Ring* and *Forlorn*. The quality of the verse correspondingly declines. We best understand the place of such poems in the volume if we think of the middle section as a flawed retrospective upon and revision of familiar styles. *Vastness* turns upon *Supposed Confessions of a Second Rate Sensitive Mind* and *The Two Voices; The Ring* upon the group of domestic tragedies that extend from *The May-Queen* to *The Wreck*. Emotion in these exercises ranges from pathos to invective to terror, unconvincingly rendered in *Happy: The Leper's Bride*. Death moves through them all, given bitter or sentimental expression. *Vastness* and *Forlorn* express the fear that rises to trouble elegiac resolutions, recalling the gloom of madness and social invective which haunts *Maud* and breaks out with passion in *Locksley Hall Sixty Years After*. *Vastness* in particular strives to analogize lost human spaces with unfathomable cosmic spaces, succinctly stating

what I see as the double pressure of nineteenth-century private and
public anxieties within the calm frame of memorial:

> Many a hearth upon one dark globe sighs after
>   many a vanish'd face,
> Many a planet by many a sun may roll with the dust
>   of a vanish'd race.   (ll. 1-2)

But calm within the self gives place to fear of disintegration. The
lines quoted above state the conclusion Tennyson intends for the
book as a whole, but that conclusion, expressed as it is at the mid-
point of the book, seems arbitrary and we do not trust it. Still the
analogy drawn between hearth and space, particular experience
and cosmic hope, is compelling, and permits the poet to work toward
a personally acceptable end.

It should also be said that the poems occupying the central section of *Demeter and Other Poems,* with the exception of *Vastness,*
touch upon marriage and remembered parenthood, on loss and be-
trayal: the themes of Tennyson's narrative poems. Marriage is
haunted by death, danger, and deceit. Its partners are threatened,
reach no peace, become separate. "Il t'amo" seems a poor gift for a
bride. Marriage seems most successful and most lovely when it becomes (contrast the endings of *The Princess* and *In Memoriam*) a
marriage to death. Thus Happy, the leper's bride, moves toward her
husband, offering him funeral flowers as invitation to the embrace.
Happy is the nadir of the volume's curve. The poems that rise from
its pathetic ugliness permit the poet to welcome spring in an increas-
ingly strong, sure voice deriving from the commemorations already
discussed. *To Ulysses* is the first of these.

Written to W. G. Palgrave, who died before reading the verses
made in honor of him and his book,[11] *To Ulysses* takes farewell of
an old poetic aspiration and name. The poet's leavetaking is explicit: to you, Ulysses, "much experienced man" (l. 1), I, the poet of
a colder clime,

>   ...once half-crazed for larger light
>   On broader zones beyond the foam,

---

[11]W. G. Palgrave, brother of F. T. Palgrave (who was closely associated with the
poet), died at Monte Video on September 30, 1888. Palgrave's book *Ulysses* had been
published the year before, in November 1887.

> But chaining fancy now at home
> Among the quarried downs of Wight,
>
> Not less would yield full thanks to you
>   For your rich gift, your tale of lands
>   I know not, your Arabian sands;
> Your cane, your palm, tree-fern, bamboo,
>
> The wealth of tropic bower and brake....
>
> Through which I followed line by line
>   Your leading hand, and came, my friend,
>   To prize your various book, and send
> A gift of slenderer value, mine.
>
> (ll. 29-37, 45-48)

Here Tennyson leaves Ulysses' name and fame to others, "chaining" his own "fancy" to the winter woods. The imaginative lands of an earlier, fuller poetry he bestows on Palgrave, who can describe them from experience, as he has already yielded the political domain of his earlier verse to Dufferin. By contrast with Palgrave he tends transplanted growths—the yucca rears its head of "half-accomplish'd bells" (l. 24) toward a pale English sun, unquelled by any winter. This seems true of the poet also, a reassertion of his earlier deliberate confinement of himself and his art to English soil, and to slender pastoral song in *In Memoriam*. The rest of *Demeter and Other Poems,* I think, fleshes out this simple, recovered sense of elegy—for the poet's work and his life lived through art. Even *Romney's Remorse* has its place in a group of poems that validate the "slender" voice, the middle voice.

Thus *To Mary Boyle* restates the lesson of *To Ulysses* and becomes an introduction to *The Progress of Spring*. Spoken to a friend in relaxed, familiar mood, the poem rejects grief:

> Let golden youth bewail the friend, the wife,
>   For ever gone.
> He dreams of that long walk through desert life
>   Without the one.
>
> The silver year should cease to mourn and sigh
>   Not long to wait—
> So close are we, dear Mary, you and I
>   To that dim gate.
>
> (ll. 53-60)

The "closeness" of death is what we hear of, and as the book goes on, the poet welcomes its advent with anticipation he once reserved for spring in *In Memoriam*. Indeed the poet's death, his recovery of poetic history, and his reconsideration of familiar forms now become analogies of spring. *The Progress of Spring,* an early poem revised for 1889 and placed after *To Ulysses* and before *Merlin and the Gleam,* celebrates spring in a recovered, Keatsian form of poetry, before giving place fully to a quiet end. For a moment the poet lives again in the sensuous landscape renounced in *To Ulysses;* for a moment an early poem announces the fullness of spring to come. The position of *The Progress of Spring* in the volume is roughly analogous to that of poems LXXXIII-XCV in *In Memoriam.* The lesson of spring is an acceptance of a gradualistic view of time. Spring teaches men to die. The poet asks spring to come from the southern sea (l. 2) and "enter also here":

> Diffuse thyself at will through all my blood,
>   And, though thy violet sicken into sere,
>   Lodge with me all the year.   (ll. 23-26)

V

These lines make a strong introduction to *Merlin and the Gleam,* a poem that subtly changes the metaphor of spring advanced above to the poet's old metaphor of the journey out, and whose position in the volume is analogous to that of *In Memoriam* CIII. Here Tennyson recovers another early form in his poetry, the ode, and with it perfects a dialogue between youth and age characteristic of his early verse:[12]

> O young Mariner,
> You from the haven
> Under the sea-cliff,
> You that are watching
> The gray Magician
> With eyes of wonder,
> *I* am Merlin,

[12]W. D. Paden discusses "the mask of age" thoroughly in *Tennyson in Egypt: A Study of the Imagery in His Earlier Work* (Lawrence, Kan., 1942).

And *I* am dying,
I am Merlin
Who follow The Gleam.

"For those who cared to know about his literary history," Hallam
Tennyson tells us in a suggestive sentence, "he wrote *Merlin and
the Gleam.*"[13] "Merlin" was, after all, the pseudonym Tennyson
had chosen for himself in 1852[14] (Magus in *The Devil and the Lady*
was Tennyson's earliest magician figure, a voice of poetic aspiration
striving against the comedy of domestic life). This Merlin, however, is
safe from seduction, and his Nimüe has become the "gleam"—poetic
inspiration, poetic power—that had compelled the poet from earliest youth. It is important to see this Merlin as unseduced—a gray
singer troubled by Amoret, so to speak, but essentially free from the
domestic deceptions and external barriers that had kept Magus from
the journey out and that ultimately destroyed Arthur's Merlin. It
is also important to realize that the poet names himself as Merlin,
as dying, and as follower of the gleam. The significance of the
italics becomes most clear when we remember Tennyson's difficulty
with naming in his early work (cf. *Armageddon, Eleanore,* and
others), and his struggle for a compelling outer voice in *In Memoriam* and *Maud.* The mage became a character in *The Devil and
the Lady,* a pseudonym in 1852, a power in the *Idylls.* Now the
name is freely confessed, its bearer a gray, winter soul attempting a
new elevation. It represents a clear sense of poetic self in a physical
shape recognized as the reality, not the mask, of age.

The poem recapitulates the poetic history which permits Tennyson to speak of himself as Merlin. Architect of Arthur's kingdom,
possessed at last by certain bad dreams, Merlin participated in The
Kingdom's fall as well as its rise. As Ricks has rightly pointed out,[15]
the poem does not exactly parallel the chronology of Tennyson's
development, but I believe that it would be incorrect to equate
chronology with history. The poem is a history of Tennyson's imagination in its important phases. Let us follow those phases briefly.

If we read stanza 2 as a description of Tennyson's earliest gift,
then the poet tells us that the gift was given from without by a

---

[13]*Alfred Lord Tennyson: A Memoir,* II, 366.

[14]See Ricks, *The Poems of Tennyson* (London, 1969), p. 1412, and my essay "Tennyson's Political Poetry, 1852-1855," in *Victorian Poetry,* 14(1976),113-23.

[15]Ricks, *Poems,* p. 1413.

"wizard" with power comparable to that of the Seraph in *Armageddon;* that it makes a place between vision and song; and that it is equivalent to a waking from sleep:

> Mighty the Wizard
> Who found me at sunrise
> Sleeping, and woke me
> And learned me Magic!   (ll. 11-14)

The Gleam touches everything—landscape and human faces—only to be dulled "by the croak of a Raven" (l. 24). It is a mistake to read this line as particularized allegory, though it may refer to many forces that restricted the young poet's capacity. We cannot name a moment as an obvious reference for the lines. We do have access, through *The Lady of Shalott,* to barbarous people who cannot hear melody, or see the magic before them, or read its representations. What is poignant about this account of the poet's rejection—his failure to be heard or read—is that the rejection makes the power of the Gleam falter. Tennyson's account of the Gleam's wandering and his pursuit of it among desolate hollows, cataracts, and water, is remarkable as a description of the romantic, mythological poetry written in the 1830's— *The Hesperides, The Sea-Fairies,* the cataracts of *Oenone.* If this is correct then the world of faery Tennyson described during his years at Cambridge is seen in retrospect as barren, misleading, and a way to desolation.

Stanza 5 tells of the poet's exodus onto the plain Hallam Tennyson associates with pastoral and *English Idyls;* stanza 6 tells of Arthur's stately melody and the tournament that identifies him. It is here that we clearly see how complex a reading of chronology in the poem can be. The transition from stanza 5 to stanza 6 can, from a chronological standpoint, suggest Tennyson's turn from pastoral to the heroic exploits of Arthur. It can also be read as a recapitulation of the Lady of Shalott's movement—that is, the singer's movement— through her landscape to Camelot. In such a reading the gleam leads the poet beyond Lancelot's essential blindness and deafness to Arthur himself:

> And last on the forehead
> Of Arthur the blameless
> Rested the Gleam.   (ll. 72-74)

It is possible to say that Tennyson's plan for his Arthuriad was in some measure well formed by 1833,[16] and that the chronology established by the poem is therefore "correct." If it is true that the abiding forms of Tennyson's poetry were established by 1833 and the time of Hallam's death, and that they thereafter needed only to be "recovered" and judged, then we might also infer that the landscape and language of Shalott, though broken in the poem, had already been completed in the poet's imagination. The Gleam darkened when Hallam died in 1833. It also darkened, we might say, whenever the vision of Arthur faded—at the end of the *Morte d'Arthur,* at the end of *Idylls of the King.* Viewing the matter this way, I would read stanza 7 as both Arthur Hallam's death in 1833, and the vanished heroic vision whenever it occurs. Such "winter" is the winter Bedivere knows in giving his king to the sea; the winter of grief for Hallam; the "winter" of old age that Tennyson now projects toward spring. It is a fact that though the Gleam wanes to a "wintry glimmer" and draws to the valley of death, it can strengthen: "slowly moving again to a melody/ Yearningly tender,/ Fell on the Shadow,/ No longer a shadow,/ But clothed with the Gleam" (ll. 89-94):

> And broader and brighter
> The Gleam flying onward,
> Wed to the melody,
> Sang through the world.   (ll. 95-98)

In recovery from "winter," from Arthur's loss or Hallam's, the Gleam spreads "through the world" in indissoluble connection with melody. The song in the world not only represents for Tennyson his commitment to songs for the world as Laureate, but the pursuit of such songs as the task of present old age. The Gleam in the world compels the old, faint singer to sing again, and, from his standpoint, makes the hillocks of dead men bloom.

At the end of his strength, Merlin "can no longer." He pursues his quest to the border of the sea but not beyond, clinging to the margin as the Gleam hovers at the poet's first sung border—the border between Ocean and Heaven. It is left to the young mariner, the Ulysses figure already clearly taken leave of in *To Ulysses,* to follow the Gleam into territories that Magus tried but failed to reach,

---

[16]*Memoir,* II, 122-25. Full commentary on the development of the *Idylls* is to be found in Kathleen Tillotson's "Tennyson's Serial Poem," in *Mid-Victorian Studies* (London, 1965), and in John Rosenberg's essay in this volume.

and that the poet dared to try in visionary fire during his youth. It is significant for the structure of *Demeter and Other Poems* that the magician keeps to the shore: he is "father" of his time only in sénd-ing another out to the quest, aware of his own frail capacity. It is left to the last poem of the volume, *Crossing the Bar,* to complete the journey in the language of promise. Stanza 9 is a poignant and brief recapitulation of the last portion of *Ulysses,* as stanza 4 is a revision of *The Lady of Shalott:*

> Not of the sunlight,
> Not of the moonlight,
> Not of the starlight!
> O young Mariner,
> Down to the haven,
> Call your companions,
> Launch your vessel,
> And crowd your canvas,
> And, ere it vanishes
> Over the margin,
> After it, follow it,
> Follow the Gleam.   (ll. 120-131)

VI

Tennyson's reconsideration of his poetic history might have ended here. I would argue, however, that although *Romney's Remorse, Politics,* and *On One Who Affected an Effeminate Man-ner* unquestionably do not match the achievement of *Merlin and the Gleam,* they have their place in a sequence that moves from the poet's just-told history to *Crossing the Bar.* For the mind of the voyager finds it difficult not to circle back upon its own insistent themes of marriage, political fault, and social pain, and to recon-sider, through the detachment of *personae,* its attitudes toward poetry, voice, and art. Romney thus confesses his failure both as husband and artist. Sir Joshua Reynolds's dictim that lured him "from the household fire on earth" (l. 39) and his own unresolved commitment to Art as separate from Life constitute a review and rejection of the early split between notions of life and art in Tenny-son's own work, a notion that he strove through the later parts of his life to defeat. Like Oenone in the last poem that bears her name,

Romney, for all his "bad dreams," recovers a vision of his own new marriage. Art is the harlot in relation to such natural bliss, the Nimüe that seduces the father from his purpose.

Against the diminished vision of Romney, Tennyson sets *Parnassus*, a poem that marks a new stage in the artist's view of his aspiration. The poet aspires to the condition of Bard—crowned, "head in the zenith," voice rolling through earth and heaven alike. But stanza 2 recognizes the vulnerability of such an elevation, and restates for good reason the humility of the poet enforced by *In Memoriam* XXXVII and XCV: "Sing like a bird and be happy, nor hope for a deathless hearing" (1. 14). Though astronomy and geology overwhelm all human effort, Tennyson permits no despair to overwhelm him, using fire (one of the few times it appears in *Demeter and Other Poems*) to make an anology between "here" and "there:"

> If the lips were touched with fire from
>   off a pure Pierian altar,
> Though their music here be mortal need
>   the singer greatly care?
> Other songs for other worlds! the fire within
>   him would not falter;
> Let the golden *Iliad* vanish, Homer
>   here is Homer there.   (ll. 17-20)

Thus fire and epic speech remain despite the prevailing elegiac frame of the volume. But since they are "there," outside the scope and beyond the margins approached by the human poet, this is a poem of freedom, freedom from the need to attain the condition of Bard "here." The Bard stands on the old longed-for border, head above all others; the poet moves toward him, but still, like Merlin at the end of *Merlin and the Gleam*, remains on the shore, as part of the shore, subject to death yet capable of forging his own elegy and monument.

The process of discrimination begun in *Romney* and *Parnassus* continues in *By an Evolutionist*. Where the pursuit of Art, Fame, and the condition of being Bard is abandoned in the former poems, only the "gold" of song remaining, body itself drops away in *By an Evolutionist*. The evolutionist is the poet, the evolution that of the soul. What is attained in the poem is a mountain to replace the mountain of the Bard erased by time in *Parnassus*. The mountain, covered with snow, is a winter place commensurate with the winter words and "chained fancy" of *To Ulysses*. Standing again at an edge, where vision from the mountain height is comparable to Merlin's poise at the border of the sea, the man disciplined by old age hears nothing of the beast, "and the Man is quiet at last" (l. 19). He reproduces in himself the ascent from beast to angel symbolized by the carvings on Arthur's Camelot. He might say, with Pater, that art "aspires to the condition of music." The refrain of such quiet, the melody that accompanies the Gleam thus perceived, is heard in the title of the poem that follows, *Far—Far—Away*. "Far—far—away" had been Tennyson's words for visions of regret since childhood. How intense the recovery of such "holy words" becomes as this volume nears its end! The song is now, as it was in childhood, a song of the border between life and death, factual and visionary experience. It is as if the phrase itself were part of "earth's green" stealing into "heaven's hue:"

> What sight so lured him through the fields he knew
> As where earth's green stole into heaven's own hue,
>   Far—far—away?
>
> What sound was dearest in his native dells?
> The mellow lin-lan-lone of evening bells
>   Far—far—away.
>
> What vague world-whisper, mystic pain or joy,
> Through those three words would haunt him when a boy,
>   Far—far—away?
>
> A whisper from his dawn of life? a breath
> From some fair dawn beyond the doors of death
>   Far—far—away?
>
> Far, far, how far? from o'er the gates of Birth,
> The faint horizons, all the bounds of earth,
>   Far—far—away?
>
> What charm in words, a charm no words could give?
> O dying words, can Music make you live
>   Far—far—away?

Dying and music are one; they verge upon one another. The idea is repeated as the bells of this poem echo against the bells of *Crossing the Bar* and in the last poems Tennyson was ever to write.

There is a pause before the end of the volume, in many ways an imperfect one, I think, as the poet typically crowds in other old associations as elements of the inclusiveness he habitually sought in completing a large work. Thus he attempts to convert the "Revolution" he has always associated with pain to "evolution" defined in post-Darwinian ways. He recovers for example, the rose that had accompanied him through his poetic life since the early farewells to Rosa Baring. I am less struck by the fact that such images recur— for they always do in a major Tennyson poem—than by the ease with which the poet's middle voice prepares for translation across the borders of life and death. The accidental, almost deceptive intrusion of the epigrams gives place to *The Snowdrop* and *The Throstle,* heralds of the new year which insist again upon the primacy of song. Then *The Oak* summarizes all that has gone before in the volume. It is founded upon a natural metaphor, fit for the poet who has called himself Merlin:

> Live thy Life,
>   Young and old,
> Like yon oak,
> Bright in spring,
>   Living gold;
>
> Summer-rich
>   Then; and then
> Autumn-changed,
> Soberer-hued
>   Gold again.
>
> All his leaves
>   Fallen at length,
> Look, he stands,
> Trunk and bough,
>   Naked strength.

From this strength, represented by *The Oak's* linguistic simplicity, the poet takes farewell of a friend, then himself. The "Farewell" to W. H. Ward, called *In Memoriam,* draws the name of the elegy like a sky over both itself and the last poem of the book. The union of Faith and Work in Ward's life, which ranges as "bells of full accord," sounds against the lin-lan-lone of *Far—Far—Away,* and then against the evening bell of *Crossing the Bar:*

> Sunset and evening star,
>   And one clear call for me!
> And may there be no moaning of the bar,
>   When I put out to sea,
>
> But such a tide as moving seems asleep,
>   Too full for sound and foam,
> When that which drew from out the boundless deep
>   Turns again home.
>
> Twilight and evening bell,
>   And after that the dark!
> And may there be no sadness of farewell,
>   When I embark;
>
> For though from out our bourne of Time and Place
>   The flood may bear me far,
> I hope to see my Pilot face to face
>   When I have crossed the bar.

Homecomings to English earth of the kind central to the argument of *In Memoriam* are past. The poet welcomes the journey out with words that unite the power of a full sea with day's end. Home now is the poet's earliest home, that space beyond the borders of experience which he celebrated and sought as a child and which he had been tempted so often to grasp for in apocalyptic terms. Now the voice of the poet reaches the condition of simplicity that costs not less than everything, a condition not that of the Bard. Heroic responses give way to quiet authority. The motifs central to Tennyson's achievement here converge to a quiet end.

VII

Two years later Tennyson asked Benjamin Jowett, master of Balliol College, Oxford, to return with him to Ida. "Dear Master in our classic town,.../ Lay your Plato for one minute down,/ And read a Grecian tale retold" (ll. 1, 4-5):

> Today, before you turn again
> To thoughts that lift the soul of men,
>   Hear my cataract's
> Downward thunder in hollow and glen....   (ll. 13-16)

The cataract evokes Oenone. Lost in the waywardness of dream, she stares at the dead vines which surround her cave. Dead as they are, they elicit memories of Paris as he once was, a vision of beauty which mocks the figure soon struggling toward her in the mist:

> and on a sudden he,
> Paris, no longer beauteous as a God,
> Struck by a poisoned arrow in the fight,
> Lame, crooked, reeling, livid, through the mist
> Rose, like the wraith of his dead self, and moaned,
>   "Oenone. ..."
>
> (ll. 24-29)

It is the shepherds who reared Paris in his youth, not the wife, who lay Paris's body to the fire. They reach back beyond the intervening years of maturity, violence, and epic endeavor to place the failed hero at his pastoral origin, and, having done so, to permit his consummation by fire. The shepherds' care exists in contradistinction to the artifice of a civilized world, to the sensuous sophistication of pastoral in the first *Oenone*. The referential civilization of pastoral —the Troy to which Oenone looks at the end of the first poem which bears her name—lies ruined, like Paris, who left his heritage to seek the world's wars. Reversing the movement of *In Memoriam* toward heroic endeavor, and the first *Oenone* toward conflict, then, Paris returns to his generic origin and finds, at the kindled pyre, a conflation of pastoral and flame. This is also true of Oenone. The image of Paris calls to her within the bitterness of her dream and she wakes, though intellectually unconscious, to follow the light of the funeral to the pyre beneath the stars. She does not know who lies within "the ring of faces reddened by the flames/ Enfolding that dark body which had lain/ Of old in her embrace" until the boldest shepherd confronts her with her failure to forgive:

> and all at once
> The morning light of happy marriage broke
> Through all the clouded years of widowhood,
> And muffling up her comely head, and crying
> "Husband!" she leapt upon the funeral pile,
> And mixt herself with *him* and past in fire.   (ll. 101-106)

Fire permits Oenone to convert dream to deed.

The Death of Oenone is a proper introit to Tennyson's last, posthumous volume. In it Tennyson asserts his need to recover the earliest images of his poetry and to phrase them in terms of his imminent death. When *The Death of Oenone* and its Dedication were written, both Jowett and Tennyson were engaged in the careful revision of a life's work. For Jowett, revision signified the correction of a scholarly edition. For Tennyson, reconsideration was the habit of a lifetime, begun with the remaking of *Armageddon* and *The Devil and the Lady* in the 1820's, evident in the central rhetorical structures of *The Princess, In Memoriam,* and *Maud.* At the end of Tennyson's life a return to visionary and apocalyptic materials was neither self-indulgent nor immature, but a poetic reality freely acknowledged. In 1891 and 1892 his interests reached beyond epitaph and poetic history, patterns that determine the quiet beauty of *Demeter and Other Poems.* Now it is the former companions of his art—shepherds, the griever, the fallen hero—who give him occasion and solace.

St. Telemachus was written in the vein of *The Death of Oenone,* altering slightly but significantly the recovery of the Ulysses theme we have already considered in *Demeter and Other Poems.* A dreamer like Oenone and likewise isolated from the company of men, St. Telemachus tends a vestigial shrine ("no longer sacred to the Sun," l. 7), caught in a dream of his own commitment. Voices come from the West commanding him to "wake/ Thou deedless dreamer, lazying out a life/ Of self-suppression, not of selfless love" (ll. 20-22), until Telemachus, following "a shape with wings" (l. 24), moves West to the recovery of himself at Rome. In the face of cruelty, his power to speak suddenly wakens, and his "dream became a deed that woke the world." In both *The Death of Oenone* and *St. Telemachus,* the vestigial recovery of youth and power is central to a deed; in both, Tennyson's concern with social pain serves the deeper theme of the recovery of poetic strength. Telemachus dies but the words he speaks do not. In *Ulysses* (1833) the first Telemachus had been left by his father to perform a social task. Now a saint with a similar name performs a task by default, in spite of himself. Dying words speak; dying acts turn us again to the beauty of whole loves. There is a strong sense of recovery in the very last pieces that contradicts the poet's wish for a quiet end in his penultimate volume. The emphasis of these short pieces is upon fire, fire conceived in the old apocalyptic way. Akbar, dreaming, significantly enough, within "the waning world of Hindostan," cries that prayer and deed should be one. He and Kapiolani tame the destructive power of fire, one by song and the other by a deed that demystifies the fear fire can impose. Their strength counteracts the terror of fire sung in *The Dawn,* and permits the notion that man is not yet fully "made." *Faith,* written at the end of the poet's life, presents fire in a way that once again permits the poet's recovery of a certain epic vision:

> Doubt no longer that the Highest is the wisest and the best,
> Let not all that saddens Nature blight thy hope or break thy rest,
> Quail not at the fiery mountain, at the shipwreck, or the rolling
> Thunder, or the rending earthquake, or the famine, or the pest!
>
> Neither mourn if human creeds be lower than the heart's desire!
> Through the gates that bar the distance comes a gleam of what
> is higher,
> Wait till Death has flung them open, when the man will make
> the Maker
> Dark no more with human hatreds in the glare of deathless fire!

The Silent Voice and *The Dreamer* strike the final notes of Tennyson's art. They are equivalent in feeling to the last poems of *In Memoriam,* in which the poet struggles toward a new sense of poetic task, and then permits the hope of apotheosis to recur. The "epic" vision of these last poems is not directed to the world or the songs of the world. Their fire is personal and sublime, pressing into the cosmic song that binds life to life beyond the known frame. Thus *The Silent Voices* rewrites *Crossing the Bar:*

> When the dumb Hour, clothed in black,
> Brings the Dreams about my bed,
> Call me not so often back,
> Silent voices of the dead,
> Toward the lowland ways behind me,
> And the sunlight that is gone!
> Call me rather, silent voices,
> Forward to the starry track
> Glimmering up the heights beyond me
> On, and always on!

The Dreamer is a winter poem. Its lines recall the lines written for Hallam in the drear early winter of 1833-1834: "Hark the dogs howl." In the poem for Hallam the shadow of the beloved passes by, away from the poet who also leaves earth below him as he seeks the voice he loves through the waste. The shadow of the beloved moves out beyond him. Now a voice of the Earth itself passes away, the troubled earth of *Maud* and the late *Idylls:*

On a midnight in midwinter when all but the winds were dead,
"The meek shall inherit the earth" was a Scripture that rang
through his head,
Till he dreamed that a Voice of the Earth went wailingly past
him and said:

"I am losing the light of my Youth
And the Vision that led me of old
And I clash with an iron Truth,
When I make for an age of gold,
And I would that my race were run,
For teeming with liars, and madmen, and knaves,
And wearied of Autocrats, Anarchs, and Slaves,
And darkened with doubts of a Faith that saves,
And crimsoned with battles, and hollow with graves,
To the wail of my winds, and the moan of my waves
I whirl and follow the Sun."

Was it only the wind of the Night shrilling out Desolation and
wrong
Through a dream of the dark? Yet he thought that he answered
her wail with a song—

Moaning your losses O Earth,
Heart-weary and overdone!
But all's well that ends well,
Whirl, and follow the Sun!

He is racing from heaven to heaven
And less will be lost than won,
For all's well that ends well,
Whirl, and follow the Sun!

The Reign of the Meek upon earth,
O weary one, has it begun?
But all's well that ends well,
Whirl, and follow the Sun!

For moans will have grown sphere-music
Or ever your race be run!
And all's well that ends well,
Whirl, and follow the Sun!

The poet drives beyond elegy in his last poem as he did in *In Memoriam,* letting fire, song, and the spin of the earth beyond its frame become the strong version of the full tide that bore him home in *Crossing the Bar.* In doing so he reverts to the earliest visionary and apocalyptic language of his poetry. This, for Tennyson, constitutes song.

1809   August 6. Born the fourth son of the Rev. George Clayton Tennyson and his wife, Elizabeth Fytche Tennyson, at Somersby in Lincolnshire.

1820   Leaves Louth Grammar School, where he had been enrolled in 1815, to be taught by his father at home.

1827   *Poems by Two Brothers* published in April by Tennyson and his brother Charles, including some verses by Frederick Tennyson. Tennyson enters Trinity College, Cambridge, in November.

1829   During the spring meets Arthur Henry Hallam, who matriculated at Trinity in October 1828. Elected to the "Apostles" in May. Wins the Chancellor's Gold Medal in June for the poem *Timbuctoo*. Arthur Hallam and Emily Tennyson meet in December.

1830   *Poems, Chiefly Lyrical* published in June. Visits the Pyrenees with Hallam during the summer.

1831   Death of the Rev. George Clayton Tennyson in March. The poet is obliged to return home without taking his degree.

1832   *Poems* published in December.

1833   Arthur Hallam dies in Vienna on September 18.

1837   Move from Somersby to High Beech, Epping.

1838   Engagement to Emily Sellwood recognized.

1840   Engagement broken.

1842   *Poems* published in May. Volume I includes poems selected and revised from the 1830 and 1832 works. Volume II comprises new work, including *The English Idyls.*

1847   *The Princess* published in December.

1850   *In Memoriam* published anonymously in May. Tennyson marries Emily Sellwood in June and is appointed Poet Laureate in November.

1852   *Ode on the Death of the Duke of Wellington.*

1855   *Maud and Other Poems.*

1859   Four *Idylls of the King* published in July: *Enid, Nimüe, Elaine,* and *Guinevere.*

1862   Dedication for a new edition of *The Idylls* written in memory of the Prince Consort, who died in December 1861.

1864   *Enoch Arden, etc.* published in August.

1865   *A Selection from the Works of Alfred Tennyson* published in January.

1869   *The Holy Grail and Other Poems* published in December.

1872   *Gareth and Lynette* published, making *Idylls of the King* as printed in *Works* (1872-1873) complete with the exception of *Balin and Balan* (written 1872-1874, published 1885).

1875   *Queen Mary* published, Tennyson's first formal drama.

1876   *Harold.*

1879   *The Lover's Tale* published in May, *The Falcon* produced in December.

1880   *Ballads and Other Poems* published in December.

1881   *The Cup* staged with Ellen Terry and Henry Irvine.

1882   *The Promise of May* produced in November.

1883   Accepts the baronetcy refused in 1865, 1873, and 1874. Tennyson is seated in the House of Lords in March of the following year.

1884   *The Cup, The Falcon*, and *Becket* published.

1885   *Tiresias and Other Poems* published in December.

1886   Death of his son Lionel at sea in April. *Locksley Hall Sixty Years After* published in December.

1888   Severe illness.

1889   *Demeter and Other Poems* published in December.

1892   *The Foresters* produced in New York in March and published in April. Tennyson dies at his home, "Aldworth," on October 6. *The Death of Oenone, Akbar's Dream, and Other Poems* published on October 28.

Selected Bibliography

The following readings were chosen to supplement the complete volumes from which the essays in this collection were taken and the bibliographical information given in the introduction. The standard edition of Tennyson's poetry is now *The Poems of Tennyson* (London, 1969), edited by Christopher Ricks. The standard biographical sources are Hallam Tennyson, *Alfred Lord Tennyson: A Memoir*, 2 vols. (London, 1897); the privately printed *Materials for a Life of A. T.* (n.d.) upon which the *Memoir* was based; Sir Charles Tennyson's life of the poet, *Alfred Tennyson* (London, 1949); and portions of Christopher Ricks's *Tennyson* (New York, 1972). Recent bibliographical studies include Lionel Madden, "Tennyson: A Reader's Guide," in J. D. Palmer, ed., *Writers and Their Background: Tennyson* (Athens, Ohio, 1973); W. David Shaw, "A Bibliographical Essay," in *Tennyson's Style* (Ithaca, N.Y., 1977), pp. 307-31; and especially *Tennyson in Lincoln, A Catalogue of the Collections in the Research Centre*, Vol. II, published by the Tennyson Society (Lincoln, 1973). Students of Tennyson are referred to the continuing publications of the Tennyson Society.

Armstrong, Isobel, ed., *The Major Victorian Poets: Reconsiderations* (Lincoln, Neb., 1969).

Bradley, A. C., *A Commentary on Tennyson's 'In Memoriam'* (London, 1901).

Brashear, William R., *The Living Will: A Study of Tennyson and Nineteenth Century Subjectivism* (The Hague, 1969).

Eggers, John Philip, *King Arthur's Laureate: A Study of Tennyson's 'Idylls of the King'* (New York, 1971).

Gransden, K. W., *Tennyson: 'In Memoriam'* (London, 1964).

Joseph, Gerhard, *Tennysonian Love: The Strange Diagonal* (Minneapolis, 1969).

Jump, John D., *Tennyson: The Critical Heritage* (London, 1967).

Killham, John, *Tennyson and 'The Princess': Reflections of an Age* (London, 1958).

Kincaid, James, *Tennyson: The Major Poems* (New Haven, 1975).

Lucas, F. L., *Tennyson* (London, 1957).

Mattes, Eleanor B., *'In Memoriam': The Way of a Soul: A Study of Some Influences that Shaped Tennyson's Poem* (New York, 1951).

Pattison, Robert, *Tennyson and Tradition* (Cambridge, Mass., 1979).

Pitt, Valerie, *Tennyson, Laureate* (London, 1962).

Reed, John R., *Perception and Design in Tennyson's 'Idylls of the King'* (Athens, Ohio, 1969).

Ryals, Clyde de L., *From the Great Deep: Essays on 'Idylls of the King'* (Athens, Ohio, 1967).

———, *Theme and Symbol in Tennyson's Poetry to 1850* (Philadelphia, 1964).

Shannon, Edgar Finley, *Tennyson and the Reviewers: A Study of His Literary Reputation and of the Influence of the Critics upon His Poetry 1827-1851* (Cambridge, Mass., 1962).

Tennyson, Hallam, *Tennyson and His Friends* (London, 1911).

Notes on the Editor and Contributors

E. A. FRANCIS, Associate Professor of English at the University of Nevada Reno and Director of Composition, is the author of articles on Tennyson and the Rossettis, editor of *Children's Literature, An International Journal,* and author of a forthcoming book entitled *Tennyson: A Reading of Fire and Dream.*

HAROLD BLOOM is Professor of Humanities at Yale University. His volumes include *The Visionary Company* (1963), *The Anxiety of Influence* (1973), *A Map of Misreading* (1975), *Figures of Capable Imagination* (1976), and *Wallace Stevens: The Poems of Our Climate* (1977). "Tennyson: In the Shadow of Keats" is drawn from *Poetry and Repression* (1976).

JEROME HAMILTON BUCKLEY is Gurney Professor of English at Harvard University. His published work includes *Tennyson: The Growth of a Poet* (1960), *The Triumph of Time* (1966), and a collection entitled *The Pre-Raphaelites* (1968).

DOUGLAS BUSH is Emeritus Professor of English at Harvard University. He is the author of many volumes, including *Mythology and the Renaissance Tradition in English Poetry* (1932), *Mythology and the Romantic Tradition in English Poetry* (1937), *Paradise Lost in Our Time* (1945), *English Literature in the Earlier Seventeenth Century, 1600-1660* (1946), *English Poetry: The Main Currents from Chaucer to the Present* (1952), *Engaged and Disengaged* (1966), and editions of the *Latin and Greek Poems* (1970) and *Minor English Poems* (1972) in *Variorum Commentary on the Poems of John Milton.*

A. DWIGHT CULLER, Emily Sanford Professor of English at Yale University, has written *The Imperial Intellect* (1955, a study of Cardinal Newman), as well as *Imaginative Reason: the Poetry of Matthew Arnold* (1966) and *The Poetry of Tennyson* (1977).

THOMAS STEARNS ELIOT (1888-1965), editor of *The Criterion,* London, 1923-1939, and Director of Faber & Faber, Ltd., received the Nobel Prize for Literature in 1948. His volumes of poetry, criticism, and drama include

Collected Poems, 1909-1962 (1963), *Selected Essays, 1917-1932* (1932), *The Use of Poetry* (1933), *Murder in the Cathedral* (1935), *Four Quartets* (1943), *Notes towards a Definition of Culture* (1948), *The Cocktail Party* (1950), *On Poetry and Poets* (1957), and *Knowledge and Experience* (1964).

JAMES KISSANE is Carter-Adams Professor of Literature at Grinnell College. He is the author of *Alfred Tennyson* (1970) and has written scholarly articles on Victorian mythology and art criticism.

F. E. L. PRIESTLEY, Professor of English at the University of Toronto and author of *Language and Structure in Tennyson's Poetry* (1973), has edited William Godwin's *An Enquiry Concerning Political Justice* (1946), co-authored *Science and the Creative Spirit* (1958), and written *The Humanities in Canada* (1964).

CHRISTOPHER RICKS is Professor of English at Cambridge University and Fellow of Christ's College. In addition to his standard edition of Tennyson's poetry, *The Poems of Tennyson* (Longman's Annotated Poets, 1969), he has written *Milton's Grand Style* (1963), *Tennyson* (1972), and *Keats and Embarrassment* (1974).

JOHN D. ROSENBERG, Professor of English at Columbia University, has written *The Darkening Glass: A Portrait of Ruskin's Genius* (1961), *The Genius of John Ruskin: Selections* (1963), and *The Fall of Camelot: A Study of Tennyson's 'Idylls of the King'* (1973).

W. DAVID SHAW is Professor of English at Victoria College, the University of Toronto. He is the author of *The Dialectical Temper: The Rhetorical Art of Robert Browning* (1968) and of *Tennyson's Style* (1976).

ALAN SINFIELD, Lecturer in English at the School of English and American Studies at Sussex University, has written *The Language of Tennyson's 'In Memoriam'* (1971).